W9-BJV-379

The Corporeal Self

PS
374
.B64
C3

The Corporeal Self

*Allegories of the Body
in Melville and Hawthorne*

Sharon Cameron

THE JOHNS HOPKINS UNIVERSITY PRESS
Baltimore and London

Salem Academy and College
Gramley Library
Winston-Salem, N.C. 27108

This book has been brought to publication with
the generous assistance of the Andrew W. Mellon Foundation.

Copyright © 1981 by The Johns Hopkins University Press
All rights reserved
Printed in the United States of America

The Johns Hopkins University Press, Baltimore, Maryland 21218
The Johns Hopkins Press Ltd., London

Library of Congress Cataloging in Publication Data

Cameron, Sharon.
    The corporeal self.

    Bibliography
    1. American fiction—19th century—History and
criticism. 2. Melville, Herman, 1819–1891. Moby-
Dick. 3. Hawthorne, Nathaniel, 1804–1864. Tales.
4. Body, Human, in literature. 5. Self in
literature. 6. Identity (Psychology) in literature.
7. Allegory. I. Melville, Herman, 1819–1891. Moby-
Dick. II. Hawthorne, Nathaniel, 1804–1864. Tales.
III. Title.
PS374.B64C3   813'.3'0936   81-47602
ISBN 0-8018-2643-8   AACR2

To
Garrett Stewart
Allen Grossman
Stanley Cavell

Contents

Acknowledgments

I am grateful to the National Endowment for the Humanities, which granted me time to write the following book; to The Johns Hopkins University, which provided additional research funds; to Ellen Mankoff, Marilyn Sides, and Elizabeth Carroll, for initial preparation of the manuscript; to Elizabeth Harvey, for endurance, editorial discrimination, and the scrupulous production of a final copy; to the staff of The Johns Hopkins University Press; to Jane P. Tompkins, for critical guidance; and finally, to the friends and colleagues—especially Eric Sundquist, Garrett Stewart, Allen Grossman, Michael Ragussis, Barry Weller, John T. Irwin, Patrick McCarthy, Kent Dixon, Albert Gilman, William Cain, Arnold Stein, Mimi Still Dixon, Jonathan Crewe, Everett Zimmerman, the late Laurence B. Holland, Henry A. Murray, Muriel Zimmerman, James McIntosh, Richard Poirier, and Robert Weisbuch—who gave this manuscript their generous attention, often at short notice and over long distance.

This was that Earth of which we have heard, made out of Chaos and Old Night. Here was no man's garden, but the unhandselled globe. . . . It was Matter, vast, terrific,—not his Mother Earth that we have heard of. . . . What is it to be admitted to a museum, to see a myriad of particular things, compared with being shown some star's surface, some hard matter in its home! I stand in awe of my body, this matter to which I am bound has become so strange to me. I fear not spirits, ghosts, of which I am one,—that my body might,—but I fear bodies, I tremble to meet them. What is this Titan that has possession of me? Talk of mysteries!—Think of our life in nature,—daily to be shown matter, to come in contact with it,—rocks, trees, wind on our cheeks! the solid earth! the actual world! the common sense! Contact! Contact! Who are we? where are we?

—Henry David Thoreau

Introduction

"*Who* are we? *Where* are we?" [1] Most philosophical explanations of identity—how the self understands its relation first to itself and second to the outside world—from the Renaissance on depend on the idea of dualism, on the notion of a separation or a split between two primary terms. The terms may be predicated as body and soul, one self and a separate other, the identity of persons as opposed to nonhuman beings, or the identity of one person at a given moment in time and space as distinct from the identity of the same person at a different temporal-spatial moment. [2] In the following pages I shall examine a revisionary notion of identity and of the philosophical dualism that attends it.

The conception is revisionary, first because it appears in literary rather than philosophical works, and in fact those aspects of the works I consider could be conceived as having an independent philosophical status. Second, it is revisionary because, although the works with which I am concerned examine the body's relation to the soul and the self's relation to the outside world (and therefore seem to invoke yet again the double terms to which I have alluded), these works then posit a third term or entity which, neither body nor soul, neither one self nor another, knits the respective entities together. The third entity, moreover, while not being material—while transcending the corporeality to include the spirit that is "outside" or "within" it—is nonetheless bodily, sometimes manifesting itself as an actual "third" person. Thus, the body of flesh and blood is complemented by a markedly different corporeality that both encompasses

[1]

and transcends it. In the works I shall discuss—Melville's *Moby-Dick* and Hawthorne's tales—what stands behind the body is another, different body. Third, the conception is revisionary because, although the central philosophical subject of *Moby-Dick* and Hawthorne's tales is human identity, these works obfuscate that fact in the presentation of their fictional subjects, professing to be about questions of interpretation. I shall be suggesting that while Melville and Hawthorne write about physically violent subjects with unabashed candor, they at the same time attempt to conceal the fact of that violence—hence *Moby-Dick*'s passionate insistence that its issues are hermeneutical, allegorical, exegetical (this while the whale body, while several whale bodies are being dismembered page after page, in unrelenting detail). If most criticism thus far has addressed itself to problems of interpretation, this is because it has followed the directives of the specific works: in the case of Melville's novel, to read *Moby-Dick* as a book about interpretation; in the case of Hawthorne's tales, to read the tales as allegories, as stories whose claims on the reader are primarily interpretive. Yet alongside the directive about how the novel and tales are to be taken are the bodily dismemberments—the anatomization of the whale and Hawthorne's "'Allegories of the Heart'" (X:268).[3] In "Sylph Etherege" characters look into the heart; in "Ethan Brand" they look for it; in "My Kinsman, Major Molineux" they trample the heart; in "Egotism; or, The Bosom-Serpent" they conceal the heart; and in "Roger Malvin's Burial" they bury the dead man's body in "the sepulchre of [the] heart" (X:356)—as if the human heart had palpable dimensions that could literally receive the verbs and the actions of the verbs addressed to them.

As the examples touched on above imply, the conception I examine is revisionary in yet a fourth way, because relations between body and spirit give rise to the literary questions "What is literal?" "What is allegorical?" and these designations of "literal" and "allegorical" are at the same time treated as if they were commensurate with the body and soul to which they also correspond. The conception is finally revisionary because, in a series of works, not coincidentally American, the identity of the self and the identity that lies outside the self (with the "outside" world often conceived as having its own body) are both connected and confused. Such notions of a self, recapitulated briefly above, therefore, collapse the distinctions on which post-Renaissance conceptions of identity have relied.

The fantasy in *Moby-Dick* is that human identities might be joined by a Siamese ligature, following which all men, fused, will be squeezed "into each other" (94:533).[4] The fantasy of Hawthorne's tales is that all selves might be joined, not by corporeal enlargement but rather by corporeal diminution in which the self is distilled to a representative bodily organ—

for example, to Ethan Brand's heart. It is simply a fact, about which I shall have more to say, that American works seem preoccupied with questions of identity conceived in corporeal terms, and that they make use of, while transcending, the philosophic dualism available to them. If, then, by pitting the great nineteenth-century American novel against the great tales of nineteenth-century American literature, I omit detailed discussion of other American literature, this is because I wish to locate the lengths to which revisionary conceptions of identity can go when we see these conceptions (as *Moby-Dick* and Hawthorne's tales allow us to do) carried to their extremes of expansion and contraction.

Yet I wish to suggest that although I concentrate on *Moby-Dick* and Hawthorne's tales, there are connections between the issues I raise here and the heart of our American literary tradition. Thus, alongside *Moby-Dick* and Hawthorne's tales there would be much to say about the way in which other American writers, or works by the same writers, are concerned with identic separations and boundary revisions, are concerned with "third" bodies, are concerned with a barely recognizable corporeality that insistently confuses distinctions between the body of the person and the body of the land. There would be much to say about the fabled man in Emerson's *Nature* who is "disunited with himself," [5] or about "the state of society" scripted in "The American Scholar" in which "the members have suffered amputation from the trunk, and strut about so many walking monsters,—a good finger, a neck, a stomach, an elbow, but never a man." [6] Or about the self in Thoreau's *A Week on the Concord and Merrimack Rivers*, who wishes to transform the sap in the trees to a current in the mind. Or about Whitman's great poem, in which the body of the self and the body of the earth are professed frenetically to be one. Indeed, there would be much to say about self-definition in Poe's *Narrative of Arthur Gordon Pym*, in which a character is composed of a first person and a second person who is ultimately supplanted by a third person (Augustus is Pym's second person supplanted by the dwarfed third person of Dirk Peters). There would be much to say about Melville's "Bartleby," a story that again posits a dualistic conception of identity in the persons of Nippers and Turkey—characters also succeeded by a third person, initially by Ginger Nut and then by Bartleby, who eats ginger nuts.

As the cannibalistic pun in Melville's "Bartleby" implies, the transformations of identity in the American works I shall discuss are primitive and crude. Insofar as the works in question domesticate identic issues—for these works are on the page rather than in the mind, and they belong to a character rather than to a self—they allow us to understand the disturbing questions they raise while leaving us bodily unimplicated in the consequences of their considerations. Yet my last statement needs to be qualified; as the discussion of *Moby-Dick* will demonstrate, it is in the disturbing way in which our relation to the texts in question raises to the surface the issue of *our* identity that the power of these works must finally be understood. That we could be more than what we are or less than what we are—that, more or less, we could be different from what we are—these are the ideas elicited from *Moby-Dick* and Hawthorne's tales. The meaning of such transformations, how they threaten and seduce, is a subject of my book, for what is at risk in the comprehension of these works is collapsed distinctions between literature and philosophy, the literal and the allegorical, the life inside the work and the life outside the work.

Poe raises these issues starkly and thus leads us to Melville and Hawthorne. In *The Narrative of Arthur Gordon Pym*, Augustus, dead of a gangrenous wound, is thrown overboard. In the process of dispensing with the body, however, we are told that "as Peters attempted to lift it, an entire leg came off in his grasp." Though Pym recoils from the event, insisting it is "loathsome beyond expression,"[7] he nonetheless manages to give it immediate, concrete expression, thereby forcing us to ask: what does it mean? In part we could say that it is a way of making a connection between Augustus and Peters—allowing the body of the one man to shift synecdochically to the body of the other, and providing a palpable emblem, a bodily part, for the transformation we are made to see being enacted. For like the parallel actions which attend this part of the tale—the shifting of the ship's cargo (Augustus becoming Peters) and the eating of Parker, the man whose body is devoured in an effort to sustain the other starving men—the leg's coming off in the hand draws unforgettable attention to the ways in which questions of shifting identity involve bodily dismemberment whose depiction is too graphic to be explained as metaphoric of identic violation unless it is, tautologically, metaphoric of itself. Melville had read *The Narrative of Arthur Gordon Pym*, and although Ahab's dismembered leg is not directly associated with the leg of Augustus that comes off in the grasp it is difficult to miss the fact that both authors probe the demarcation of identities in emphatic, if repellent, corporeal terms.

I shall suggest that *Moby-Dick* takes *monster* bodies apart in order to examine of what they are made; and that Hawthorne's tales take *human* bodies apart in order to reveal of what they are made. In the two chapters that follow, I discuss the relationship between this opposition. In addition, I shall suggest that while *Moby-Dick* ostensibly asks: what is the self's relation to the world that lies outside of it, the self acknowledges that world

[4]

only in the process of trying to appropriate it. Insofar as the world is imagined, it is imagined so as to be converted into the character who envisions it. *Moby-Dick* dismembers the outside world of which the whale is an emblem, with the hope that, as a consequence of the dismemberment, the self could magically take the world—now sufficiently partialized—into its own body. Contrarily, in Hawthorne's tales, the world outside the self is conceived as irremediably exterior to it. Hence the need for allegorical correspondence, for the world outside the self must be *known* in a relationship and not *had* in a possession. Insofar as Hawthorne's characters seek to come into relation with the world's essence, they do not violate the world's bodies; rather they violate their own, attempt to distill themselves into a representative essence with the hope that this essence—made sufficiently small, made even invisible—could come into correspondence with the body of the outside world. The claim of these reductions and partializations is, as I suggested a moment ago, that they are allegorical. Although it will be one of the purposes of the chapter on Hawthorne to examine the meaning of such a claim, suffice it to say here that since Hawthorne's tales show us human bodies coming apart, they make use of a convention that not only accounts for (offers us instructions about how to read) the human dismemberments of which they tell, but also tries to make them literary, to make them, as it were, "not real."

It will be my contention that behind the dismemberment of the whale bodies (in which the imagined mutilations seem *literal*) and behind the reductions of the human bodies (in which the imagined mutilations seem *allegorical*) lie the following (same) questions: what is the relation of my body to what lies inside of it, to that which I cannot see (call it essence or soul)? what is the relation of my body to that which lies outside of it (call it the world of other human bodies, or call it the natural world, the world of foreign bodies, those not kin to my own)? Granted, there must be connections between the body and (my) non-corporeal essence and between myself and other beings—connections not contingent upon palpable substance (as philosophical and theological tracts, long before Descartes, take elaborate pains to show)—since I do not conceive of myself as wholly, even primarily, defined by my body, what exists in lieu of the body, on whose substance I can count? [8]

Although the questions Hawthorne's characters typically ask in the tales—how is part of the self integral to the whole self, which it also represents?—seem solipsistic rather than relational, these questions bear impassioned witness to the understanding that the world outside the self is (to commit a tautology) emphatically outside it. Since, in the simplest sense, the world can be neither had nor known, the proper object of anatomization must be the self. Thus, although on the face of it, Hawthorne's tales, asking as they do about the self's relation to itself, seem more primitive than Melville's avowed concern about the self's relation to the outside world (as the concept of *one* entity is more primitive, reductive, developmentally "earlier" than the concept of two entities), the real state of affairs is exactly reversed. For however obsessive Melville's descriptions of the whale or the outside world, the eloquence of these descriptions, as Ishmael acknowledges early on in the novel, is ultimately narcissistic. Eloquence describes the externality so as to domesticate it. Describes it, as it swoons toward it, so as to make it part of the bodily self in question. Thus, I shall consider *Moby-Dick* first, for although the date of the novel's publication follows that of most of the Hawthorne tales I discuss, in its representation of the problem of identity and of identic boundaries it comes chronologically "first."

If *Moby-Dick* and Hawthorne's tales are philosophical and psychological counterparts in raising primitive concerns, as I have already intimated, they do not do so in isolation. It is not incidental that works as radically different as Melville's encyclopedic novel and Hawthorne's finely chiseled tales should take as their subjects the problem of human identity. The problem of human identity considered explicitly as a bodily problem, a problem that revolves around knowing the boundaries of the body, while not an American phenomenon, has a characteristic American form of expression conceived in terms as uncultivated as the discovery of a new land and the need to create a national literature. I shall develop these observations in the chapter on *Moby-Dick*, and shall couch them, where they belong, in that tradition of criticism exemplified by such studies as Quentin Anderson's *The Imperial Self: An Essay in Literary and Cultural History*, Richard Chase's *The American Novel and Its Tradition*, Richard Poirier's *A World Elsewhere*, and, earlier, by D. H. Lawrence's *Studies in Classic American Literature*. The critics to whom I allude customarily distinguish the American novel from its British counterpart by suggesting that the American novel depicts the self outside the confines of a social context. It is part of the purpose of the following discussion to particularize this observation, suggesting that in at least one strain of American literature the distinction is cruder and more palpable than the critical commentary has yet acknowledged, that American fiction is concerned not simply with definitions of the self but also, more specifically, with problems of human identity predicated in terms of the body.

Why American works should focus on what is integral to the body and what is exterior to it is of course a matter of speculation. One could see corollaries here between a child's first discovery that his body is his own, excluding other bodies, and the discovery of men struggling to distinguish their own literary subject. If this comparison seems stretched, we might recall Piaget's sensible observation in *Genetic Epistemology*[9] that the development of persons and concepts has a hierarchical order, so, to express it in numerical terms, the concept of one must precede the concept of two, and the concept of two that of three. The assumption is in fact frequently, if implicitly, made that psychological development has a literary corollary. We see the assumption operating negatively in the denigration of American literature, in the assessment that it is "not up to" the formal coherence of the more respectable British fiction, that it is adolescent or, worse, childish. Although much American literature is indeed deliberately primitive, the relegation of that literature to an imaginary second class is prompted by a value judgment that dismisses what it does not have the terms to understand; that is, the judgment is prompted by the inadequacy of the criteria being invoked to assess the literature in question and not, as usually specified, by the inadequacy of the literature. If, instead of dispensing with the literature for its unwieldy lack of conformity to traditional literary standards, we attempt to see what it is doing, it is immediately clear why "identity," conceived in surreal bodily terms, should be taken as an American subject, and, more to the point, why the authors I discuss should wish, by analogy to the human developmental process, to define identity, as we all first do, in bodily terms. The mind works by analogies, deducing what it cannot see from that which it can. The body is what one can see, is the thing (the only thing) that can be owned. Thus, given the particular concern with definition of one's own (national) space, with problems of territorial expansion, with a subject uniquely delineated, one's relation to one's body (though far from being analogic), since it is the most palpable relationship we have, suggests analogies for these secondary problems of owned subject. The authors about whom I write may be seen to fall back not simply on the first stage of a development *model* (the problem of definition; the learning of what something is), but on a developmental *subject* (specifically, the definition of the human body).

I touch suppositionally on the idea of an "explanation" for what I shall describe in the following pages. Matters of causality are, in the end, not definitively to be determined. I would, however, like to point to the recurrence of the subject of the body as we see it in works other than *Moby-Dick* and Hawthorne's tales. Earlier, in *Mardi*, Melville anatomizes the human body directly. So in connection with Samoa, the man forced to turn physician to himself and amputate his ailing arm, the question is put to us:

> Now, which was Samoa? The dead arm swinging high as Haman?

Or the living trunk below? Was the arm severed from the body, or the body from the arm? The residual part of Samoa was alive, and therefore we say it was he. But which of the writhing sections of a ten times severed worm, is the worm proper?[10]

So in the case of the man whose spinal cord has snapped—that is, in the case of the man in possession of his whole body but lacking sensation in any of it—we are brutally shown that when the body is made to move by a force external to it, this movement is as detached from the self as Samoa's cut-off arm: "wonderful to tell, his legs refused to budge; all sensation had left them. But a huge wasp happening to sting his foot, not him, for he felt it not, the leg incontinently sprang into the air, and of itself, cut all manner of capers" (*Mardi*, p. 506). So also in *Mardi* we are told that a man may be separate from himself not because he is dismembered (a part of the body cut from the outside) or because he is paralyzed (a part of the body cut from the inside), but rather because he is too close to himself. He can feel but not see the whole of who he is: "Though your ear be next-door to your brain, it is forever removed from your sight. . . . It is because we ourselves are in ourselves, that we know ourselves not" (*Mardi*, pp. 296–97).

Turning momentarily from Melville and Hawthorne, we see a similar confusion about how to distinguish the boundaries that rope the self off in the writings of Charles Brockden Brown. In *Wieland*, voices heard from inside (as in hallucination) are undifferentiated from voices heard from outside (as in ventriloquism). In fact, the phenomenon of the voice—that which exists but is not visible—offers an exemplification of why the self has trouble knowing the boundaries between itself and the world. For since there are things inside the body that the self fails to know in palpable or bodily terms, why may there not be things outside of the body—someone else's voice, for example—that could also belong to one's own body, while failing to be perceptible in palpable or bodily terms? As *Moby-Dick* and Hawthorne's tales painstakingly point out, it is just because the self has a non-bodily part (a soul, an essence, a voice in the mind) that the problem of personal identity, or the confusion of boundaries, so persistently occurs. The split within the body (between the corporeal entity and the non-corporeal essence, between the body and the voice in the mind) generates a corollary split outside of the body, between one entity and a separate other. This split is or can be real. One body is, after all, separate from a unique other. But the real can be problematic. Are the voices Wieland hears in the body or outside of it? Are they his voices or someone else's? This question about boundaries, hallucination or ventriloquism, voices not clearly *in* the body nor clearly outside of it, prompts the hallucinatory

[8]

idea that one body could actually turn *into* another, as, for example, Pym turns into Augustus and Augustus into Peters. For if the voice outside the body is indistinguishable from that within it, the body from which that second voice comes may also be indistinguishable from one's own body. Such a confusion is the subject of Brockden Brown's *Edgar Huntly*, where a man chasing a sleepwalker becomes himself the sleepwalker. And the transformation of one body into another (we have learned to call this gothic, perhaps out of repulsion at a rendition of our earliest confusion) exactly characterizes Poe's tales. Poe, I suppose, would offer the most clichéd example of the exploration of identic bodily boundaries—of people converted to bodily parts (Berenice to her teeth) or transformations of one body into another body (Ligeia into the second wife or Morella into her daughter, Eleanora into the natural landscape, the wife into the wall, William Wilson into his double)—although I believe that Poe stylizes, sentimentalizes, or exaggerates, and so finally discredits as threatening, the transformations he is supervising. Hence, he calls their status into question, whereas Melville and Hawthorne leave these transformations and boundary confusions just real enough to terrify.

Concern about the body is obviously not limited to the confines of American literature, but we have only to glance at a book like Leonard Barkan's *Nature's Work of Art* and its subtitle, *The Human Body as Image of the World*, to note that the body in English literature is treated not so much as a palpable entity but rather as a figure or "image." The deflection from the body's palpable substance, as we see it through Barkan's critical eyes, may issue partly from the fact that his study grounds itself in the sixteenth century but it also issues from the fact that in English literature, as Barkan explicitly says and as his examples eloquently illustrate, the sense of the body is figural, "is used . . . as a figure for the world's complexity, whether cosmic, political, or architectural." [11] Conceived as such, the body has analogic status; it is, as it were, divested of its palpability, or, rather, its palpability is put into the service of something else.

By contrast, we see the prominence of the body and the confusion about its corporeal demarcations illustrated not simply in nineteenth-century American fiction, in the works of Brockden Brown, Poe, Melville and Hawthorne; we see it also in twentieth-century American literature, in Faulkner's *The Sound and the Fury*, for example, which has as its subject not simply a fragmented perspective, the same story told over by four different persons, but, in addition, a central character who has no present body, no narrative or voice of her own. She has only recollected or filtered substance. And this in a novel that simultaneously insists that Caddy (the absent body) both bodily nurtures the other characters and—in the other

[9]

use of the body—betrays them by her promiscuity. We also see the body's prominence in *Lolita*, that greatest parody of the American novel, which is similarly a tale about a little girl whose body is possessed, is appropriated and raped, and who, moreover, exists not in her own right (we only once in the novel hear her speak without the screen of praise that simultaneously presents and covers her up), but rather exists unclearly separate from the man who has confected her. In *Lolita* and *The Sound and the Fury* problems of bodily identity take on twentieth-century attributes. By invoking these modern works here I mean simply to suggest that from its earliest roots, through the forms that come to parody them, American fiction focuses not simply on the body, but on the body's coming apart, on the way in which it is partialized—half corporeality, half ineffable something else. The splits are addressed again and again through strategies of allegory and literalization. Is Lolita in the body? Is she in her own body? "I was always 'with Lolita' as a woman is 'with child,'" [12] Humbert Humbert proudly tells us. And what does it mean to be "in" one's own body?

We see concern with a body that can be aggrandized or anatomized not simply in American fiction or in American poetry, in Whitman's magnifications of the bodily self (the body sponging up the life of the whole world) or in Dickinson's bodily reductions (the self fractured to the eyes, the feet, the heart, to a "Cobweb on the Soul"); we see it also in American philosophy and psychology, in the scrupulous examinations of the body as they comprise the work of William James or, earlier, that of Jonathan Edwards. Indeed, Edwards's central task in his major—his most moving—work, *Religious Affections*, is to define the "signs" that will discriminate what is generated in the body from what, though perceived in and by the body, contrarily comes from outside of it:

> All such kind of things as we perceive by our five external senses, seeing, hearing, smelling, tasting and feeling, are external things: and when a person has an idea, or image of any of these sorts of things in his mind, when they are not there, and when he don't really see, hear, smell, taste, nor feel them; that is to have an imagination of them. [13]

Yet existing in the mind, phenomena may also be in the world, may call into question our pedestrian distinction between the respective placements considered as alternative when it is too assuredly clear:

> It is now agreed upon by every knowing philosopher that colors are not really in the things, no more than pain is in a needle, but strictly nowhere else but in the mind. But yet I think that color may have an existence out of the mind with equal reason as anything in body

[10]

has any existence out of the mind, beside the very substance of the body itself, which is nothing but the divine power.[14]

Although the subtlety of Edwards's deliberations rebukes hasty analysis, I mean by my passing reference en route to my two authors pointedly to be suggesting that while my discussion will focus explicitly on Hawthorne and Melville and on a circumscribed number of their works, the impulse to define the body and its palpable boundaries (1) has a specific American manifestation, (2) often becomes a subject more philosophical or psychological than traditionally "literary," or rather becomes a subject that cannot be understood in traditional literary terms, and (3) illustrates that the subject of identic boundaries conceived in bodily terms raises, almost by definition, the problem of enlargement and diminution, and thus of bodily size. One could say that Melville, in enactment of his own theme, cannot write a novel as traditional novels had been written, but rather makes it ostensibly an encyclopedia of hermeneutic strategies, as if the words contained between the covers of the book could *be* and so *mean* all. Similarly, Hawthorne cannot tell a tale as traditional tales had been told; often Hawthorne's stories exemplify a minimalist's art, or they divide within themselves. It is the traditional complaint against them that their morals are severed from their plots. Actually, however, the impulses toward formal expansion or diminution exaggerate and enact the desire of one author to enlarge the bodily self and of the other author to diminish the bodily self. For these memberments and dismemberments—as Hart Crane would have said, these "transmemberments"—veering in opposite directions, depict the body by redefining its actual corporeal limits.

All language is allegorical, is not the thing about which it speaks. Yet works that themselves explicitly distinguish what is allegorical from what is literal (and that make claims tantamount to the assertion that what they say has no bodily consequences), works that simultaneously take as their subject the dismemberment of the body (in Melville's case of whale bodies; in Hawthorne's case of human bodies) are, as I suggested earlier, deflecting attention away from the violence of what they do. In this respect it is unimportant how a given work announces its subject, for the anatomization of the whale bodies or alternatively of the human bodies, however elaborately their authors distinguish the strategies employed toward the respective enterprises, amounts to the same thing. When the action of allegory is the dismemberment of the human body, what the work chooses to call itself and how it chooses to interpret itself are secondary or immaterial in the face of what it does. Yet if I suggest that allegory can distract from the palpability of a given subject, I mean also to suggest that allegory

[11]

Salem Academy and College
Gramley Library
Winston-Salem, N.C. 27108

does indeed address itself—is especially equipped to address itself—to that part of the human self which does not have visible or palpable characteristics. It is simply a fact that we allegorize our bodies all the time when we refer to the heart or the mind and imagine these to be neither organs nor bodily regions, although organs and bodily regions may well stand for them—may necessarily stand for them—as their only available representation.

I would like to suggest that Melville and Hawthorne take the problem of what is literal, and what allegorical, and pitch it to exaggeration, even to disintegration. They refuse to accept the definition of the two words as they have customarily been understood. They are thus in a particularly strong position to illustrate the fissures and dualisms that are the inevitable consequences of imagining that one could pry the allegorical from the literal, the body from the soul. These consequences, I shall suggest, haunt novel and tales, respectively. Hence, we do not read Ahab and Ethan Brand allegorically. We read them reading themselves, with all the reductionism and overdetermination (not in a critical but in a psychological sense) that these processes involve. Hence, Melville and Hawthorne make a generic or definitional crisis (how to distinguish what is literal from what is allegorical) into a philosophical one (how to distinguish body from soul), and, as I have suggested earlier, they also attempt to cure the distinction between the respective separations by predicating a third (bodily) entity. Thus, with respect to these works, formal interpretation, of the sort we have come to expect in literary studies, is not the surest access to them. This is not because they resist it; as I have acknowledged, they invite, even prompt it. But as a consequence, they are similarly immune to it—having worked problems of interpretation out so well in and through their systems—in these particular cases, having fathomed questions about the relation between the literal and the allegorical until such questions, ingrown as the characters' psychology, are indistinguishable from it. In these texts, problems of "identity" are not problems of characterization, at least not as that word is understood in traditional literary terms. The rebuke of characterization is manifested in various bodily partializations: Ahab addresses not the whale but rather its severed head (" 'speak, thou vast and venerable head' " [70:405]); Aylmer "handle[s] physical details, as if there were nothing beyond them" (X:49), devoting himself to the birthmark as if it were a whole person. Ideas of character are questioned in the fictional making of a man, as the witch in Hawthorne's "Feathertop" constructs a body without a spirit, or as the carpenter in *Moby-Dick* is asked to construct a body with a "chest modelled after the Thames Tunnel" (108:599). That the soul can imagine it houses a second body (as Roderick

[12]

Elliston does in "Egotism; or, The Bosom Serpent") or as Ahab imagines such a body in the feeling of the phantom leg—these are assaults on the idea of character.

"And here's his leg!" the Pequod's carpenter morosely says after a conversation with his irascible captain. "Yes, now that I think of it, here's his bedfellow! has a stick of whale's jaw-bone for a wife!" (108:601). "He'll stand on this. . . . It looks like a real live leg, filed down to nothing but the core; he'll be standing on this to-morrow; he'll be taking altitudes on it. . . . So, so; chisel, file and sandpaper, now!" Such good-humored mockery issues from the carpenter's exasperated puzzle at Ahab's making the leg synecdochic for his whole human body. Neither support to keep him up nor solace to lie along his side, to Ahab the leg represents the inscrutability of a self. His conversation with the carpenter, which I shall examine in the first chapter, suggests a connection between the wooden leg made by the carpenter, the carpenter's "live leg" which Ahab urges him to "put . . . in the place where mine once was," and the phantom leg "so long dissolved" but still felt by the soul (108:600), for all are to Ahab enigmatically related in an identity. Soul, body, a third corporeal entity. "What was that now about one leg standing in three places?" the carpenter asks. "How was that?"

1 Identity and Disembodiment in *Moby-Dick*

[Moby-Dick] is not a peice of fine feminine Spitalfields silk—but is of the horrible texture of a fabric that should be woven of ships' cables & hawsers. A Polar wind blows through it, & birds of prey hover over it.

—Herman Melville

"No man can ever feel his own identity aright except his eyes be closed" (11:87). This Ishmael says to the reader early in *Moby-Dick* as he and Queequeg lie in bed together at the Spouter-Inn. The remark, like so many of those uncommented upon enigmas in the novel's initial pages, turns out, upon scrutiny, to show us how Melville literalizes questions about identity—as it is construed by the body with its eyes glued open to receive the world, as it is construed with its eyes glued closed, knowing itself by the thoroughness with which it walls out all that is outside. The querying of identity is not simply a persistent theme, but, as I shall suggest, the subject of *Moby-Dick*, that most nerve-racking of novels, whose demented strangeness seems to implicate us in the understanding of it. As with someone else's bad dream, whose images are so primitive as to repel our inclination to attend to them, we normalize the novel at the risk of failing to comprehend it. What we would comprehend, were we to give ourselves over to its images, is the repetitive and feverish question: of what are bodies made? Concern about the body's composition manifests itself with respect to the idea that bodies are incomplete. At the conclusion of "Extracts," Ishmael says to the Sub-Sub, comparing this world to a heaven in which bodies might be durable as well as whole: "Here ye strike but splintered hearts together—there, ye shall strike unsplinterable glasses!" (Extracts:8). The concern manifests itself with respect to the idea that the body's incompletion may have to do with the invisibility of its essence. Hence the inability of the mourners in "The Chapel" to say where their dead are buried—to say where particular bodies are—to say where essence is when it is deprived of a body. More than incomplete, bodies may seem insubstantial *because* their essence is invisible. Hence the image of Narcissus who falls toward the water in death because "he could not grasp [his] tormenting, mild image" (1:26), could not touch as well as comprehend it. For bodies contain essences (as the common notion of the body as a vessel suggests), and this idea about containment when it is literalized, as the novel attempts to literalize it, causes tragedy in the end.

As if to jar our complacence about how bodies are to be fathomed, the novel's initial chapters introduce us to Queequeg's odd customs: his scalping of other bodies, the catalog of the foods his people put into their bodies, the worship of Yojo (a representative body), Queequeg's lounging on the bodies of the sleeping sailors on board the Pequod's deck—as if bodies could be benches, commodities without essences, dead to the world in their own right. These pictures of the body unsettle from the very beginning our illusion of its familiarity as the novel sets it before our eyes. If through Queequeg's customs Melville would make the body foreign, make us see it from outside, in showing us the three mates and how they inhabit their bodies, he simultaneously domesticates the image of the body. The relationship of Starbuck, Flask, and Stubb is, as the critical commonplace goes, hierarchical, and the hierarchy is expressed first and foremost by the respective ways in which the mates inhabit their bodies. Starbuck, the godly man, represents the Biblical proverb that "the body is a temple of the Holy Ghost": "His pure tight skin was an excellent fit; and closely wrapped up in it, and embalmed with inner health and strength, like a revivified Egyptian, this Starbuck seemed prepared to endure for long ages to come" (26:157–58). At a further remove from an inside, Stubb is described in terms of his pipe, though it be external to the outermost part of his person. Flask is depicted in terms of the world that lies outside of bodily confinements or comforts—in terms of "carpenter's nails . . . made to clinch tight and last long" (26:163)—for Flask is a man so hard that as the whale is to him "but a species of magnified mouse" so his own body is a mere "brace" against the world that lies outside of him (26:163). These three images of progressive distance from bodily habitation complement the earlier image of the body as seen from the outside, as Queequeg's anecdotes represent it. Indeed, I would like to say in passing that, although the four characters to whom I have alluded are generally regarded as central, it is because their representations remain static that it is possible to see them as such; whereas in fact the more important issues of identity rather have to do with characters, or with relations between characters, who are subjected to redefinition and for whom static limits are challenged or denied. It is because Starbuck, for example, can distinguish—and rest content in—the difference between inside and outside that Melville both esteems and leaves him, as it were, alone.

It is not simply the body's representation from outside nor its habitation from within, but rather the relation between inside and outside itself at which we are asked to look. This idea may at first seem abstract. The novel is quick to literalize it. Thus, we see Ahab's thoughts because Melville makes us privy to them—privileging an inside to which we would otherwise have no access—and also because we are told they are written on Ahab's brow by "some invisible pencil . . . tracing lines and courses upon the deeply marked chart of his forehead" (44:267)—inside becoming outside (the mind's chart a virtual map of the nautical outer world through which he works his way) by manifesting itself there. The previous externalization finds its counterpart in Ishmael's only half-comic speculation that a king's head is anointed with oil "with a view of making its interior run well" (25:156). Attempts to depict what lies inside the person as visible on the body, or to internalize what lies outside the body and hence to ask where an "outside" goes when it is no longer visible, are common enough notions when they are conceived as metaphors, but Melville deprives us of metaphoric consolation and makes us see the self's relation to its own body as *literal*. The hope seems to be that, were one to literalize these relations, as the examples I have pointed to try to literalize them, one might see through to the question of identity, might see it as if it were palpable, and so comprehend it. The image of seeing through the body, whether from inside or from outside, is given direct expression in the novel's second chapter as Ishmael, walking the streets of New Bedford, looks for a place to house his body, for an inn to spend the night: " 'In judging of that tempestuous wind called Euroclydon,' says an old writer," who is, in fact, Melville,

> "it maketh a marvellous difference, whether thou lookest out at it from a glass window where the frost is all on the outside, or

whether thou observest it from that sashless window, where the frost is on both sides, and of which the wight Death is the only glazier." True enough, thought I, as this passage occurred to my mind. . . . Yes, these eyes are windows, and this body of mine is the house. What a pity they didn't stop up the chinks and the crannies though, and thrust in a little lint here and there. (2:34)

The idea about seeing into the body, astonishing enough in its own right, is complicated in *Moby-Dick* by an even more fantasmal idea that one could enter others' bodies, could inhabit others' bodies as, for example, a soul inhabits a body. Thus, the relation between interior and exterior, body and soul, is in the novel's inventive hands turned into a wish about more improbable habitations, as if, could one penetrate the body—go through the windows of that house, through the truly unsplinterable glass—one might heal the incompletions within this world rather than in some other, might heal them actually rather than in conception.

How Melville literalizes embodiments and disembodiments will be the subject of the following pages. Before proceeding, however, I would like to situate my work in the context of the novel's previous criticism. While discussions of *Moby-Dick* are as diverse as the novel itself, they nonetheless tend to polarize at the following areas of investigation: (1) the examination of the novel's formal properties, its sources and inventions;[1] (2) the attempt to understand the novel as revisionary social criticism, whether this criticism acts itself out in general terms by being a book about community uncompromised by social institutions, whether it instigates a complex drama between pastoralism and industrialism, or whether it allegorizes America itself;[2] (3) an inquiry into the novel's passionate insistence that various antitheses—innocence and evil, love and death, the natural world and the human one, the ego and a transcendent sublime[3]—must be related, and into the novel's simultaneous acknowledgment that this is a backbreaking imperative precisely because of the interpretive difficulty of understanding such relationships; and (4) the designation of Ishmael as the novel's world-interpreter, the man at different times character and narrator who, uniting the bifurcated roles, becomes a dependable explicator.[4] Diverse as they may be, the representative concerns to which I have alluded have one thing in common. They all attempt to grapple with the difficulty of the novel's surface, whether that difficulty be a formal or a social one (for queries about the novel's response to society are of necessity concerned with forms and behaviors, however deep their roots), or whether the difficulty positions itself with respect to how surfaces and appearances are rightly to be interpreted so that they may be brought into proper relationship. It is indeed because of investigations of the perplexities raised by the novel's surface that we understand *Moby-Dick* as well as we currently do.

What have not been investigated, and the subject to which I turn, are the concerns to which the formal, social, and epistemological issues give way. I see the tension in the novel to exist between the hermeneutic issues that comprise the novel's surface and the more primitive issues of identity to which that surface is forced to cede. The novel enacts a pull between the hermeneutic procedures (the attempts to allegorize the world, to symbolize and metaphorize it, to make multiple fables of it, to examine its social forms or the forms of representation) and the literalizations that are left when these processes exhaust themselves or cancel each other out. As has probably become apparent by my use of the word *literalize*, I mean that Melville displaces ideas from an explanatory status and confers on them the status of immediacy or palpability, that he poses questions of identity in emphatically physical terms, asking: can things be taken literally? Can they be taken bodily? What would it mean so to take them? Differently put, then, the novel's tension is between the spirit and the letter, one exegetical in its focus, the other affixed to the bodily thing itself. The novel dramatizes a return to the letter, to the literalization that kills.

I shall be suggesting that the novel's interpretive questions are secondary to its more primitive questions about identity. Throughout my discussion I shall want to focus on the connections between literalization and embodiment, on the novel's crazed but repetitive notion that two persons could exist in one body and, alternately, on its suggestion that bodies may be disassembled—as the whale is disassembled—so that *(a)* what is inside could be viewed, and *(b)* what is inside could be removed. The taking apart of the whale, chapter after chapter of it, deflects from the more compulsive dissection and reconsitution of the novel's characters, again as if, could one just take bodies apart, one might see of what they are made. Could one put bodies together, they would perhaps be reconstituted as self-sufficient. Thus, the reflexiveness of Ahab's taunt in "The Candles"—"'in the midst of the personified impersonal, a personality stands here'" (119:641)—indicating as it does the proximity of disparate states (the fine line between personal and impersonal), becomes emblematic of the concerns of the whole novel. I shall be suggesting that Melville picks at that line between personal and impersonal, asking how otherness is coerced into identity, or, alternately, how otherness is thrown out of identity's bounds. For the ways in which characters desire other characters to embody them confuse our concepts of projection and embodiment as concepts, try to turn them into the real thing.

[19]

Ahab and Pip:
Those Are Pearls That Were His Eyes

The complexity with which Melville brings characters together may be
seen with respect to Pip and Ahab. " 'Like cures like'" (129:672), Ahab
says to Pip, as if in explanation of his attraction to the little black boy. It
will be remembered that Pip, who has jumped into the ocean and been
deserted for a few moments by Stubb, caught up as the latter is in the passion of the whale-kill, is driven crazy by the abandonment. But Ahab is
wrong. Pip's madness is not like his own. It is in fact the very antithesis of
his own, and in guarded recognition of the difference (" 'There is that in
thee, poor lad, which I feel too curing to my malady'" [129:672]) Ahab
knows that in his attraction to Pip lies the danger of its dissipation. In the
scene I have begun to describe, Pip and Ahab are in the latter's cabin, and
when Ahab moves to return to the deck, Pip takes his hand to follow. As
Ahab first tries to entice Pip to stay below (" 'as if thou wert the captain.
Aye, lad, thou shalt sit here in my own screwed chair; another screw to it,
thou must be'") and later bosses him into obedience (" 'Weep so, and I will
murder thee!'"), it is apparent that their separation is compelled by the fact
that Pip is a check to Ahab's madness. Therefore, Pip must be screwed to
the chair, kept in his place—any place will do that is away from
Ahab—and Pip's response to the injunction speaks directly to the fear that
causes the order and implicitly to the tragic consequences of obeying it:
" 'No, no, no! ye have not a whole body, sir; do ye but use poor me for
your one lost leg; only tread upon me, sir; I ask no more, so I remain a
part of ye'" (129:672).

The entire two pages of "The Cabin" revolve around the subject of
incompletion, of selves that require a necessary other not only to be whole
but in order to be at all. We learn this lesson, see the lengths to which
abandonment can go in the reduction of identity, when Ahab leaves Pip
for the deck. Then Pip seems literally *beside* himself, no longer housed in
his body. Then he tries to comprehend how one loss generates another:
" 'Here he this instant stood; I stand in his air,—but I'm alone. Now were
even poor Pip here I could endure it, but he's missing'" (129:673). Pip's
statement is complex as both psychology and metaphysics. Ahab cannot
be Pip where being is understood as graft rather than relationship. But if
literal completion is impossible, Ahab's subsequent repudiation of Pip (his
repudiation of relationship) has murderous consequences. For although
two cannot be one where "being" would involve the reduction of a self,
one cannot be at all—cannot acknowledge itself as being—unless it is

completed from without, unless it is allowed human proximity. Forbidden this proximity, Pip disappears to himself. He cannot abide solitude, and thus must be absent to himself so that he will be kept from perceiving the absence *outside* his person. The accompanying excisions—Ahab abandoning Pip because, as I shall suggest, Pip cannot be within him; Pip beside himself because Ahab will not be without or proximate to him—spatialize, as the novel's prepositions imply, the reduction of identity when it refuses relationship.[5] That the self needs to be completed in the way made possible by relationship in order to be at all seems to be the point Melville would drive home. In Pip's plea that Ahab survive his mutilation by treading on him, Melville literalizes the point, for Pip's offer to let Ahab use his leg makes into a bodily thing the problem of relationship for which it stands. Pip will be what Ahab is not. Two will be one. The idealism of that union, echoing chapters back against the poignantly early marriage of Ishmael and Queequeg at the Spouter-Inn, will triumph over the malignancies of a severative world.

But of course that is not how it works out. And, in fact, in "The Doubloon," Pip's comments on the dangers of such a union, his seeing of self-transcendence as violation, complicates the idea that characters can go outside themselves, if not actually to complete each other, then to create an analogic wholeness. In the crossing of these two ideas (and of the two scenes that bring them into play, which I now wish to explore in detail)—that selves can go outside of their delimited boundaries, and that such projection is impossible except as projection—Melville does not so much cancel the two ideas as bring them into unresolved relationship. The crossing of antithetical notions—Melville's antithetical notions about the hope for curing identity, where cure would involve its enlargement to incorporate other people, and his chastisement of that hope—is emblematic of the contradictory claims made by the entire novel.

In "The Doubloon," it is clear that Ahab has suddenly found a way to coin the image in the mirror and reify it as currency. We know something about the perversion of this egotistical sublime as we regard Ahab scrutinizing the coin, his vision self-reflexively in possession of the whole world:

> 'The firm tower, that is Ahab; the volcano, that is Ahab; the courageous, the undaunted, and victorious fowl, that, too, is Ahab; all are Ahab; and this round gold is but the image of the rounder globe, which, like a magician's glass, to each and every man in turn but mirrors back his own mysterious self." (99:551)

Although discussion of the doubloon passage is central to any interpretation of the novel, the connection it insists upon between symbol as private currency and money (that symbol purified of private meanings, that is, made public) and the way in which private and public here get confused (as, indeed, Melville means momentarily to confuse Pip and Ahab) has not been fully discussed. For the doubloon's meaning is first projected by the various characters and then consigned value. In the conjugation of Pip's verbs ("'I look, you look, he looks; we look, ye look, they look'" [99:555]), we see that the denomination of the doubloon, like that of all coins, is determined arbitrarily by an image cast onto the neutral metal, an image whose own significance validates it. We see, in addition, however, that in distinction from other coins the doubloon has no common (public) meaning, for its denomination is fixed by eyes at variance with each other, and in the private symbology that comes into play with the engagement of more than one connotative system. Consequently, those who project meaning or value onto the coin in the form of their own image of the world then want to possess the coin, (re)appropriate it, but now with its private value acknowledged and made public, reified by others as monetary value or "currency" rather than as arbitrary image. It does seem as if although value is declared out of the idiosyncrasies of private interpretation, it is not made good until its meaning has been acquiesced to by others. I take this to be the significance of winning the coin.

Thus, despite the solipsism of projection, success is imagined paradoxically as validation by others. And although for most of the crew the doubloon has obvious monetary significance, winning the coin also means being validated in Ahab's eyes: "'Whosoever of ye raises me a white-headed whale . . . he shall have this gold ounce, my boys! . . . Skin your eyes for him'" (36:218). Therefore the coin's monetary or public value (what the coin is worth) is subordinated to its symbolic or private value (one man's evaluation of what the coin is worth). In the double claims made by the coin—that meaning may be projected outside of a public context, and that it must nonetheless receive sanction within the parameters of that context—we see the crux of the ensuing problem, which Pip puts this way:

> "Here's the ship's navel, this doubloon here, and they are all on fire to unscrew it. But, unscrew your navel, and what's the consequence? Then again, if it stays here, that is ugly, too, for when aught's nailed to the mast it's a sign that things grow desperate." (99:556)

As reference moves from idiosyncratic connection to the commonplace of surface interpretation—those meanings taken for granted because seen from the outside (in this latter case, the Pequod seen by another boat, and responding to the agreement of fixed nautical signs)—we see that part of what troubles Pip is not the disparity of public and private meanings, but rather the smoothness of their link, as if it were precisely the seamless conjunction of meanings outside the self and within it which made them so difficult to pry apart.

What lies within the self, what outside? What connects inside to outside, and, as in the case of the visible navel, can the place of connection be fixed? These are precisely Ahab's questions. They are the questions of the entire novel. But, articulated by Pip's compressed rhetoric, the questions rise to the surface. What disturbs Pip is not simply the connection between public and private meanings—between what is felt from the inside and interpreted from without—but what drove him mad in the first place, and, as I shall suggest, what drives Ahab mad too; that the self is cut loose to separate identity from the communal body that breeds it. As meanings, public and private, have their indecipherable link, so the isolated self is connected to others by those invisible ties for which all of the lines in the novel, in lieu of that original cord, so insistently yearn. Yet the mind that puzzles relation unclarified by identity asks: what constitutes connection sufficient to keep life sane (" 'But, unscrew your navel, and what's the consequence?' "); what goads the self to desire a finite life apart from those bodies with which it might try to fuse (" 'Then again, if it stays here, that is ugly, too' ")? As Pip's words turn over these questions, we see the issue of interpretation give way to a quandary about identity, to which the interpretive questions are secondary.

Thus, the coin that initially seemed to raise the subject of projection in an *interpretive* framework, to ask how visions are cast out upon the world, now in an *identic* framework, and in light of these new images of birth, which query the relationship between internal and external, asks how the self is cast out upon the world. As if in imitation of the double subject he is scrutinizing, Pip vacillates between a consideration of the crew's fate (" 'They are all on fire to unscrew it' ") and intersecting questions about the unscrewing of his own fate (" 'But, unscrew your navel, and what's the consequence?' "), focusing on an appropriate pun (as in "screwy"[6] or a "loose screw") for a mind undone by the communal body from which it has been cast away. What is involved in the fears Pip voices above, of course, is not simply a pun, but also a joke current in the nineteenth century that if you unscrewed your navel, your bottom would fall off.[7] Melville would not only have been alluding to this joke, he would with macabre humor have been retelling its well-known consequences—would have been insisting that the result of the ostensible metaphor of the navel's unscrewing was the body's literal falling apart. He would, moreover, half disassociating himself from the joke on which he

[23]

plays, have been making the joke horrific by suggesting that birth was such a disembodiment.

The question of birth and generation, enveloping the question of interpretation, shows us, by example, how we are to understand the dilemma of the entire novel. It also explains how the two issues of interpretation and disembodiment—of the coin's multiple meanings as each man separately looks, and of Ahab's imperative that the men skin their eyes, take themselves out of their eyes, make their eyes into his—on which the novel so repetitively harps come into relationship. As I suggested earlier, the question about interpretation, about private meanings and public ones, exists only in the larger context of a question about disparate bodies. Thus, although Ahab's leg is terribly cut off, this mutilation is in fact synecdochic for the more radical excision that hones him from the original body that first created him and then cut him away. Such a construction seems inevitable, given how frequently in the novel the image of lost or unknown parents with whom Ahab would be reunited is invoked as the antidote that would bring his madness to an end. Ahab wants to be nourished by the universe, as a child is nourished by its parents: " 'Thou art but my fiery father; my sweet mother, I know not' " (119:643), Ahab apostrophizes the lightning in 'The Candles." His sweet mother, the world clothed in beneficence, in love rather than power, might save him. In fact, he has been saying all along that if only he could turn love to power, make power " 'come in [the] lowest form of love' " (119:641), he would worship the world that he will now annihilate.

What is my genesis? Where do I come from? Why do I come? To these questions there is no answer. Ahab's reasoning in the wake of the ensuing silence is as follows: if the world gave birth to me, it will nourish me. If not, why would it have given birth to me? And if it does not nourish me, I will kill it. What Ahab desires is a world untortured by ambivalence and ambiguity. What he gets is the weave of contradictory feelings (that which makes up his nature) and the ambiguity of the world outside himself (that which makes up its nature). This has been the tenor of the discussion of the novel, with the emphasis on the ambiguity of the world, throughout the history of its criticism. Yet it is because we have separate bodies that what is outside us is unknown, is not made of our substances, is thus, by definition, alien. For the only familiar meanings are the ones generated from within, those to which we are attached; and that we possess our own meanings so that they inhabit our bodies is an idea that haunts these pages, illustrated as it so often is by the depictions of the body as a receptacle (" 'Oh God! that man should be a thing for immortal souls to sieve through!' " [125:659]) or a vacant space (" 'I'll order a complete man after a

desirable pattern, . . . [the] chest modelled after the Thames Tunnel'"
[108:599]).

Thus, the real question is not, as it deceptively appears in the novel,
"what do things mean?" but rather, "why am I not attached to those meanings—why am I separate from the reality I am therefore forced to know?"
Not being separate would replace knowledge. Being would replace cogni-
tion, and indeed all of the attempts to impose meaning outside of one's
body—whether foisting it upon the coin or, in Ahab's case, making his
men the material part of his will—are gestures toward that substitution.
The question of birth, of how the self is delivered from the world's body
with which it forever longs to reunite, locates the problem at its origin. To
unscrew one's navel is to perish, to be severed from the body of the
nourishing world; not to do so is to perish also, never to cut oneself to the
hardness of separate identity. Birth is at once delivery to particular shape,
to the separateness that makes Ahab Ahab, and delivery to determinate
limit (*limit* here defined as an end to the separate self, to an outside from
which it is excluded).

In Pip's case, the fall into the ocean duplicates the first severance of
birth, but a difference attends the duplication. This difference is one of
consciousness driven out of its mind by comprehension of the rift. It is as if
Melville were suggesting that we survive the devastation of our birth
because we do not remember it. The novel replicates the consciousness for
us, imagines what it would feel like (Walter Benjamin in reverse),[8] and in
the terror that rushes around the thought suggests that, were we to feel our
birth as well as to know of it, there would be, for us as for Pip, no way
back, consciousness walling itself off from those other beings to whom ties
would be, if at all, only fragilely imagined. Indeed, if we regard Pip at the
moment he is left to the world's mercy, regard and compare him to Ahab
in a comparable stance of affliction (as Melville surely means us to do), we
see in the awe of the narrator that when Stubb's "inexorable back was
turned upon him," intent instead on chasing the precious gold, Pip is set
adrift on a rimless ocean of sorrow. And meticulous as Melville always is
in the distinctions he would have us consider, we are told that what drives
Pip to the depths of reason is not the actual danger into which he is fallen,
nor the arduousness of keeping afloat, but the pure horror of abandonment, the realization that there is nothing between self and world to fend
off one and shield the other, no mediating agency, not even the dubious
intercession of others.

Nowhere in the novel, not in any passage devoted to the goring of the
whales or to the perils of the crew, does Melville give us such an
unadulterated vision of violence as in those few sentences that detail the

[25]

sacrifice of Pip's mind. In the enormity of that loss we see the passive universe that robs Pip of his reason is the very same as that which rises before Ahab in the specter of the white whale: "Now, in calm weather, to swim in the open ocean is as easy to the practised swimmer as to ride in a spring-carriage ashore. But the awful lonesomeness is intolerable. The intense concentration of self in the middle of such a heartless immensity, my God! who can tell it?" (93:529). Who can live to tell it? Who can stand to tell it? Pip is stabbed to silence by what he feels, unable to tell for himself the terror of his selfhood. It is a terror Melville will take over seven hundred pages to try to tell; something about the rapidity with which it comes to Pip that he is alone (he knows it as he hits the water, long before he has time to know whether he will be rescued) and the thoroughness with which solitude turns into a castigation of self, drives speech out almost as if at that moment it threatened to intercede between mind and the unrelieved consciousness of its isolation. As Pip is cast away from the lines of human desire, all longing, whether for immortality or power or knowledge, longing even for the salving presence of others—all are nothing before the huge indifference of the world. This is the antithesis of a Narcissus fall in which the self is lost in fusion with the universe. In Pip's fall, self and world are rent, opposites turned toward each other as if to epitomize the central symbolic posture of the novel's characters.

Although there is the deservedly well-known passage in which Pip is compensated for his isolation and insanity—we are told he sees "God's foot upon the treadle of the loom" (93:530)—the form compensation takes is manifestly disconcerting. It records a vision of divine power rather than of divine love, of God's foot rather than of His face. One could say that much as Melville tries to invoke the miracle of the sights the rest of us are spared, the fact is that my way of putting it is expressive of Melville's attitude. That Melville has a clear sense of where the interpretive emphasis of Pip's experience should fall is revealed in the locally ambivalent diction of the chapter in question. We are told Pip sees "wonderous" sights, and we are told he sees "eternities," but in the very same sentence these eternities are declaimed as "heartless." Melville's insistence on Pip's isolation from, rather than on his transcendence of, the human condition he survives is revealed in the following chapter, "A Squeeze of the Hand," which works itself into a passion in a hopeless effort to salve the terror previously scripted. And lest we have any doubt that terror comes from transcendence, that isolation overwhelms wonder, we are diligently reminded by the pathetic recurrence of Pip's own emphasis on a solitude so terrible it is actually self-annihilating. Thus, in "The Cabin," in a passage to which I have already alluded, Pip solicits Ahab's presence as that completion without which he cannot be, and this plea comes chapters after Melville's half-brave, half-bitter attempt to describe isolation as compensated for by sights that are "wonderous."

Although Pip is unaccommodated, a mere nuance in the midst of a heartless immensity, his response is not to become heartless himself, but rather to mourn his fate, the fate of all men for whom mortal greatness, and trivial life itself, is but disease. Grief is a capitulation to the ruthlessness of the world, that which accedes, however unhappily, to its power ("'Oh, the gold!'" Pip says, voicing sorrow at the gratuitousness of the sacrifice, "'the precious, precious gold!'" [99:556–57]), a lament where a curse might be. In fact, grief is the one feeling we do not see Ahab experience—do not except once, when, in "The Symphony," Ahab says to Starbuck, "'Oh, Starbuck! is it not hard, that with this weary load I bear, one poor leg should have been snatched from under me? . . . I feel deadly faint . . . as though I were Adam, staggering beneath the piled centuries since Paradise'" (132:684). Ahab remembers his wife. He remembers the world he has abandoned, and for the first time he states the reason for the abandonment in terms that we can pity: "'Is it not hard.'" This is the source of his grief, and because it is stated as grief—the cry of a man intolerably chastened by the indifference of the world—it loses the quality of obsession and shrinks to the size of the human world of compassion which could minister to it. For, as has been frequently observed, the moment Ahab feels grief as human, he also feels consolation as sufficient: "'[S]tand close to me, Starbuck; let me look into a human eye; it is better than to gaze into sea or sky; better than to gaze upon God. By the green land; by the bright hearth-stone! this is the magic glass, man; I see my wife and my child in thine eye'" (132:684). In this image the self looks outward without violating what it sees, and what it sees is multiple. The reflection in Starbuck's eyes recalls Ahab's wife and child as if, gentled by grief, doubleness and multiplicity imply the world's beneficence and not any longer its blasphemy. No longer conceived as deception, then, doubleness is complement or supplement. But the very grief that opens the world to conflicting interpretations proves in the end too confusing. It deflects understanding, where understanding is imagined as single.

Hence, grief must be repressed, stamped out, cast down. My verbs are not arbitrary, but are in fact suggested by that confrontation between Pip and Ahab, in which it becomes clear that Pip is the grief that completes Ahab's rage, makes of it a wholeness rather than a partiality. It is precisely this grief, rather than Pip's ability to predict ruin, that Ahab will find intolerable. I should like to speculate that, as the scene in "The Cabin" suggests, Pip is that part of Ahab which is driven out of the latter's mind, and, if my idea is correct, then the phrase "Pip is driven out of his mind" (Stubb calls Pip an "unearthly idiot face"; Ahab calls him "crazy") takes on the urging of a pun. Melville invokes not this phrase, but rather the following sentence: "The sea had jeeringly kept his finite body up, but drowned the infinite of his soul" (93:530). In the case of Melville's sentence, or of my colloquial equivalent, what matters is the separation of body and soul, of mind and the body that houses it. In fact, Ahab, contemplating his relationship to Pip, draws on a metaphor of incorporation: " 'True art thou, lad, as the circumference to its centre' " (129:673). And in 'The Log and Line": " 'Thou touchest my inmost centre, boy; thou art tied to me by cords woven of my heart-strings' " (125:659). In this light, Pip's "strange mummeries" (113:622) are akin to the workings of an unconscious mind, a capitulation, at another level entirely, to the heartless devastations of the world. Indeed, as we recall, in trying to induce Pip to remain "screwed" to the chair, Ahab is invoking Pip's metaphor for the doubloon (" 'this doubloon here . . . they are all on fire to unscrew it' " [99:556]), and that he should be privy to Pip's language when the latter speaks in soliloquy is not surprising, given how thoroughly Melville means us to see these characters as halves of the same consciousness. Thus, Ahab knows Pip's words because he knows Pip's thoughts, and it is just these thoughts that he is at such pains to drive out of his mind.

Unlike Starbuck, with whom Ahab has moments of sympathetic union, Pip is everything Ahab is not, and, most intolerably, at least to Ahab, he is a reminder of the latter's incompleteness. In externalizing that half of the mind and that half of the body which Ahab has lost, externalizing and embodying it in the disparate character Pip, Melville complicates his initial insistence that we are severed from each other in a fracture impossible to heal. What replaces the desired fusion of bodies which would make interpretation unnecessary is their imperfect complementarity both within and outside the self—grief and rage united within Ahab, grief and rage able to face each other outside, to tolerate the fact that feelings have separate sources in one person not identical with another. In the latter case, selves could complete each other in the glue of an analogic bond. But accepting the analogy means accepting the substitution of analogy for the desired real thing, and this means acknowledging as incurable—and the metaphor of illness as inaccurate—our severance from each other, for which that severed leg so ostentatiously stands. But Ahab focuses on the lost leg as on an idea he will not relinquish, although he will not hear of any substitution that could stand in place of the imagined completion. For the worst crime that could be committed against him—by the world or by Pip—would not be, as it might initially have seemed, to multilate him, but rather to inauthenticate him, to make him take into his person something not his. Hence his rejection of Pip's body. In fact, rage at the lost leg, so unremittingly dwelt on, throws out of focus for critics, as well as for the novel's characters, the simple meaning of the incompletion for which it stands. The body is an incompletion, and it desires a wholeness it does not have. As I have suggested, the substitution for this wholeness would come in the form of analogy or relationship, in an acknowledged connection with other selves. In the generosity of Melville's image ("'do ye but use poor me for your one lost leg . . . I ask no more, so I remain a part of ye'") we see the lengths to which compensation can go. The other completion to which I have alluded might happen within the self in the reconciliation of disparate emotions that will nonetheless not reduce to the same thing. Instead, grief is purged from the body, is that feeling rage will not have in its midst, because it threatens the uniformity of conception it would both invade and divide. Thus, the command to Pip to stay down below involves the repudiation of a particular relationship and of the fact of relationship itself, the refusal to allow grief and rage to face each other when they will not reduce to an identity.

Ahab flees from the generosity of the offer, and Pip's subsequent cry indicates how thoroughly Ahab has pushed Pip away, wrenching himself free, this time for good: "'Hist! above there, I hear ivory—Oh, master! master! I am indeed down-hearted when you walk over me!'" (129:673). Pip had wanted Ahab to walk "on" him, to give Ahab a cushion for the hardness of the world. Instead, or, as I have suggested, as a consequence, Ahab has banished him. In the transformation of one preposition into another, of "on" into "over," and in the pun with which Pip voices his grief ("'I am indeed down-hearted when you walk over me'"), we see that the part of Ahab momentarily risen to conscious acknowledgment is relegated to an inaccessible depth. Ahab will push his heart down, will have no heart, just like his mechanical man. As the chapter comes full circle, leaving Pip sunk in the hold and predicting disaster (the oysters who will come to join him), having moved from its hint at reconciliation to despair at its impossibility, we see, as has been so frequently acknowledged,[9] that this circular pattern of contradiction is the narrative thrust of the entire novel. But circularity as a way of dealing with contradiction is a psychological as well as narrative strategy, and it is to this subject that I shall momentarily turn.

I want first, however, to comment briefly on the line from *The Tempest* that I have appropriated for this section's title: "Those are pearls that were his eyes" (I.ii.399); second, to comment on my earlier assertion that the

[29]

doubloon is a symbol that confuses the issue of the projection of vision, the ceding of vision, the ceding of self for which vision becomes synecdochic; and third, to comment on Melville's ambivalence about the kinds of fusions (between one character and a part of his own body, between one character and another, between a character and the outside world) imagined possible. These three ideas, which thus far in my discussion have surfaced in unexplained proximity, are in fact directly related.

It is in obvious recollection of the sight imagery in *King Lear* (that is, to make our recollection of it inevitable and therefore obvious) that in *Moby-Dick* the meaning of vision, of characters looking at each other or outward at the world, figures both imitatively and, I shall suggest, in a revisionary way.[10] Prefacing the story of Pip's jump from the whale boat, there is a sustained allegorical passage in "The Castaway" that talks of the "panic-striking business" in which Pip loses his mind. Before the incident is rendered, we are given an image that emblematizes the scene that Melville will then present dramatically. We are told the fall "had most sadly blurred [Pip's] brightness," by turning it into "blaze." And we are told of the event in ornate, even oracular style, as if its impersonality only randomly included Pip:

> But Pip loved life, and all life's peaceable securities; so that the panic-striking business in which he had somehow unaccountably become entrapped, had most sadly blurred his brightness; though, as ere long will be seen, what was thus temporarily subdued in him, in the end was destined to be luridly illumined by strange wild fires, that fictitiously showed him off to ten times the natural lustre with which in his native Tolland County in Connecticut, he had once enlivened many a fiddler's frolic on the green; and at melodious even-tide, with his gay ha-ha! had turned the round horizon into one star-belled tambourine. So, though in the clear air of day, suspended against a blue-veined neck, the pure-watered diamond drop will healthful glow; yet, when the cunning jeweller would show you the diamond in its most impressive lustre, he lays it against a gloomy ground, and then lights it up, not by the sun, but by some unnatural gases. Then come out those fiery effulgences, infernally superb; then the evil-blazing diamond, once the divinest symbol of the crystal skies, looks like some crown-jewel stolen from the King of Hell. But let us to the story. (93:526–27)

What at first glance is odd about this passage is the way in which it wants to offer us an emblem for an event before it narrates the event itself, wants to *obstruct* event with emblem, although this reversal of order, this insistence on meaning prior to meaning's having an object, is, for Melville, an unusual narrative occurrence. It is an occurrence that therefore asks us to pay special attention to the way in which it reveals its own meaning—emblem both prefacing event and ultimately swallowing it up.

What is additionally odd, and the phenomenon on which I wish to focus, is the way in which the entire passage refuses to make an explicit connection between Pip's eyes and his being, and, at the same time (because of that initial verb, which speaks of the event as having "blurred [Pip's] brightness," and because in the rest of the novel Pip exists only as a seer), the way in which the passage suggests that being is synecdochic for eyes. This way of expressing it, making the "I" stand for the "eye," where *eyes* would be the whole, where part would subsume its context (like emblem subsuming event), is reiterated in Ahab's desperate query about whether his eyes will survive his being (whether eyes will *become* his being?) when he lies at the bottom of the sea: "'Will I have eyes at the bottom of the sea, supposing I descend those endless stairs?'" (135:712). Pip's eyes turn to pearls, or to something similarly hard, to diamonds or coral perhaps (we are told that he sees "coral insects, that out of the firmament of waters heaved the colossal orbs" [95:530]). Whether or not Melville had that line from *The Tempest* ("Those are pearls that were his eyes") in mind is unclear, although much more than *King Lear*, *Moby-Dick*, like *The Tempest*, is a text about reconciliation to the human community, in this case, to the *idea* of a human community, since it has in point of fact been annihilated. That Melville had this particular Shakespearean line in mind may seem dubious until it is recalled that both Ahab and Pip worry the transformation of self into eyes, and, in Pip's case, bring surrealistically together the idea of world and eyes, for which those words "colossal orbs" do double duty.

It is through Pip's eyes that we see the solipsism of the others. It is also through his eyes that we see the direct equation of being and seeing, as if in the grammatical litany ("'I look, you look, he looks; we look,'" etc.) "look" were something into which being is translated—as if it were appositional to the pronouns—or through which it directly manifests itself. Ahab would have no eyes except to look inward (or so he tells the carpenter) in spite of the fact that, in a passage to which I shall momentarily turn, he cannot help but look outward, and in looking outward feel annihilated. In the prominence of the novel's concern with eyes (of the characters' desire to have eyes become equivalent to being, eyes that do away with body and world alike by calling attention to the corporeal organ that makes the connection between them—where connection just might mean identity) we see that *Moby-Dick* revises rather than reiterates *King Lear's* understanding of the meaning of vision. Although I shall have more to say on this subject, I would like to comment in passing that *King Lear* provides much

[31]

of *Moby-Dick*'s power—the latter text embracing Shakespeare's idea of tragedy while transforming its terms, turning the fairy tale of the love test into a Biblical test of rage, the location of Britain with its oddly unspecified geography into a less demarcated sea, and swelling the mad scenes on the heath into the proportion of novel size. Of course, the novel has many sources, a cacophony of half-familiar voices, orchestrated from many texts but weirdly brought together here as if subjugating their plurality by feigned issuance from a single source. This compositional mode in which the novel speaks, as it were, in tongues—but tongues made comprehensible by a translation willfully unfaithful to the original—is consonant with the practice I have observed elsewhere, the insistent incorporation of many into one. Throughout the operatic extravaganza, however, the voice of *King Lear* is dominant, albeit the power of its appearance lies in the transmutation, in what Melville makes of what he reads, in how *King Lear* enters his mind and is turned out differently embodied. Thus, while *King Lear* considers others as monsters (his daughters, humanity itself), *Moby-Dick* talks of actual monsters (whales), literalizes the idea of monstrosity, exploring character as an otherness.

But Melville's revisions of Shakespeare's text are not created in a single design. In *King Lear*, characters will not see, where to see would be salvation, would put an end to the idea of converting an other into the self by revealing the former as he is. *Moby-Dick* reverses this hope, shows seeing either as falsification, as a foisting of the self's configuration onto the world, or as a disfigurement of the world when it is taken in through the eyes. In *Lear* the fool teaches the king. He is that complementarity or other who, in lieu of Cordelia, Lear will have by his side, as Pip is that human other Ahab will have in his midst. But whereas the fool's alliances are with Cordelia, representative as he is of someone truly external, Pip is not a discrete character; he is part of Ahab's mind. Pip is not only part of Ahab's mind, but the part that has been cast out of it. Thus, his very existence as a character throws into question the connection between relation and identity, or, put another way, between body and mind. *King Lear* is a family tragedy that dramatizes the terror of natural relationship. *Moby-Dick* allegorizes the idea of family, enlarges it to embrace the Pequod's crew, and draws that fact to our attention by Pip's discourse on the navel. In *King Lear*, love, violated and abused, may provoke madness, but it also has the power to cure it. *Moby-Dick* is a tragedy not of the relations between persons, but rather of persons who keep themselves from relationship because relationship is not equivalence. By "equivalence" I do not mean to imply equal value, but rather am invoking the logical or algebraic sense of the word in which two disparate identities cannot be the same. As

[32]

Wittgenstein says in the *Tractatus:* "To say of *two* things that they are identical is nonsense" (5.5303).[11] Indeed, it is around just this issue of equivalence that the two texts posit the image of sight, and simultaneously part company with respect to their understanding of it.

In *King Lear*, characters refuse to see, would repudiate their eyes, for what they would see, were they to look, would be their separation from other characters. In *Moby-Dick*, characters would have eyes be all, would turn self into eyes, as if, if eyes were all, the world might be internalized— taken in through the eyes—or the self externalized, as it is in the reciprocity of those crossed images in "The Doubloon." Thus, my earlier reading of Ahab's imperative to his men in "The Quarter-Deck" to " 'Skin your eyes for him' " (36:218) depends upon an emphasis on the line's ostentatious physicality—on the conversion of being first into Ahab's vision and second into Ahab's self—and this is insisted upon by the corporeality of Melville's description of bodily transformation: of the men into Ahab, of Ahab into the men. In "The Quarter-Deck" we are told that Ahab would contain his men in "the Leyden jar of his own magnetic life" (36:224). Reiterating this corporeality in a converse image, we are reminded that in the passing of the chalice Ahab's "spirits were simultaneously quaffed down with a hiss" (36:225). Ahab would fill his men with spirit to the "brimming," would fill his men with spirit until it " 'forks out at the . . . eye.' " That we are meant to read "spirit" as Ahab's non-corporeal essence (as well as the actual grog the men drink) is reinforced by language that makes emphatically if unidiomatically bodily the idea that spirit will " 'spiralize in ye' " and, reaching the finite top, will " 'fork out at the serpent-snapping eye.' " Perhaps the most brazen idea of bodily revision interrupts the chapter "The Quarter-Deck." " 'Take off thine eye!' " (36:221), Ahab mutters to Starbuck, meaning, at the level of colloquialism, "remove your eyes from my person." At another level, however, Ahab seems to be suggesting that eyes are a piece of clothing, an accommodation of which man could be undressed. Could dismemberment be disrobement, could Ahab remove another's eye—could he skin the crew of its eyes—they might put on his own.

The multiple instances of characters talking about their eyes, about eyes as equivalent to existence itself, culminate in "The Candles," where in half-hysterical equation of being with vision and in Hamlet-like distress, Ahab asks: " 'Open eyes; see, or not?' " The question that equates vision and being (and that is uttered as Ahab looks outward at lightning that is besieging the ship) does so in reversal of an earlier image—earlier by a few sentences—in which vision is regarded as catastrophic, that is, as being's annihilation: " 'Take the homage of these poor eyes, and shutter-hands. I would not take it. The lightning flashes through my skull; mine eye-balls ache and ache; my whole beaten brain seems as beheaded, and rolling on some stunning ground'" (119:642).

What I would like to focus on is the way in which Ahab conceives of looking outward at the world as a mutilation of himself. That the world can come in at the eyes or the self be cast out at the eyes, and that such images are ways of externalizing the self or internalizing the world, is perhaps obvious. But the notion is important and is in fact revisionary—not only of the meaning of the sight imagery of *King Lear* but also of Melville's earlier insistence that self and world, Pip and Ahab, could be joined as complementarities, but *only* as complementarities. It is important because it seems to negate that earlier insistence and to hope, as Ahab hopes, that such separation is not necessary, that it may not even be possible. For seeing creates the fusion between self and world, and seemingly makes it inevitable. In fact, in Ahab's thought about death's reducing men to mere eyes (this is how I understand Ahab's question about eyes at the bottom of the sea, since this is the only part of the body in which he expresses any proleptic interest), Melville hints that after death one could take the world in—become the transparent eyeball as the self loses its body—through transcendence rather than through decay, or that the self could assume the world's body, again through transcendence rather than decay. In the context of these reflections, Ahab's wild notion about being beheaded as a consequence of looking at the world would be the first step toward such a disembodiment. "'I burn with thee; would fain be welded with thee'" (119:643), Ahab says a moment later. He is perhaps contemplating disembodiment, although the fervor of the assertion suggests he has forgotten what a moment earlier he feared—that the disembodiment of the self as a consequence of its fusion with the world is equivalent to the self's dismemberment, that is, to its annihilation.

Thus, to look at the world is to be drawn out of one's body, not to have a body, or, as in the case of Ahab's image of the head, to have the body come apart. For Melville, as for Ahab, it is unclear whether this state is to be longed for or abhorred. One way to reconcile the apparent contradiction introduced by "'see, or not,'" between seeing as equivalent to being and seeing as being's annihilation, would be to conceive of the self as able to be in lieu of its palpable body. Perhaps this is what Ahab is contemplating when he intones, in "The Candles," "'I burn with thee.'" But this momentary rapprochement notwithstanding, one thing is clear: seeing and being are in the previous images equated. *Projection* is too casual a word for an appropriation that converts the world into the self (takes it into the body) or the self into the world (diffuses it through the world's body by taking that self apart).

In the metaphysics of this context, Pip's lexical conversion of doubloon to navel would draw an explicit connection between looking at the world and fusing with it. The self would be what it sees—would make the world not simply into its own image, but in fact into itself. For, as I have suggested, sight in this novel has meanings antithetical to those in *King Lear*, as if Melville were taking Shakespeare's meanings, terrible in their own right, and making a dark comment upon them, suggesting that under the influence of what was later to be called Romanticism, vision is no longer conceived as pure, and therefore can no longer be conceived as redemptive. Hence, characters in the novel do not avoid sight, but rather solicit it, as if eyes provided the opening that would sabotage distinction, through which the self could leave its body or could become commensurate with the world's body. Given what human eyes do, then, the idea of eyes turned to diamonds or stones able to reflect the world—to *reflect* rather than take it in (and here reflection would work both ways, mirroring feelings from within and events from without)—is redemptive even as an image, though it must be added here that it is precisely at this diamond hardness, at the perceived hardness of limits, which forbids the world's entry to the self or the self's access to the world, that Pip loses his mind. These two images of vision, of eyes hardened to diamond brilliance (to brilliance and to grief) and of eyes appropriating the world (taking it into the body or being disembodied by it) are, in fact, disparate emblems of being. In the array of their antithetical implications, Melville, with no comment, places them side by side.

Moby-Dick; Or, The Whale

The traditional way in which the novel's oppositions have been interpreted might be expressed in the following formulation: if we understood contradictions properly, we would also be able to reconcile them, to conceive of them simultaneously as a poise or a balance, a reciprocal suspension of all one-sidedness.[12] Such a sanguine interpretation takes account of lucky moments like the one in which Ishmael is able to imagine—without faulting as contradictory—the idea of "resting at last in manhood's pondering repose of If" (114:624). It does not, however, take account of the brutality with which oppositions in the novel customarily fail to recognize each other or, if they do, acknowledge each other for the purpose of doing violence to each other. In this connection Philip Rahv is instructive when he insists that a Melville rescued from his contradictions (that is, from our construing them as problematic) is "canonised."[13] Leslie Fiedler similarly warns: "Multiple ambiguities undercut the simple polarity" between good and evil, Ishmael and Ahab, contradictions and their reconciliation "which the book superficially suggests."[14] It is the complications of this undercutting to which I shall turn.

I have suggested that the novel's ability to bring contradictions into relationship by depicting them circularly is not simply a rhetorical strategy but an epistemological one as well. Narrative enacts circularity as a way of teasing itself into a consideration of otherness which, if faced with outright, it would repudiate. This fact is important, for it suggests that the reason Ahab shrinks from acknowledging contradiction within or outside himself is that he is assaulted by its extreme poles (rage or grief, power or love, evil or innocence), between which traffic is, by definition, unthinkable. The chapter "Brit" shows us how it is done, offering a lesson not only in rhetoric but also in psychology. It begins by suggesting a tentative relationship between the ferocity of the sea and the quiescence of the land, then shies away from the connection only to find its retreat stopped by a collision of the two worlds it was doing its best to keep apart.

The chapter's structure may be discerned in the sequence of its images. It is inaugurated by a first sentence that points to the pervasive cannibalism of the whales—or rather of the sea as a single organic economy— as they feed on meadows of brit (the spawn of herrings and other young fish):

> As morning mowers, who side by side slowly and seethingly advance their scythes through the long wet grass of marshy meads; even so these monsters swam, making a strange, grassy, cutting sound; and leaving behind them endless swaths of blue upon the yellow sea. (58:361)

Immediately, as if to soften the implications of the analogy to human mowing, Melville cushions it with a footnote that insists that the statement is "true" rather than metaphorically descriptive: "part of the sea . . . bear[s] that name ['Brazil Banks'] . . . because of this remarkable meadow-like appearance, caused by the vast drifts of brit continually floating in those latitudes, where the Right Whale is often chased." Then as if in deliberate shift away from the question of how the image is to be taken—away, that is, from the relationships between the movements of whales and the movements of men—the narrative voice obscures the question, suggesting that the whales look more like "lifeless masses of rock than anything else." Arguing the incomparability of whales with any other form of life, Ishmael maintains that it is difficult to believe these "bulky masses" can be "instinct, in all parts, with the same sort of life that lives in a dog or a horse" (58:362). To anticipate a bit, the argument of the whole chapter, once it has retreated from the danger of the initial comparison, is as follows: you cannot make the analogy between the whale and other forms of life. But this logic gives way to the confession that you cannot make it easily, since once it is made, its implications are irretrievable. The argument persists in the assertion that because the sea will murder and kill, it is an otherness so transcendently terrible as to belie comparison with man.

In the assurance of that denial, the narrative voice grows bold, addressing outright the cannibalism on which the preceding paragraphs have touched. For now the sea itself seems monstrosity personified; and the personified sea—here terrific as a whale—is an image of self-engorgement: "not only is the sea such a foe to man who is an alien to it, but it is also a fiend to his own offspring; worse than the Persian host who murdered his own guests. . . . Panting and snorting like a mad battle steed that has lost its rider, the masterless ocean overruns the globe" (58:363). The horse with whom, a page earlier, the sea's comparison was denied is invoked with no acknowledgment of the attending contradiction. We could say that the narrative voice is at liberty to investigate ferocity precisely because it has freed itself from the fear of analogic reprisal. But the very freedom that sanctions knowledge of horror pushes the narrator to the premonition that his knowledge is a consequence of inherent familiarity with its object, that the sea is, in fact, a mirror for the ferocity inside. Thus, "Brit," like so many other chapters in the novel, contains a readjusted understanding of the relation between interior and exterior. It is almost as if Melville were arguing that since the self is incomplete, it must find analogues in the world, analogues rather than identities. Not to do so is to become Ahab, a man victimized by his idea that completion could exist in the totality of his own person.

"Brit" consequently shows us a mind revising its concept of the relation between interior and exterior, shows us that if one shrinks in revulsion from all that is antithetical to life, it is because the object of revulsion lies not without but rather within the self:

[37]

> Consider, once more, the universal cannibalism of the sea; all whose creatures prey upon each other, carrying on eternal war since the world began.
>
> Consider all this; and then turn to this green, gentle, and most docile earth; consider them both, the sea and the land; and do you not find a strange analogy to something in yourself? (58:364)

The acknowledgment of the connection between man's brutality and the sea monster's is neither intellectual nor aesthetic, as the image of the mowers threatened to make it. Fleeing from any precipitous recognition that would do its work on us in judgment and therefore superficially, we bump into it from the other side, and learn by the thoroughness with which we experience horror that in fact it is our own and at ourselves. The ability to escape an easy reductionism, and to work away from a point of intolerable comparison by following it around to the other side, is a crucial strategy adopted by the novel as a cure for the violence of extremes that cannot come into unmediated contact. Against the strain of the initial analogy of mowers as whales and mowers as men, presented and then revoked, the chapter offers a demonstration of how to draw oppositions into relationship. For if, with respect to Pip and Ahab, Melville had chastised the latter for wishing an impossible connection, he here chastises the reader for imagining the antithesis to that impossibility to be no connection at all. Relationship—whether between persons or between persons and offending world—will be felt. Relationship will *be*, whether or not it is felt. What is brutal about the chapter "Brit" is not so much its violent imagery or the violence of the subject on which Melville discourses as it is the violence with which it brings that philosophical point home.

Interestingly enough, the chapter concludes by hedging the insight at which it has so arduously arrived. Its last sentence once again takes up the illusory stance that the worlds of horror and peace can be kept separate:

> For as this appalling ocean surrounds the verdant land, so in the soul of man there lies one insular Tahiti, full of peace and joy, but encompassed by all the horrors of the half known life. God keep thee! Push not off from that isle, thou canst never return! (58:364)

I shall have more to say about the seeming regression to an earlier point of view, but let me speculate for the moment that this way of stating the problem as if it were one of concentricity underlines the mind's desire for the separation of good and evil, which it now knows it may not have.

Between "Brit" and "The Grand Armada," fear of interiority changes to a yearning for it. In "The Grand Armada," we are told the Pequod is "hemmed" in by a "living wall" of whales (87:496). The whales' proximity, even the enclosure of the ship, is surprisingly not felt as a constriction. Distracted from the question of aggression or its source, Ishmael turns to the nearby whale cubs not simply "domesticated" but "nursing . . . as human infants" (87:497). "Though surrounded by circle upon circle of consternations and affrights . . . these inscrutable creatures at the centre freely and fearlessly [did] indulge in all peaceful concernments" (87:498–99). The double image—of the whales encircling the Pequod and of the Pequod encircling the whales, of peace at one's center (with center defined as inside the self, the "insular Tahiti" of "Brit") or with peace at one's center (with center defined as outside the self, in the image of nursing whales with whom Ishmael identifies by analogy "amid the torpedoed Atlantic of my being" in "The Grand Armada"—reproduces between chapters the two pictures played out within the single chapter, "Brit," reiterating itself thus:

> The lake, as I have hinted, was to considerable depth exceedingly transparent; and as human infants while suckling will calmly and fixedly gaze away from the breast, as if leading two different lives at the time; and while yet drawing mortal nourishment, be still spiritually feasting upon some unearthly reminiscence;—even so did the young of these whales seem looking up towards us, but not at us, as if we were but a bit of Gulf-weed. (87:497)

Looking upon the men not as brit but as gulf weed, not as food but as transparency, as object of meditative stupor, the difference between men and whales momentarily dissolves. For in the musing of the whales, as in the musing from the masthead, men and whales do not remain within; they rather straddle their respectively circumscribed worlds.

How differently Ahab deals with contradictions may be seen in "The Symphony." The chapter begins by evoking the tranquillity of the world as feminine, just as its counterparts of fire, power, and destruction, have been invoked as masculine. In a naturalization of forces worthy of Wallace Stevens, Ahab suddenly sees his desired parents flung down to the earth from the realm of the invisible gods, where in "The Candles" he had hopelessly addressed them. The humanizing of powerful agents, the ability to conceive of them as both human *and* absent, momentarily at least, drives hatred from his heart. Appropriately, and prompted perhaps by a knowledge of Pip's self-chastisement in the cabin once Ahab has abandoned *him* ("'have ye seen one Pip? . . . hang-dog look, and cowardly! . . . Shame upon all cowards'"), Ahab experiences grief from his culpability, feels the inadequacy of being human, rather than its outrage. So he weeps, the lone tear of a man grief has not quite abandoned. But when Starbuck suggests they turn back, Ahab remembers his revenge and, more to the point, disclaims it as his own: "'What is it, what nameless, inscrutable, unearthly thing is it . . . making me ready to do what in my own proper, natural heart, I durst not so much as dare? Is Ahab, Ahab? Is it I, God, or who, that lifts this arm?'" (132:685).

Like the order to Pip to remain screwed to the cabin chair, putting literal space between himself and the otherness that would contradict it, the driving of remorse out of the mind by the fury that he first attributes to God and then sees as rebounding to invade his own actions is prompted by his inability to allow opposite states to exist together. Yet knowledge of his culpability lingers. We hear it, in the following passage, in his explicit question about the fate of murderers. And, in that same passage, we hear it in the shifts of subject, as if changing the subject could transform or dismiss it:

> "Where do murderers go, man! Who's to doom, when the judge himself is dragged to the bar? But it is a mild, mild wind, and a mild looking sky; and the air smells now, as if it blew from a faraway meadow; they have been making hay somewhere under the slopes of the Andes, Starbuck, and the mowers are sleeping among the new-mown hay. Sleeping? Aye, toil we how we may, we all sleep at last on the field. Sleep? Aye, and rust amid greenness; as last year's scythes flung down, and left in the half-cut swaths—Starbuck!" (132:685–86)

The image of the meadows and the mowers, encountered first in "Brit," is equally surrealistic when seen in the context of Ahab's longing for peace. In "Brit," the mowers were monstrous. Here they seem drugged, themselves cut down and wasted. Perhaps it is simply that they are asleep, and the idea of quiet, prompted at first by the mildness of the day, leads to a premonition of death. Each time Ahab returns to the stasis of his initial picture, picking up and turning over that word *sleeping*, as though in its reiteration he might penetrate the travesty of man's power, it is clear that thought would beg meaning from the silence of the image, would prod it to interpretation. But while sleep suggests death, suggestion will yield no further picture or knowledge; it therefore comes to rest in the limits of analogic provocation. As Ahab muses on the world that ripens into consequence, on the green world of death, it is clear that death is the ultimate contradiction, the final offending incompletion. He desires rescue from the vision, a cure to mortal conclusion, and his appeal to Starbuck, however implicitly articulated, might be regarded as the gesture of a man who still imagines human salvation from the consequence of mortality. In the space where an answer would be, Ahab reinvigorates the chase. He will cancel the pastoral vision, turn rot into rust, flesh into machine, into mere steel that, flung to the ground, betrays no human cry of pain. He stiffens

[40]

himself so he cannot be made stiff, and in the mechanization of that last image, of "'rust amid greenness,'" we see his cherishing of the idea that death will age without canceling, discolor without destroying, that the self can still be—notwithstanding Starbuck's silence at the hopelessness of this idea—can retain its mortal body, altered but not perished, and in the conservation of its essence, sacrifice nothing at all.

"'None does offend, none, I say none! I'll able 'em,'" Lear maintains, rushing off to kill. "Brit" and "The Symphony" provide the images whose unacknowledged relationship generates tragedy. Mowers and mown, killers and killed, driven apart by more than three hundred pages as the two chapters are that depict these antithetical images, are never allowed to come into direct relationship. Neither are Pip and Ahab, once Ahab has banished him to the cabin. The question of such relationships, of rage and grief, killers and killed, of why relationships are not identities, is, as I suggested earlier, the subject of *Moby-Dick*. Thus, when Ahab is unable to repress his ambivalence (when his feelings of grief are at war with his desire for revenge), he projects grief from his mind, allocating it to Pip, as he projects rage from his mind, attributing it to God. What is left once the self has been purged of its impulses is, of course, nothing—the whiteness of which Ishmael speaks with reference to the whale's mysteries, or the vacancy directly attributed to Ahab (44:272). But while "nothing" would seem to be the absence of identity, for Ahab it comes (falsely) to constitute identity, for "nothing" is the one state in which differences are not perceived. In the context of these resignations, we see that questions about identity are not simply problematic for the novel's characters, as I have been maintaining, but that they are also problematic for Melville, as he too seems to imagine his characters as part-people, people who only as complementarities comprise wholes.

The questions may be reiterated thus:

1. Why am I not identical to the world—that is, why must I be in a position to (have to) understand the world from which I differ?
2. Why am I not identical to myself—that is, made of a single substance, purged of ambivalence and contrary desires, as Ahab tries to purge himself of Pip, or of that aspect of himself which is drawn toward Starbuck rather than Fedallah (the man birthed in Ahab's dreams and seen by the eyes of the Pequod's crew), or as the Pequod's men purge themselves of female sexuality?

For while, from Ahab's perspective, Pip is that part of Ahab which must be repudiated, from Melville's perspective—housing grief in a separate body, as elsewhere he has housed audacity in the separate body of Bulk-ington—such quarantines of disparate feelings to the confines of isolate bodies seem suspiciously to partake of the desperation felt by the characters, as if something about contradictions made them intolerable to conceive within a single body.

Psychologists, notably those of the Kleinean school, have written much of part-objects, and they define these part-objects as what an infant sees when he is still so attached to the mother that he experiences her totality as defined by the breast rather than by her whole person. The consequence of the infant's distortion leads first to the delusive belief that the part *is* the person, is the totality for which it stands, and second, as a consequence, to the infant's attempt to try to incorporate the part into his own person, to imbibe and to have it, no longer as a separate thing. Leaving entirely aside the question of whether such a psychological description corresponds to an actual phenomenon, I would like to suggest it is an accurate metaphor for Melville's conception of his characters' relations to the world. The characters, like ourselves, cannot see the whole world. They and we are a crew birthed from its navel and somehow related to it in an unfigurable connection that ceases to be problematic when the incomprehensible otherness that can neither be seen nor understood is absorbed into the self.

In "A Squeeze of the Hand," the desire for such absorption is given voice and a picture, as fusion is made possible by a mystical sexuality: "Come . . . let us all squeeze ourselves into each other; let us squeeze ourselves universally into the very milk and sperm of kindness" (94:533). Indeed, Ahab's quest for the whale might be regarded as a quest for the source of the sexuality yearned for outright in the imperative cited above. The sexuality I have called mystical partakes of sexual apparatus—sperm being both unprocessed whale oil and sexual seed—at least in a synonymic way, but it is not the real thing. The real thing is banished early in the novel. The paltry examples of women in *Moby-Dick*, Biddy and Charity, are introduced to be dismissed. The women are occasions for transferring sexuality to some other, person-transforming, person-eliding realm. In fact, Biddy and Charity are not so much parodies of women as they are phantoms—even more so than Fedallah, for all practical purposes, minus bodies as well as minds—as if Melville wanted to establish early the object of desire elsewhere.

Once the women are banished, to be replaced by the homosexual fellowship (the ensuing marriage between Ishmael and Queequeg),[15] we see that the power of the homosexual relationship lies in the discrepancy between its representation of transport—its life-saving gift—and its

[42]

exemption from the turmoil of ordinary life. Much of what endears Queequeg to us, as to Ishmael, is the way he fulfills an unspeakable fantasy in
which a mystical partner makes the ultimate sacrifice, sullying neither it
nor himself in the world's banalities. In an early dream that would
expound the union Ishmael tells us that a "supernatural hand seemed
placed in mine," attached not to a person but rather to a "nameless,
unimaginable, silent form or phantom" (4:53). Eventually, for Ishmael, the
phantom will be infused into the landscape. For Ahab, it will become
spirit-spout. The transformation amounts to the same thing. Yet Ahab
cannot have the spirit-spout, as Ishmael cannot have the landscape — cannot have possession of spirit-spout or landscape, with that word *possession* designating incorporation into one's person as well as understanding.

" '*My* line! *my* line?' " (134:706), Ahab intones when told of Fedallah's
death (caught as the latter is in the strangle of the whale line), and at this
point in the novel the two characters are so fused as to be practically indistinguishable. But Melville keeps Ahab alive a day longer so that, as has
been prophesied, he can witness his own death in the image of Fedallah's
person:

> Lashed round and round to the fish's back; pinioned in the turns
> upon turns in which, during the past night, the whale had reeled the
> involutions of the lines around him, the half torn body of the
> Parsee was seen; his sable raiment frayed to shreds; his distended
> eyes turned full upon old Ahab. (135:715)

Here the body is half-torn because one half of it remains in Ahab's briefly
attenuated life. Consonant with Melville's linking of Ahab with Fedallah,
when the whale line subsequently snaps to separate the two characters,
Ahab experiences the severance as a mutilation from inside (" 'What breaks
in me?' "), cut as he is from his counterpart and from the desired whale
itself. Clinching our understanding of the meaning of Ahab's death, at the
conclusion of the death (at death's claiming the other half of the body)
Ahab addresses the whale: " 'chasing thee, though tied to thee. . . . *Thus*, I
give up the spear!' " (135:721). The explanatory "thus" does not tell simply
how the death occurs, it tells why the death occurs, tells that death reunites
Ahab with the Fedallah momentarily split off from him, and unites
him — ties him securely for the first time — to the whale whose possession
has goaded the action of the entire chase.

Ahab dies strapped to the back of the whale with which he desires to
become one — dies *in* and *of* the fusion he self-confessedly desires.[16] While
Melville punishes Ahab for the fusion, he nonetheless allows him it. The

"allowance" I am discussing is apparent in more than the novel's ending. It is obvious in the many ways in which descriptions of Ahab and the whale are metaphorically proximate, and it is apparent in the novel's title, which lexically demarks the sort of possession or embodiment hoped for by the central characters. In the context of the novel's issues, the title does not simply serve as frontispiece for the story of Moby-Dick. It rather insists that the thing itself has been captured in and as narrative. Melville spells it out twice: *Moby-Dick; Or, The Whale*, suggesting that the novel's mythic title has got possession of the thing about which it is trying to tell—has got it inside its body, has got it *as* its body. In context of the attendant issues, this is not a neutral fact. For that equational "or" resonates against the novel's other attempts to equate internal and external—whether the desire for equivalence manifests itself with respect to people coming into proximity (Ahab and Pip), or of opposite feelings coming into proximity (grief or rage), or of self and world coming into proximity (Ishmael and the whale, in whose skeletal insides, domesticating the Jonah tale in "A Bower in the Arsacides," Ishmael leisurely wanders). The novelistic convention of giving narrative a double title is complicated, then, by the ways in which *Moby-Dick* appropriates the convention and asks it to be reinterpreted. The reinterpretation would go as follows: it would equate our names for objects with the palpability of those objects, as if designation and object, world and the subjectivity voicing it, really could be the same. It would equate a particular whale, one to which the novel has given a name, with all whales, again canceling distinctions by large generic claims. It would make the stories of the men on the Pequod into a single story, as Ahab in fact succeeds in doing: "They were one man, not thirty" (134:700). It would suggest the object of desire could be contained in a body, and therefore by inference might be possible to possess.

Much of the novel repeats the reflexivity promised by the title. In fact, Ahab's desire to be one with the whale, to reduce his life to its dimensions, is parodied by Ishmael—the ostensible alternative to Ahab,[17] for however diverse their respective temperaments or fates, the characters remain variations on the same theme. To consider the novel as Ishmael's story *or* Ahab's implies a discrete creation of character which Melville's craft refutes at great pains. We could say that it is not that Ishmael avoids the risks taken by Ahab, but rather that he better knows how to ward off their fatal consequences. It will be recalled that Ishmael at watch on the masthead, mesmerized by the sea, is jolted back to his senses in the following recognition: "But while this sleep, this dream is on ye, move your foot or hand an inch; slip your hold at all; and your identity comes back in horror. Over Descartian vortices you hover" (35:214–15). The obvious mean-

[44]

ing of the passage—the way it has conventionally been interpreted—is to conceive of Ishmael's horror as generated by his understanding that he has nearly *lost* his identity. But there would be another, antithetical way to interpret the words: to move your hand or foot is suddenly to become aware of your identity, of the impossibility of ever losing it. Of course, what Ahab and Ishmael want is not to be absorbed into the landscape, but rather, as one would expect, to retain identity, and, as in "The Gilder" Ishmael explicitly says, to absorb the landscape into the self: "Oh, ever vernal endless landscapes in the soul. . . . Would to God these blessed calms would last" (114:623–24). But the purpose of the statement is really to displace a wish. The point of the adjective is that it have something to modify, that it have "landscapes" to modify, and this way of expressing it suggests that modification might fix landscapes, make them integral to the soul. Thus, Ishmael's desire, and the fall in "The Mast-Head" which almost brings it to consequence, is the *antithesis* of Pip's fall into the ocean, with which, in the critical commentary, it is analogously compared.

In light of the desire to internalize the landscape, it is not incidental that at the novel's beginning we are similarly absorbed by a landscape, as, at the Spouter-Inn, we are shown a painting made of "unaccountable . . . shades and shadows":

> But what most puzzled and confounded you was a long, limber, portentous, black mass of something hovering in the centre of the picture over three blue, dim, perpendicular lines floating in a nameless yeast. A boggy, soggy, squitchy picture truly, enough to drive a nervous man distracted. Yet was there a sort of indefinite, half-attained, unimaginable sublimity about it that fairly froze you to it, till you involuntarily took an oath with yourself to find out what that marvellous painting meant. (3:36)

Although there would be a way of reading this description as a parody of the novel's terror (as the word *squitchy* directs us), humor and parody are finally subordinated to that which invites Ishmael to follow the painting's "pull." Adrian Stokes has suggested that art always involves seduction, and that part of a painting's hypnotic effect lies in the way it makes the viewer's eyes all, makes his eyes epitomize all:

> Though they always have the strong quality of coordinated objects on their own, the world's artifacts tend to bring right up to the eyes the suggestion of procedures that reduce the sense of their particularity and difference; even, in part, the difference between you and them, though the state with which a work is manifestly concerned be the coming of the rains, or redemption and damnation, or the long dominance of the dead. . . . The depicting of incident thus

receives a somewhat generalized imprint, offers a relationship that at first glance saps the symbolism of an existence vividly separate from ourselves. As we merge with such an object, some of the sharpness that is present when differentiation of the inner from the outer world is more accentuated, the sharpness and multiplicity from the introjectory-projectory processes, are at first minimized. Yet I shall note, on the other hand, that under the spell of this enveloping pull, the object's otherness, and its representation of otherness, are the more poignantly grasped.[18]

If the picture at the Spouter-Inn momentarily transfixes us, the novel's entire first chapters, culminating in "The Lee Shore," act, as the picture does, first to frame the "inside" of the novel, and subsequently to draw us toward it. Even more so than Father Mapple's sermon, that other preface to the novel's events, the picture at the Spouter-Inn overcomes us by its inexplicability. It is in gazing at the painting that we become subsumed by our incomprehension, become eyes that take in image while being denied understanding of it. This fact is important, for it translates us into a position illusorily equivalent to that of the characters. Such equivalence would express itself not so much through our incomprehension as through the covert equation between vision and incomprehension.

In "The Lee Shore," Melville plays with our incomprehension and further unmoors us, so that we read of Bulkington's fate as if it were our own. It is simply a characteristic of that allegorical figure Bulkington that he stands between the frame-story and the novel, or, to put it differently, that he stands between us and the characters. It is as easy to read his fate as an allegory of our own—at least while the novel does its work on us—as it is to read it as an allegory of those characters who are ostensibly fleshed out:

> But as in landlessness alone resides the highest truth, shoreless, indefinite as God—so, better is it to perish in that howling infinite, than be ingloriously dashed upon the lee, even if that were safety! For worm-like, then, oh! who would craven crawl to land! Terrors of the terrible; is all this agony so vain? Take heart, take heart, O Bulkington. Bear thee grimly, demigod! Up from the spray of thy ocean-perishing—straight up, leaps thy apotheosis! (23:149)

After the initial hundred pages or so, we are fed to the "infinite" of the novel, and it is hence only in the next chapter that Ishmael can speak of being "fairly embarked" (24:150). In the context of these issues, the much-discussed "pasteboard mask" takes on new meaning. If man will strike, strike through the mask, he might disassemble (this is the fantasy) the *visible* wall or frame. The issue here is not primarily one of seeing the hidden substance but rather of taking the visible substance apart (as Ishmael's dissection of the whale illustrates), as if it were an obstruction in whose place the self might be.

How much the world is conceived as a spatial barrier—positing otherness where a self might be—is revealed in the chapter "Ahab and Starbuck in the Cabin," as Starbuck tries to direct the former's attention to the oil casks that are leaking, and Ahab turns the conversation around to his own body, to which he directly alludes as a cask.[19] Ishmael sets the scene for us: "According to usage they were pumping the ship next morning; and lo! no inconsiderable oil came up with the water; the casks below must have sprung a bad leak" (109:602). "'What we come twenty thousand miles to get is worth saving, sir,'" Starbuck reminds Ahab. "'So it is, so it is; if we get it,'" the latter replies. Starbuck, hearing his words in Ahab's subjective "usage," intercepts the captain thus: " 'I was speaking of the oil in the hold, sir.' 'And I was not speaking or thinking of that at all. Begone! Let it leak! I'm all aleak myself'" (109:603). In drawing a direct connection between the leaks in the oil casks (Starbuck's subject) and the leaks in the body (Ahab's subject), we see how thoroughly Ahab equates the dismemberment of the world's objects with the dismemberment of his own body:

> "Aye! leaks in leaks! not only full of leaky casks, but those leaky casks are in a leaky ship; and that's a far worse plight than the Pequod's, man. Yet I don't stop to plug my leak; for who can find it in the deep-loaded hull; or how hope to plug it, even if found, in this life's howling gale?" (109:603–4).

The representation is harrowing in direct relation to its specification of fear in terms of bodily inadequacy—much as Ishmael tried to express it in the image of the house and its unpluggable holes, which he wishes to "lint" up (2:34). Yet although the body has holes, they are inadequately sized. "You cannot put a shelf or chest of drawers in your body," Ishmael laments on the masthead, for "the soul is glued inside of its fleshly tabernacle, and cannot freely move about in it, nor even move out of it, without running great risk of perishing" (35:210). Even if you wished to clothe the soul inside the body (since you cannot clothe the soul outside the body), there is no room between body and soul where protection—here literal clothing—might be. Thus, although the world comes in at the body, amorphously comes in, "a watchcoat" won't fit. *Moby-Dick*, focusing on the body's orifices, on what can go in and out of them, seizes upon these particular facts about the body (that its holes are unpluggable—cannot keep the self in, cannot keep the world out) as if such facts were its generative fault.

[47]

What is terrifying about Ishmael's and Ahab's representations alike is their genesis in those fears we have either learned to socialize or else to repress, and in either case to take out of the amenities of language. Melville gets them back in—these questions about the body—as if he were unafraid of the thoughts in which they are going to have to mire themselves. Because a play like *King Lear* raises questions about identity in a human context, its questions, of necessity, are civilized by that context, are, at their crudest, concerned with the horrors of *adult* sexuality. *Moby-Dick*, in distinction, displaces the subject and foists it onto an ostensible consideration of monsters (much as we saw "Brit" do); hence, it is not bound by human conventions, and can raise, unreprimanded, with an unacknowledged but savage zeal, questions about identity as they articulate themselves primitively in our minds.

We see these questions spatialized in Ahab's cry to Pip, "'Oh God! that man should be a thing for immortal souls to sieve through! Who art thou, boy?'" (125:659). The dizziness of Ahab's question, its sense of lost footing, is a consequence of the fact that the soul is invisible, is hidden by the body of which it is an ostensible part. Perhaps Ahab's dizziness is a consequence of the fact that Ahab, looking at Pip, can no longer tell the difference between inside and outside. Melville, putting Ahab face to face with Pip (that incarnation of Ahab's soul), seems implicitly to suggest that, could one externalize the soul and see it, could one give *it* a body, as Pip does here, one could reify otherness in a discrete object with which one might therefore merge. Indeed, it is because the whale can make otherness *have* a palpable body *outside* of the self, as otherness (here conceived as a soul) cannot have a palpable body *within* the self, that the whale's body becomes for Ahab equivalent to what it also represents. Another way of putting this is to say that Ahab reduces otherness to the size of the whale body, for the whale body, however large, is possible to conceptualize, as the whole world is not, and is therefore possible to possess.

In such a fluid conception of bodies, the self's exterior and its interior are incapable of distinction: who can "stop to . . . find [one's leaks]; or how hope to plug [them], even if found." But while Ahab's image voices its fear at loss of the self's parts—at their leaking into the world—fear obscures the way in which this particular image of exit allows the self a wanted "out." As I have suggested, the corollary to the idea of false embodiment—believing that otherness can be reduced to a single body—is the expulsion from Ahab's body of those feelings he wishes alien to it: grief allocated to Pip, rage to God. For if you cannot become Bulkington, cannot absorb the landscape, then you must postulate a reductive singularity within and without yourself, achieving singularity by doing away with characteristics legitimately—but intolerably—part of the two identities in question. Unable to stand parts of himself he would repudiate as "other," Ahab first projects them outward, lets them leak into the world—in the concreteness of his image conceives of such exorcism as physically possible. These parts, once outside his person, are attributed to another body. Thus, Ahab conceives of them as having a body manifestly different from his own, and then construes that body as evil *because* it is outside of himself, *because* it is not his own. The hope would be to vanquish otherness and the evil with which Ahab now identifies it.[20] Then the alien body could be reappropriated, but purged of its unwanted attributes: made beautiful rather than monstrous, mystical rather than sexual, elemented of a single feeling rather than of ambivalent ones. From the cleanness of such a body, one might actually wish to be born.[21]

What are the relations between interior and exterior, part and whole, representation and thing represented? The novel asks these questions with respect to its readers as it ushers us into the narrative, first fixing our attention in a manner of which we are barely conscious, until, in the chapter on Bulkington, whether by analogue or antithesis, our identities come back to us in horror. It asks these questions with respect to narrative, as the chapter "Brit" demonstrates, where the analogy between man and monster is dismissed even as it is introduced. But when this analogy is brought back, its return insists on the connection between man and monster *and*, more to the point, on a new connection between reader and character. For now characters are insinuated to be mere analogues for the novel's central subject, namely, the reader: "Do you not find a strange analogy to something in yourself?" (58:364). Lest we reject the connection, it is didactically insisted upon, as analogy becomes metaphor, enacting, as well as expressing, the relation between internal and external, and suddenly incorporating us into the body of its text:

> Consider all this; and then turn to this green, gentle, and most docile earth; consider them both, the sea and the land; and do you not find a strange analogy to something in yourself? For as this appalling ocean surrounds the verdant land, so in the soul of man there lies one insular Tahiti, full of peace and joy, but encompassed by all the horrors of the half known life. God keep thee! Push not off from that isle, thou canst never return! (58:364)

Both analogy (that of land and sea) and metaphor (the soul's "insular Tahiti") show the meaning of typology, in its broadest sense, not as exegetical foreshadowing, the Old Testament of the New, but rather as natural foreshadowing: nature, the divine soul; earth, the heaven that is to come.[22]

This transformation from analogy to metaphor, type to antitype, phenomena outside the self to phenomena within (character conceived as "outside," reader as internal to him), like the novel's title, cannot be a neutral rhetorical strategy in a text whose subject is the danger of such transformations. In addition, the concluding metaphor does not so much reverse tenor and vehicle as it jars our sense of their meaning. If the figure of the insular Tahiti "stands" for something, it is for an idea the novel as a whole insists is impossible—an impossibility violently reiterated by the particular chapter "Brit." If the ocean stands for barbarism, we have just been told we cannot keep it outside ourselves; we must "consider it" not simply as analogy but as an actual part of ourselves. If it "stands for" the world of otherness, we must travel in its midst. As Pip reminds us, " 'If it stays here, that is ugly, too.' " And if it stands for the novel, we, like Bulkington, have long ago been drawn away from the land here invoked as the place of safety. "Brit" is exemplary of the narrative technique of the novel, as both chapter and entire novel introduce terms for the separation of interior and exterior and then baffle their relation. The ending of "Brit" is not a simple dialectical inversion of the terms initially introduced. Were it so, its argument would go as follows: "Man's connection to the monstrous is preposterous. Man's connection to the monstrous is inescapable." But, as I have suggested, there is a third and unanticipated proposition that circles around to the chapter's beginning while at the same time being more expansive than it, for it *contains* the respective positions that have evolved in the course of the argument—contains and transcends them by turning its attention to us: "Do you not find a strange analogy to something in yourself?"

On the question of embodiment—ours, now, into the text—there is at least one more thing to say. We are "taken in" by the end of "Brit"—both designated as its subject and tricked by its seemingly antithetical claims. To bring these two occurrences together: we are first made part of the narrative totality—in its designation of us as its subject—and then expelled from the enclosure of meanings by their apparent inconsistency. For meanings at odds with each other create the opening that becomes our "out." The opening would be the narrative contradiction (the initial claim that we can escape the ocean's monstrosity; the concluding claim that immersion in it is inevitable; the unexpected coda that, to preserve the "insular Tahiti," escape it we can and must), which suddenly permits us to be critical of an argument that had heretofore seemed airtight. Thus, "Brit" first embodies us, making us part of what we interpret, and then, in the divergence of its claims, calls that embodiment into question.[23] In the enormous compression of the chapter's last paragraph, where terms encircle each other, it is easy to miss the contradictory assertions I have pointed to above. In the last paragraph we are yet again being enjoined not to acknowledge a relationship that the chapter itself has argued is inevitable. One way of making sense of this contradiction is to see that since relations (however we care to specify them) between internal and external, or between selves and others, are neither single nor palpable and hence cannot be embodied, the strategies that represent these relationships will similarly be fluid, and to understand at the same time that they are never so fluid (Ahab's description of "leaky casks" notwithstanding) as to offer up that one image—of self becoming other—at which all of the characters, and at which the readers made into characters, wait to be transfixed.

Duplicates in Mind

In "The Sphynx," Ahab, gazing at the whale head, comments on the subject of analogy as he tries to penetrate to the invisible connection between two things lacking palpable body—mind and atoms: " 'O Nature, and O soul of man! how far beyond all utterance are your linked analogies! not the smallest atom stirs or lives on matter, but has its cunning duplicate in mind' " (70:406). It is, as I said, to Ahab that Melville gives these words, although the former manifests seeming incomprehension of the way in which they constitute an analysis of his own predicament. Ahab's words ought to make him stop in his tracks, ought to enable him to see what they are. He has, after all, been speaking of that in nature which corresponds to man's soul; for it does seem as if "nature" and "soul" are different entities entirely and not conjunctive properties of the same thing, "man." "Your linked analogies" would then articulate a kinship between nature and soul, and in a punning characteristic of the doubleness of language on which Melville draws to render Ahab's complexities, "duplicate in mind" would mean that even the smallest, most insensate atoms had correspondences in the human mind, and also, perhaps astonishingly, can conceive of their own likenesses—the latter now understood in the colloquial twist that makes good the pun. For insensate nature to have duplicates in mind and in the mind, to conceive of correspondences and to bear them out, this was what we thought Ahab was pondering.

If these were his thoughts, he might well start at the implication that the desire to probe the face behind the mask is a mere indication of an unarticulated desire to know the harder secrets of his own being. Thus, the self would look at nature to see its own likeness, would look outward to see itself. For if one could see the face behind the mask, one would have in possession a mirror image of one's own face, an image with a duplicate in mind. What Ahab would see, were he listening to his words, is that man is not an otherness to the world he sees opposing him, but is made in its very image. Sharing the same fate as well as an ignorance of what prompts it, Ahab would see that the perception of kinship disquiets an earlier idea, naive as it is predictable, that knowledge of essences will bring peace. But while it disabuses the notion that knowledge could bring content or enlightenment, it promises in its place the beneficence of shared fate, soul and nature resisting interpretation and comparably related to the inexplicability that formed them.

This is not, however, what Ahab understands, because it is not how he interprets his own words. If it were, the quest for vengeance would come to a halt. It could be argued that Ahab voices his apostrophe to nature and soul by conceiving them both as attributes of man alone. At the same time, insofar as he acknowledges the world at which he looks, the tenor of his response to it is to believe that even the smallest atom has cunning in mind. That is the stress of the analogy, as I imagine Ahab understands it, though it is certainly not its literal meaning. Thus, while Melville means us to see the kinship of the initial comparison (an epithet close to the one Ahab invokes when he asks the world to parent him), Ahab sees his own words point to the cunning or malevolence of those atoms, penetrating, as he now speculates, even as far as the mind. Ahab cannot properly interpret what he says because he is still imagining the object of interpretation as inside himself—neither separable nor visible, as one's own person is never visible (except in a single view, and that through the reversal of a mirror), cannot see itself as whole. To point to Ahab's apparent understanding in this passage is to suggest yet another way in which the novel frames questions of interpretation in questions of identity. I would like to speculate that the linking of interpretive and identic issues is not unique to *Moby-Dick*, but is a characteristic phenomenon in a dominant strain of the American novel.

Moby-Dick and many of the novels that precede and follow it are haunted by primitive psychological and epistemological confusions presented in an entanglement whose strands resist separation. They refuse to respect ordinary characterological boundaries and seem to predicate embodiments for the purpose of violating or dissolving them. Indeed, the dissolution of a self often occurs at the precise moment when a character, in order to know the world, thinks he can become one with it. Perhaps this is why American novels frequently evoke discomfort, seem so much more nerve-racking than their British counterparts. Like *Moby-Dick*, that novel which banishes duplicates (in the sense of duplicities or contrarieties) from the mind, or tries impossibly to retain duplicates (in the sense of replications) within the mind, American novels do not tell stories as much as offer paradigms for the problem of relationship—specifically for the relationship between identity and epistemology, between what a self is and what it is able to know.

How are selves to be conceived? How are selves to be differentiated? How does a character predicate identity, and how does he make the boundaries around it "stick"? (The latter question would be particularly relevant for the characters in Poe's and Brockden Brown's fiction.) The primitiveness of these questions and the way in which they result in characterological peculiarities—in selves who resist the distinction of discrete character—may be specified for American fiction as follows: (1) the persistent inability to accept identity as a given, and (2) the querying of a thing's essence, whether it be located in the world or in the self, or in the reflexive relationship between the two. It is at this juncture that two senses of identity come into play: the first defined from within, as that which is constant, the same with (as) itself; the second defined from without (though on the basis of the integrity I have posited), defined by an outside that metaphysically distinguishes the identity in question from all other beings or things. It is precisely these disparate understandings of identity, however, that get confused in the American novel, for when interior and exterior are no longer separate, self and world *are* "duplicates in mind."

No novel of whatever nationality has privileged access to the question of identity, and English and Continental novels tell stories of characters' identities along their own lines; that is, they usually construe identity as a priori defined, or as capable of receiving definition within a social context. In *Moll Flanders, Tom Jones, Jane Eyre, Pride and Prejudice, Daniel Deronda*, and most of Dickens, for example, the very question of disguise, on which so many of these novels hang, is possible precisely because identity is presumed stable enough to be hidden. Although many British novels are concerned with the forms that characterize relationship and finally come to define it, the problems they consider are predicated on an acceptance of the very structural distinctions that a novel like *Moby-Dick* calls into question. Even a novel like *Tristram Shandy*, which parodies stable conceptions of the self, reifies the stability it ostensibly mocks. Parody and humor finally separate the narrative voice from the instabilities it is promulgating. To deride a stable sense of self is to be sufficiently detached from the subject of derision to permit the luxury of pointing to someone else's folly—even if the "someone" be one's own self at a different moment in time. Thus, Sterne's parodic insistence that the self is an arbitrary construction puts the identic instability advanced by the narrator emphatically *outside* himself.

Of course, doubles and complementarities, like identic instabilities, exist in all fiction. Yet in European fiction, in Dostoyevsky and Gogol, for example, characters inhabited by others are generally haunted by them. They feel terror rather than pleasure at the otherness in their midst. In *Moby-Dick*, on the other hand, Ahab experiences his externalized counterpart, Fedallah, with neither pleasure nor horror. He seems undisturbed by the question of Fedallah's relation to him, unconfused by the man Melville means us to see as problematically at once inside and outside of him. In addition, in most European fiction, where doubleness exists, it normally occurs within only one (the central) character, whom we are meant to conceive as afflicted by its presence there. But in *Moby-Dick*, the pairings of character, whether between Ishmael and Queequeg, Ahab and Fedallah, Starbuck and Ahab, or Pip and Ahab, are, as the examples suggest, multiple, and a consequent norm. Finally, we could say that most of the "others" in pre-twentieth-century British novels, with the possible exception of *Jude the Obscure* and *Wuthering Heights*, are symbolically part of the self in question. They are not psychologically part of it. Thus, splits in most British fiction are about analogues rather than identities. Frequently there is no necessary recognition on the part of a particular character that the "other" is related to him. It is the reader who customarily perceives the existing connection. In a text like "The Secret Sharer," for example, the captain's double is never understood to be literally a part of him, whereas the disturbance of literality is at the heart of primitive American structures, which is perhaps why Ahab is never concerned about his relation to Fedallah. He accepts Fedallah as that part of himself which exists outside himself, as a duplication of self that never threatens the self's integrity; he accepts Fedallah as a manifestation of an identic status quo.

Distinctions like the ones I am making belong in a context that I touched on in the Introduction, and that I would like to recapitulate in part. Richard Poirier's *World Elsewhere* gives voice to the idea that "to be 'outside American society' is . . . to be in the great American tradition."[24] Poirier suggests that American figures cannot be characterologically construed because they are not conceived in traditional characterological terms, but rather are fragmented. While Poirier remarks on stylistic deformations that posit character outside of and against the exigencies of the social world, Edwin Fussell, in *Frontier*, maintains that characters are divested of realistic status, have realism usurped by the prominence of the landscape—in this case by the mythic prominence of the American West.[25] Fussell suggests that the frontier is a metaphor for a particular kind of "paradoxical monism"[26] characteristic of the American mind. A meeting of civilization and formlessness, the land lies ahead to be explored and is simultaneously conceived as regressive or behind, in the sense of embryonic or generative. I would like to suggest that what makes characters in American novels especially difficult to discuss—to put Fussell and Poirier together momentarily—is their desire to merge with and so become the land, at the same time that the equation of self and landscape is, as we have seen in *Moby-Dick*, tantamount to death. The desire to merge with the landscape is in these novels a consequence not so much of the fact that self and society are opposed (for in a text like *Moby-Dick*, society would have to be acknowledged before it could be annihilated), but rather of the fact that the land *is* the body that the self hopes to become—to become, not to possess.[27] Thus, characters are always what, in another context, F. O. Matthiessen called "diagrammatic abstraction[s]."[28] The self must be a diagram or abstraction, because as particularity or person it would be confined within flesh and blood walls.

From the vantage of different perspectives, the critics to whom I have alluded see the American novel as breaking from social tradition, and, in the process, creating non-mimetic versions of "character." In addition, they conceive the exploration of the wilderness as having analogues in (for) the American mind. I would like to extend this notion, and to suggest that in American fiction analogues get confused with and converted to identities. They stop being emblems for social change, and instead initiate revisionary notions about the boundaries between persons. Thus, the idea (now a commonplace) about the American desire to repudiate conventions of British fiction or to flee from society constitutes an explanation that itself socializes characters' desires to diverge from and overcome the reality that predicates persons as discrete who, because they are discrete, must come into social relationship.

In imagining a history for these related explanations, the departure from England comes first, and the subsequent importance of establishing a national identity, of cultivating the land and giving meaning to the act. Such imperatives then become metaphors, as Fussell and Poirier, for example, suggest. But there seems to be a point where the metaphors no longer appear to be perceived as metaphors, when they generate the idea that expansion could take place *inside* the self by a revision of *its* boundaries. Such a confusion seems attested to by texts like *Moby-Dick*, which enact

[55]

boundary revisions and expansions between persons, as if such enactments were an unacknowledged but central obsessive task. This enactment could be called gothic, as it is called with respect to Poe. But by whatever name it goes, the point to which I wish to draw attention is the way in which the cultivation of new physical territory makes the self imagine that it can—not analogously but actually, and somehow at the same time—magically be enlarged. The self appropriates history—the birth of a new nation, the necessity of its expansion—and converts it to interior structure. The self hangs on the idea of history to modify its own structure, as if this modification were part of history's providential design. Fiction provides the apparent means for accomplishing the disintegration of limits intolerable to the self. In the context of desired fusions, it is interesting to note that just as the distinction between persons and land is, in nineteenth-century American fiction, susceptible to transformation, so nineteenth-century literary forms are comparably fluid: for Whitman, essays and tracts becoming poems; for Thoreau, the *Journal* becoming philosophy, and philosophy, fiction; for Emerson, essays creating a voice with enough diversity and dimension to suggest that they are peopled by a plurality of characters—the fabled one man "disunited with himself." But because novels, in distinction from poems and essays, replicate reality in an ostensibly mimetic way—that is, create stories peopled by multiple characters (as poems and essays usually do not)—they simultaneously engage that reality *as if* on its own terms. Hence, in readjusting those terms, they come closer than poems and essays (which speak either "about" the relation between persons or from "outside" of that relation, since generally in the lyric there is only one voice) to redefining identic boundaries.

In American fiction, since the self cannot adequately or stably be defined, neither can distinctions between selves. How one differentiates identities depends upon one's stance, upon whether, for example, one speaks from within the subject being defined or from outside its boundaries. Confusing the distinction, Isabel tells us in *Pierre*, "there can be no perfect peace in individualness,"[29] and Mrs. Glendinning tells us why: "who can get at one's own heart, to mend it? Right one's self against another, that, one may sometimes do; but when that other is one's own self, these ribs forbid."[30] *The Confidence Man* is even more hopeless about the possibility of stable identity: "'the difference between this man and that man,'" Melville says defiantly, "'is not so great as the difference between what the same man be to-day and what he may be in days to come.'"[31] The very idea of identity, however, is contingent upon a dependable outside from which the self differentiates itself, as the very idea of interpretation insists upon a plurality of perspectives, a relativism against which a clearly delineated self or a particular interpretation takes a stand. Thus, questions of identity and interpretation not only intersect but are themselves defined by the contrast that makes sense of them. *The Confidence Man* offers the most extreme example of unstable identities, hence, of the difficulty of interpretation. In this respect it is not an atypical text, in the context of either Melville's literary career or other American novels. On the question of the interplay between interpretive issues and identic ones, on the question of well-defined subjects, American literature has an embarrassment of riches. " 'I am called woman, and thou, man, Pierre,' " Isabel says, emphasizing for our regard this mystery of the subject, " 'but there is neither man nor woman about it.' " [32]

The lack of specificity designated by the word *subject* is more than random. The American novel often vacillates between positing its subject fleshed in human terms and positing it hewn from the land itself. Indeed, the most frequent configuration of subject may be construed as a fracture or a confusion (particular novels variously calling to mind the metaphor of a blur or a split) in which the subject draws its features partly from the human visage and partly from the face of the land. This is true in Poe's *Narrative of Arthur Gordon Pym*, in which the disaster in the mind and the disaster outside of it come together in the vortex of the novel's conclusion, as it renders the distinction gratuitous. It is true in *The Sound and the Fury*, in which for Quentin land itself is equivalent to sustenance, that which he takes into his body, conceives of as if it were food: "There was something about just walking through it. A kind of still and violent fecundity that satisfied ever bread-hunger." [33] It is true of *Moby-Dick*, in which the "insular Tahiti" in the ocean and the less locatable one in the heart become impossible to tell apart. It is true in Thoreau's *Journal*, that novelization of a life in which the man wants to write sentences that "lie like boulders on the page" [34] and, hearing Heywood's Brook falling into Fair Haven Pond, asks, "What is it I hear but the pure waterfalls within me, in the circulation of my blood, the streams that fall into my heart?" [35] It is true in the parodic *Lolita*, in which the desecration of "the lovely, trustful, dreamy, enormous country," [36] so ravishingly reproduced, is indistinguishable from that of the little girl. In American fiction, ideas about otherness and civilization of the land get mythically confused. It *is* a mythic confusion that confounds person and land (as, for example, one could say British gothicism confuses persons and houses), and in this respect Hart Crane in *The Bridge*, Williams in *Paterson*, and Whitman in *Leaves of Grass* are not inventing such a confusion, but rather learning how to replicate it, imitating not only American poets but also the

American novelists who wrote alongside them. Person or land, it barely seems to matter, as if American novels had abandoned all interest in representational coherence. The content of the representation is immaterial, or it changes its material, more concerned with designating and destroying boundaries than with the content that makes them up.

Bone Dust

The significance of boundary destructions and of the subsequent dismemberment of bodies comes to light in "The Deck," when Ahab, contemplating essences—of time, of the coffin–life preserver, of the meaning of all physical objects—remarks, as he hears the carpenter hammering out the coffin:

> 'There's a sight! There's a sound! The greyheaded woodpecker tapping the hollow tree! Blind and dumb might well be envied now. . . . Rat-tat! So man's seconds tick! Oh! how immaterial are all materials! What things real are there, but imponderable thoughts?" (127:666)

Ahab thus moves from acknowledging phenomena that are invisible to concluding that nothing is real *except* phenomena that are invisible and that therefore cannot be embodied. These conclusions about disembodiment, about only the immaterial being real, lead him to think that since identity is not constrained by bodies, he can violate the bodies in his midst, either by imagining there is no difference between one body and another or by imagining that the self can be honed to a single piece of representative anatomy. We shall see how these assumptions amount to the same thing. The first idea is revealed in Ahab's notion that he and Pip are of the same body, that one body could contain the other, now in a literal way. Thus, at the end of "The Deck," he seeks Pip's counsel. "'I do suck most wondrous philosophies from thee! Some unknown conduits from the unknown worlds must empty into thee!'" he says of the mad boy. Here Pip is thought of as a container into which wisdom is poured and from which it can also be sucked, and this idea of others' bodies as hollow—to be filled up or emptied—is complemented by the idea that bodies can be "splice[d]" (36:219), or soldered to each other: "'Ye are not other men, but my arms and my legs'" (135:716), Ahab says to his crew. The latter conception of others as appendages of one's body (wholly different from the analogic completion Pip had offered Ahab earlier) is echoed by the narrative, with its chapter called "Leg and Arm," in which the captain with the sawed-off arm is put forth by Melville as a counterpart to the captain with the sawed-off leg. Just in case we do not get the point, do not take the novel's tragedy as a literalization of the point, we are shown that when the self tries to incorporate the other, this incorporation is a form of mutilation and disfigurement, and results in that particular disembodiment the name of which is death.

All men are incomplete, are incomplete by definition, and the point is literalized in the person of the blacksmith, who, wholly innocent, has nonetheless lost "the extremities of both feet" (112:616). It is literalized with respect to Stubb, who, after a quarrel with Ahab, says, "What the devil's the matter with me? I don't stand right on my legs'" (29:174), and who in a subsequent dream has his own leg "'kicked . . . right off'" (31:176). It is literalized by Pip, who fantasizes the body's incompletion as a mutilation he deserves. Speaking of himself as if in the third person, he orders the following punishment: "'Jerk him off; we haul in no cowards here. Ho! there's his arm just breaking water. A hatchet! a hatchet! cut it off—we haul in no cowards here'" (125:658–59). Literalized finally and most brutally in "A Squeeze of the Hand," that chapter which, as we recall, begins by imagining a transcendent wholeness in which men are so fused as to be "squeeze[d] . . . into each other" (94:533), and which then turns its attention to the deprivations and excisions, to the mutilations of this world. With unacknowledged curtness, the chapter punishes its earlier fantasy, punishes the wish behind the fantasy, as if, in fury at its unfulfillment, it would mutilate the wish itself. The chapter thus concludes: "This spade is sharp as hone can make it; the spademan's feet are shoeless; the thing he stands on will sometimes irresistibly slide away from him, like a sledge. If he cuts off one of his own toes, or one of his assistants', would you be very much astonished? Toes are scarce among veteran blubber-room men" (94:535).

In the context of such excisions, and the way in which Ahab conceives of them as curable, thinking that bodies could contain other bodies or else could be grafted together, Melville gives a different picture of completion as he depicts Ahab's farewell to Starbuck in "The Chase—Third Day." That reconciliation, made and then averted, does not simply reiterate the earlier scene in "The Symphony," where the bond between the two men could, if acknowledged, stave off tragedy; rather, it makes the bond *physical* in the convention of a handshake. Ahab will reject this form of connection as analogic and so inadequate, but before he does so, Melville makes him go through its motions, as if to point out to us the way they represent relation, the representation formalized into convention not because it is devoid of meaning but rather because it epitomizes meaning. "'I am old;—shake hands with me'" (135:713), Ahab says to Starbuck before he turns from Starbuck and the life of which the latter is an emblem. The handshake is inadequate because Ahab dreams of more complete connections. Thus, one conclusion of the idea that all is "immaterial" is that bodies could be fused. A corollary to this idea is the notion that since the self is not housed in the body, it will survive its death by becoming a distillation or an essence: "By heavens! I'll get a crucible, and into it, and dissolve myself down to one small, compendious vertebra" (108:601). Part of the crew, or dissolved to representative essence. Body stretched to the whole world (literalizing the expression of the body politic) or shrunk to a single bone.

In light of the previous remarks on embodiment and its literalization, it is of more than passing relevance that Melville offers us a carpenter whose task it is to make a man. "Bless my soul," the carpenter says on the subject of the bone dust that makes him sneeze, "it won't let me speak!" (108:597). But speak he does about the intricacies of identic construction, and Ahab speaks back, as if Melville were taking the questions: "of what is man made; what constitutes identity; how can something unseen be definitionally bounded?" and answering them from scratch, and more important, in *isolation*, divorced from the consideration of fused bodies about which I have elsewhere spoken. Thus, as Ishmael attempts to get the whale's dimensions to produce understanding of its essence, Ahab thinks he can force an answer by conceiving it as literal. Here the logic would be as follows: if an answer could be literal, then logically it would be possible; it also might be visible. But the problem with the conversation is that Ahab and the carpenter, no duplicates of mind, speak to each other from the exiles of different positions. Ahab's queries are philosophical. Unable to comprehend the relation between physical objects and their meanings, he tries to pry the two apart as if to grasp the distinction between them, whereas the carpenter is fully rooted in the materiality of the physical world, sees its meaning *in* its physicality. Contemplating his ideal man—at first glance a wholly material construct—Ahab orders him up as follows:

> Hold; while Prometheus is about it, I'll order a complete man after a desirable pattern. Imprimis, fifty feet high in his socks; then, chest modelled after the Thames Tunnel; then, legs with roots to 'em, to stay in one place; then, arms three feet through the wrist; no heart

at all, brass forehead, and about a quarter of an acre of fine brains—and let me see—shall I order eyes to see outwards? No, but put a sky-light on top of his head to illuminate inwards. There, take the order, and away.

Now, what's he speaking about, and who's he speaking to, I should like to know? Shall I keep standing here? *(aside.)*

'Tis but indifferent architecture to make a blind dome; here's one. No, no, no; I must have a lantern.

Ho, ho! That's it, hey? Here are two, sir; one will serve my turn.

What art thou thrusting that thief-catcher into my face for, man? Thrusted light is worse than presented pistols. (108:599)

What is being dramatized when the carpenter hands Ahab a lantern, thinking finally he has understood what Ahab wants, and the latter meets it with incomprehension, is not only the discrepancy between Ahab's meaning and the carpenter's understanding of it, but also the discrepancy between Ahab's desire to *have* palpable embodiments of things and, when they are present, his finding of them inadequate. Thus, Ahab's wish to have things be embodied so he can see and possess them is countered by his rejection of actual embodiments when he finds they are not made to the mind's specifications. The rejection is simultaneously complicated by Ahab's concomitant terror that existence and hence identity are both contingent upon palpable embodiment and, paradoxically, irrelevant to it: "'Would now the wind but had a body; but all the things that most exasperate and outrage mortal man, all these things are bodiless, but only bodiless as objects, not as agents'" (135:710). Turning from the wind back to the body with which it is directly compared ("'Run tilting at it, and you but run through it'"), Ahab faults the body for the very palpability he has elsewhere seemed to crave. The novel's central issues come together in Ahab's conversation with the carpenter, and they may be stated as follows: the question of whether or not things can be embodied; Ahab's ambivalence about whether or not he wants a body; his dependence upon his body, want it or not; and, finally, despite the fact of the body, the inability of flesh to define identity in any substantive or satisfying way. Ahab's discussion with the carpenter addresses these questions, as it simultaneously transforms philosophy into pain. "I thought, sir, that you spoke to carpenter," the workman says after the frustrated exchange about the lantern:

Carpenter? why that's—but no;—a very tidy, and, I may say, an extremely gentlemanlike sort of business thou are in here, carpenter;—or would'st thou rather work in clay?

Sir?—Clay? clay, sir? That's mud; we leave clay to ditchers, sir. (108:599)

Ahab has been conceiving the carpenter as God, and this fact is clear, first in his designation of the carpenter as a "manmaker," and second in his question to the carpenter about why the latter does not work in clay—and in our knowledge that he does work in dust. "'The fellow's impious!'" Ahab comments about the remark on ditches, dismissing all interpretations that debase his religious imputations. He continues:

> Look ye, carpenter, I dare say thou callest thyself a right good workmanlike workman, eh? Well, then, will it speak thoroughly well for thy work, if, when I come to mount this leg thou makest, I shall nevertheless feel another leg in the same identical place with it; that is, carpenter, my old lost leg; the flesh and blood one, I mean. Canst thou not drive that old Adam away? (108:600)

The focus on the wooden leg—akin to the leg Pip had offered Ahab earlier—isolates for our consideration the object of the novel's scrutiny. Melville displaces the question of the leg, removes it from between the two characters, and in synecdochic focus—as if to query Ahab's essence—removes it from Ahab himself. In fact, in Ahab's conversation with the carpenter, the flesh and blood leg is exactly what is absent, although *it* is what engenders sensation, as the visible wooden leg, though present and palpable, is without defining feeling. Thus, the real (and missing) leg is representative of that part of our being that does not show in our bodies, that does not have a body, while nonetheless seeming to comprise us, to represent us as our essence. Heretofore Ahab had asked: what lies behind the world's masks, or inside the body's hollows, where feelings and soul are hidden? But in taking the body apart, Melville's discourse on the leg dismisses these spatial conceptions. The philosophical puzzle—the lost leg, the flesh and blood one, intruding in the identical space as the leg made out of wood—posits a new metaphysic. It suggests that identity is not "beneath" visible appearance (as in Ahab's submerging of Pip), nor "outside" of that appearance (as in the characters' projection onto the coin), nor "behind" visible appearance (as in the image of mind or "pasteboard mask"), nor even caged within it (as in the concentricities of "Brit"). Rather, identity is *part* of (that is, inseparable from) the thing in question.[37] Yet the terms of Ahab's query ("Will it speak thoroughly well for thy work, if, when I come to mount this leg . . . I shall nevertheless feel another leg in the same identical place with it?") show us the way in which embodiment can come to seem at odds with existence, not because something is missing (though that is in fact the case here), but rather because the body of flesh and blood is not identical to life and, as a consequence, life is experienced as if it were (or could be) separable from it.

In this respect our bodies always betray us, making us feel as if something were missing. For although real flesh and blood represent and distinguish identity, they are nonetheless not equivalent to identity. The absence of equivalence can come to look like absence, period. Can come to look like deprivation. Can come to look like disfigurement. Yet essence or identity is not in fact separate from flesh, and it is the *lack* of separation rather than, as it had seemed, the fact of it that Ahab laments a moment later: "Here I am, proud as Greek god, and yet standing debtor to this blockhead for a bone to stand on! Cursed be that moral inter-indebtedness which will not do away with ledgers. I would be free as air; and I'm down in the whole world's books" (108:601). What Ahab has been bragging about is disembodiment—*is* air—that sensation in the absent leg makes it superior to the wooden one. But as he is the first to acknowledge, words themselves come from palpable bodies. Indeed, Ahab's cursing of mortal indebtedness (that is, the cursing of dependence on the body, on all the world's bodies, on its objects and artifacts, on its infinite containments) imagines an alternative that is itself bodiless, does not know how to flesh itself out. Conception is indebted, then, to the very palpable forms of which it most wishes to be free. Bodies are immaterial, with respect to a fantasized, higher materiality (itself a spatial conception, the name of which perhaps is God), and the latter invisible substance both cannot formally be imagined and, at the same time, seems to lurk "between" or "in" the world's forms, in its most indivisible parts, in its interstices and its atoms. Yet it is just Ahab's inability to separate flesh from the meaning from which he thinks it differs (the world's *refusal* to divide into spirit and body), to gratify the spatial notions that have characterized the novel thus far, that defines the problems addressed by *Moby-Dick*, and, in the discourse on the leg, reveals them to be unsolvable. For the idea about existence and invisibility—the equation of existence and invisibility—causes tragedy in the end.

What cannot be seen is the body's meaning. Meaning cannot be seen. That it is there but invisible, not separate from the body, and simultaneously not equivalent to it, is precisely what drives Ahab crazy. "Look," he says to the carpenter,

> put thy live leg here in the place where mine once was; so, now, here is only one distinct leg to the eye, yet two to the soul. Where thou feelest tingling life; there, exactly there, there to a hair, do I. Is't a riddle?

I should humbly call it a poser, sir.

Hist, then. How dost thou know that some entire, living, thinking thing may not be invisibly and uninterpenetratingly standing precisely where thou now standest; aye, and standing there in thy spite? In thy most solitary hours, then, dost thou not fear eavesdroppers? Hold, don't speak! And if I still feel the smart of my crushed leg, though it be now so long dissolved; then, why mayst not thou, carpenter, feel the fiery pains of hell for ever, and without a body? (108:600)

It is in how scarily Melville literalizes the novel's whole dilemma—one to the eye but two to the soul, as Ahab has tried to literalize and so solve it—that we see the novel's subject cast in relief, or, to alter the metaphor, into the anxiety of the original terms that generated it. We may be in danger of missing Melville's point precisely because he does literalize it. How can the question of the missing leg not be a metaphor, for us if not for Ahab? But it is not. For one to the eye but two to the soul is what has prompted the entire line of philosophical argument which catches on the division between body and soul, visible and invisible, internal and external. It is what prompts our sense of the body as disguise, as that which hides the soul. It generates our fantasies of imprisonment—of being caught inside a body that comprises without representing us, characterizes without defining us—and it inspires our conviction that what is missing is that which could embody not us but rather some outlined or heightened meaning. For one reason we desire identity (or its meaning) to be visible is not simply so it will show in our bodies. It is rather so it will show *outside* our bodies, will abolish the distinction between inside and outside (call it body and soul), as later it might abolish the distinction between inside and outside, conceived of now as designating one body and a separate other.

Thus, could meaning be seen—that is, could it be separately embodied—it would represent us as an epitome, and, moreover, magnet-like, could be wed to other epitomes, as anything external can always be placed proximate to any other external phenomenon. Indeed, the metaphor of a magnet is a repetitive image in *Moby-Dick*. It describes first Ahab's attempts to magnetize the minds of his crew (35:224) and second his attempt to keep the magnet of his purpose affixed to Starbuck's brain (46:284). Finally, it is literalized in the figure of the compass that Ahab smashes—perhaps as a competitor to his own magnetizing powers—at the novel's end. The magnet is thus that image through which Ahab desires to externalize his will—to fix it to others' wills, to obviate the difference between one will and another by drawing the two together. In that proximity, relationship might become identity; two might become one. For in the human world we know, place bodies together though we may, the proximity never means the dissolution of two into one. Did essence lie *outside* the body, or were it *equivalent* to the body, proximity might be identity.

It is in an attempt to make meaning literal and visible that the self projects its image into the coin: the attempt to draw meanings out of body that engineers all the novel's lines, whose meaning Pip exposes in the chapter on the doubloon as navel. Ahab's complaints about dichotomies and disembodiments notwithstanding, he in fact desires a split between objects and their meanings, though he would prefer meaning to lurk in front of the objects rather than to hide behind or within them. Front of but separate from them; in this respect the fantasized disembodiment would not diffuse the identity in question, but would rather differently reify it. " 'Faith, sir,' " the carpenter says. " 'Faith? What's that?' 'Why, faith, sir, it's only a sort of exclamation-like' " (127:666). Ahab would have it be a thing.

I have touched on some of the ways in which the novel is itself a disembodiment. Although the title suggests that meaning could be given a body, an identity, and a name, the novel elsewhere despairs of that fact, specifically in the person Bulkington, who seems not to need a name, as elsewhere he has not needed a body, or rather has traded his body in for an apotheosis Melville alludes to but cannot name. Indeed, insofar as we are put into uneasy equivalence with Bulkington, we are deprived of our bodies. What we are left with is not our minds, but rather the minds of the characters we are asked to inhabit. I should at this point register my skepticism at the idea that all texts are self-reflexive, or that readers are always to be treated as if they were characters. But these notions are relevant with respect to *Moby-Dick*, for the reader is continually bullied into an equation with the characters from whom he would just as soon be disassociated. Insofar as reading is a certain kind of (mental) activity, the reader's body is sacrificed to his mind. Insofar as it is a certain kind of relegatory activity, the reader's mind is sacrificed to the dominance of the characters' minds. What makes *Moby-Dick* a special case with respect to these observations is that it takes such castings out, such disembodiments, as its subject. Put differently, its subject is characters who are driven out of their minds—whether this be Pip out of Ahab's mind, or Pip out of his own mind (now in the colloquial sense of that word), or Fedallah out of Ahab's mind. These displacements, of character from mind, of one character from another's mind, of one's own character from one's own mind, or of a character's mind from his body, affect the reader until the reader's mind is unmoored or dislodged from any sense of fixed character.

While the novel's pages, it is true, are bounded by Ishmael's voice, even his first announcement, "Call me Ishmael," asserts an arbitrary and hence problematic distance between identity and its designation. If Ishmael *is* a fixture—the one whose stable identity demarks the novel's boundaries, punctuating its beginning and end—he is orphaned not only from the fates of the other characters but from our fates too. He is the one who does not look at the doubloon, perhaps because Melville knows he would see only what the others do. Indeed, Ishmael sees Ahab look at the coin, but then the narrative moves directly to Starbuck's vision, and from Starbuck's to Stubb's, from Stubb's to Flask's and Queequeg's, each character introducing the next and putting Ishmael at an illusory but crucial remove from the projection for which Melville kills his characters. In the end, it is Stubb who witnesses Pip's analysis of the action, as if to reiterate yet more strongly that although Ishmael cannot help but have an indirect relationship to this incident, as to all the others in the novel, here it is so indirect as to be immaterial. For if nowhere else in the novel, then most emphatically here, Melville wishes to keep his narrator in the dark. Ishmael is the lone character who does not lose his body to death. But he does become pure voice, relinquishing his life as a character. "'Who art thou, boy?'" Ahab asks Pip. "'Who's he speaking to?'" The carpenter asks of Ahab. "'What's he speaking about?'" Because metaphysically the "who" precedes the "what" and must determine its nature, the characters do not answer to the attempts to embody them representationally. So the novel seems culpable of enacting the very wishes for which it kills its characters.

Let me summarize my argument. I have suggested that the fall to selfhood is regarded as a disembodiment—the self's expulsion from the body of the no longer nourishing world—and this disembodiment is dramatized by Pip's fall into the ocean and, in "The Doubloon," by his reflections on the meaning of that fall. I have further suggested that while in *Moby-Dick* the birthing of the self is explicitly connoted as terrifying (actually it is remembered with grief by Pip and with rage by Ahab, and is depicted in the present tense as neither of these alternatives, but rather as a kind of romantic sublime), this is not because the self is absolutely detached from all others, but rather because it is ambiguously attached. Hence, identities are related to each other, though they are not related in an equivalence. The self's own identity is not an equivalence, not elemented of a single substance, but rather is woven of contradictions—in Ahab's case of rage and grief—though, of course, there are ways to simplify the complications of relationship. One form such simplification takes is to turn others away when they are "likes" rather than identities, as in Pip's relegation to the cabin. Another form of simplification is to repudiate contradictory emo-

[66]

tions, making God epitomize rage and Pip epitomize grief. The final simplification is to steel the self against mortal contradiction, to turn self into scythe, man into machine. I have further suggested that the characters' inability to accept themselves as incompletions—that is, as people who come into relationship rather than into identity—is complicated by the way in which the narrative rearranges its characters, treating them as part-people, whose incompletions could be healed by structural rearrangement. These rearrangements are multiple, and none in itself will do, for the moment wholeness is imagined, its particular embodiment is recognized as finite, hence as incomplete.

Such problems of identities regarded as structural inadequacies revolve around spatial confusions—specifically, around the confusion of what constitutes a single entity, and hence of how internal is related to external, visible to invisible, one body to another, analogues to what they analogize. A chapter like "Brit" demonstrates the problematics of relationship, as if Melville were insisting that if Ahab understood typology, he might also understand complex spatial relations, might understand that the self and what lies outside it do not constitute a static configuration, but that the very notion of inside and outside, monster and man, character and reader, ocean and land, peace and turmoil—the very notion of antithesis—falsifies their shifting relations. Thus, the ocean is "outside" in the sense of "exterior to" or alien, and "outside" in the sense of "outermost part of." But Ahab sees no difference between the world and the mind that conceptualizes it. Rather, either world and self have nothing to do with each other or else they are identical. Like other American characters, he understands the fluidity of shifting relations to promise the conversion of relationship to identity. Indeed, Ahab's spatial confusions, his ways of visualizing the essence of a body, whether the world's or his own, as "behind," "inside," or "absent" invoke spatial concepts that obscure his disappointment not so much in meaning's not being visible *in* the body as in its not being separable *from* the body. Separable as a symbol would be separable if it *were* what it represented—as the whale might represent the world, or a single vertebra the self; as the doubloon might represent the meeting of self and world, might show private becoming public, symbol taking on meaning and codifying it into value.

So Ahab casts Pip away and Pip's offer of his leg; he disparages analogy because it cannot be embodied, and is therefore not the real thing. But, as we have seen, he repudiates not only what is invisible and analogic, he—in an "identical" manner—repudiates what *is* palpably embodied, the wooden leg the carpenter offers him, because *it* is not the real thing, is a *visible* embodiment that fails to correspond to the invisible feeling behind it. In the rejection of both offers of completion (because from each, albeit oppositely, something remains missing) we see that Ahab's ideas about essence are separate from the objects he contemplates. Thus, I have argued that although Ahab claims this separation or disembodiment of meaning is what maddens, meaning's disembodiment is exactly what he desires and what the text enacts.

I would like to look, for a moment, at the question of epistemology—the subject on which most discussions of the novel rest—and to suggest its relation to the question of disembodiment as I have here been considering it. William James defined knowledge as "an ultimate relation between two mutually exclusive entities." But the familiarity of relationship of the sort James was describing does not, oddly enough, have the effect of making the known thing visible. Rather, it has the effect of making that thing seem to disappear. The link between knowledge of a phenomenon and the dissolution of its outlines—the phenomenon's no longer seeming foreign (hence its not seeming at all)—is a commonplace, for example, with respect to the idea of words whose meaning is well known, as Michael Polanyi describes: "The familiar use of a word, which is our subsidiary awareness of it, renders it in a way bodiless or, as is sometimes said, transparent." [38] To be in such full possession of a phenomenon that we are unconscious of its existence suggests that questions of knowledge and unconsciousness or (to focus on the word *bodiless*) that questions of knowledge and inhabitation are linked. Polanyi makes explicit the connections between unconsciousness and inhabitation: "We may say, in fact, that to know something by relying on our awareness of it for attending to something else is to have the same kind of knowledge of it that we have of our body by living in it." [39] That knowledge is equivalent to being—specifically to the perception of being as absent—may seem on the face of it like a perverse formulation. Knowledge should sharpen the edges around objects rather than making them disappear. But William James helps us out again here, for, in the following passage, with his meticulous description of bodily sensations, he invokes the idea that the body most fully aware of itself feels the totality of its own person but is simultaneously dead to what lies outside its boundaries:

> Sometimes, indeed, the normal consolidation [of the body] seems hardly to exist. At such moments it is possible that cerebral activity sinks to a minimum. . . . The eyes are fixed on vacancy, the sounds of the world melt into confused unity, the attention is dispersed so that the whole body is felt, as it were, at once, and the foreground of consciousness is filled, if by anything, by a sort of

solemn sense of surrender to the empty passing of time. In the dim background of our mind we know meanwhile what we ought to be doing: getting up, dressing ourselves, answering the person who has spoken to us, trying to make the next step in our reasoning. But somehow we cannot *start:* the *pensée de derrière la tête* fails to pierce the shell of lethargy that wraps our state about. Every moment we expect the spell to break, for we know no reason why it should continue. But it does continue, pulse after pulse, and we float with it, until—also without reason that we can discover—an energy is given, something—we know not what—enables us to gather ourselves together, we wink our eyes, we shake our heads, the background-ideas become effective, and the wheels of life go round again.

This is the extreme of what is called dispersed attention. Between this extreme and the extreme of concentrated attention, in which absorption in the interest of the moment is so complete that grave bodily injuries may be unfelt, there are intermediate degrees.[40]

In James's description of the way in which focused consciousness makes the body *stop* seeming physical (so much so that "grave bodily injuries may be unfelt"), it is clear that there is a relationship between intensity and lack of distinction between self and the object of its perception. It is almost as if James were suggesting a connection between intensity and identity, as if concentrating something *in* attention had the effect of actually interioriz-ing it. What would be interiorized would, of course, be invisible. Invisible but adamant. In *Varieties of Religious Experience,* it is no accident that the metaphor for this combination is, appropriately enough, a magnet, that which attracts objects outside the self and mysteriously draws them inward. In the cogency of an image Ahab would be the first to appreciate, James tells us that we do not perceive our bodies when we do not perceive the difference between our bodies and what lies outside of them. Thus, absorption in the world enables us to interiorize it:

It is as if a bar of iron, without touch or sight, with no represen-tative faculty whatever, might nevertheless be strongly endowed with an inner capacity for magnetic feeling; and as if, through the various arousals of its magnetism by magnets coming and going in its neighborhood, it might be consciously determined to different attitudes and tendencies. Such a bar of iron could never give you an outward description of the agencies that had the power of stirring it so strongly; yet of their presence, and of their significance for its life, it would be intensely aware through every fibre of its being.[41]

If being for James has meaning to the precise degree that the self *(a)* loses consciousness of the difference between body and world, and *(b)* effects a fusion between the two by drawing the world into the self through an invisible force, the *absence* of being is similarly conceived by that earlier American psychologist, Jonathan Edwards. The interesting point of similarity is that for both men, body has meaning (rather than perceptibility) either as it incorporates otherness or as it is expelled in its midst; that is, only at those moments when it comes into relation with the world:

> When we go to expel body out of our thoughts, we must be sure not to leave empty space in the room of it; and when we go to expel emptiness from our thoughts we must not think to squeeze it out by anything close, hard and solid, but we must think of the same that the sleeping rocks dream of; and not till then shall we get a complete idea of nothing.[42]

Thus, questions of identity hang on the self's engagement with the world. Insofar as this engagement is with an essence that cannot be specified, the self will lose the sense of its own essence, or will have to conceive of it metaphorically—as separate from its body—in the psychological terms of an unconscious, in the religious terms of a soul, or in the philosophical terms of an ideal. In James's as in Edwards's description of the self's relation to the world, two steps are involved: (1) the disassociation of meaning from the world's physical bodies, and (2) the attempt to reify meaning anew by providing the idea of identity with a different body. The initial divestment does not, of course, do away with bodies; that would be impossible. Rather, it suggests that the way to overcome the difference between bodies and the objects outside of them is to take them into the self—but purified of their palpability—as the soul is conceived of as within the self, or as an unconscious is so conceived, or a typological ideal.

Moby-Dick comparably exteriorizes our fantasies about the discrepancy between material phenomena and spirit—exteriorizes in the sense of addressing them. This philosophy always does. And it interiorizes these concerns, foists them into particular bodies. This literature always does. Thought of in these terms, the very conversion of philosophic issues into story is a way of suggesting that they could be remedied, that narrative could have an answer, could, through continuity, discover completion, now understood in the sense of making man whole. Indeed, pulled between disparate forms of representation—between narrative and drama (specifically, the drama associated with tragedy), between epic and (in its hymns to bodilessness) lyric, the novel itself refuses specific embodiment, enacts the tension between various forms of literary embodiment, attempts in its own body to make these disparate forms fuse. If identity could be disembodied, as the chapter "The Whiteness of the Whale" tries to disem-

body it, as Fedallah disembodies Ahab, as the extracts at the novel's beginning disembody the whale, as Ishmael on the mast-head hopes for his own
disembodiment, as the novel's dramatic moments disembody speech
(removing it from the narrative that elsewhere acknowledges the connec-
tive tissue between the two), as the strictly roped-off gams seem to exist for
the explicit purpose of pointing to and hence creating the disembodiment
in the rest of the text, and finally as Ahab's missing leg disembodies identity, such ways of conceiving identity would both wrench it from its context and in the process make it palpable.

The attempt to pry meaning apart from epitomic objects is perhaps
what Lawrence had in mind when he spoke of Americans as killers—a
diagnosis Melville literalizes (as, below, when the Pequod goes down,
Tashtego stands hammering the ship's flag to the disappearing spar),
literalizes, and makes repellent. For although in the following passage the
killing is inadvertent, because it is the last killing in a book so full of
mutilation, it becomes representative of the sacrifice of the world's bodies
to the mind that would grasp their meaning:

> A sky-hawk that tauntingly had followed the main-truck down-
> wards from its natural home among the stars, pecking at the flag,
> and incommoding Tashtego there; this bird now chanced to inter-
> cept its broad fluttering wing between the hammer and the wood;
> and simultaneously feeling that etherial thrill, the submerged
> savage beneath, in his death-gasp, kept his hammer frozen there;
> and so the bird of heaven, with archangelic shrieks, and his impe-
> rial beak thrust upwards, and his whole captive form folded in the
> flag of Ahab, went down with his ship, which, like Satan, would
> not sink to hell till she had dragged a living part of heaven along
> with her, and helmeted herself with it. (135:722–23)

That meaning is inseparable from objects is not, however, what we
think as we try to get a grip on the novel, to nail it once and for all, as if
were we in possession of the novel's meanings—could we demark someone else's meanings, as Ahab tries to demark God's—we might discover
them to be our own, or discover that we have our own. Might in the midst
of this discovery lose our bodies to our minds, and our minds to the meaning that consumes them, become etherealized as spirit, but spirit made
visible—as concrete as James's iron magnet or Edwards's rock. So Melville
wrote *Moby-Dick* and called the representation wicked. So we call it the
greatest American novel, valorizing this narrative that dooms its embodiment of meaning to failure at the same time that it sharpens our hopes that
such an embodiment could be. What appalls is not the idea that this story
could stand without interpretation, but rather the idea that our lives (what

would be their content but a version of what we have read here?) will stand without interpretation, will be mere unexplicated outline: desire, pursuit, death.

"'Is it not hard,'" Ahab says to Starbuck, concentrating on what resists embodiment and hence interpretation, "'that with this weary load I bear, one poor leg should have been snatched from under me?'" Hard to stagger under the world's weight without knowing how to represent it, not knowing how to separate meaning from the body that shows it forth. Knowing, in any case, that the body is not all, that something is missing, and always will be missing; that we always will be, as the saying goes, in a joke it is surprising the novel does not itself make, without a leg to stand on. For we inhabit our bodies by conceiving of them as inadequate, first because they are incomplete—they enclose without fulfilling us—and second because, although they contain life, they are nonetheless not equivalent to it.

Here it is almost as if Melville were taking Shakespeare's idea about the reduction of identity (the poor bare forked animal), and showing us how it looks, shucked of all context, where context would be provocation or cause. This is perhaps the most crucial difference between the novel and the play. In *King Lear* we see the unaccommodation happen, see Shakespeare undress Lear, strip away possessions and people, turn him out on the heath and query his identity. This is the unaccommodation, and questions about the minimal forms of man's essence are examined in its light. *Moby-Dick* is deprived of such a context, since we are repeatedly told that Ahab's motive for rage is insufficient to its fact, may even be incidental to that fact, as it never is in *King Lear*. Thus, although the adventure in the novel would seem to contradict my idea about the absence of context for Ahab's rage, the story, such as it is, is not about provocation, but rather about Ahab's response to the *absence* of provocation, as if Melville wanted to consider the question of man's essence or of his sufferings—as other American texts do—unadulterated by the impurity of context.

For Melville, man's essence has no form, is terrible because it is invisible. On the heath, looking at the fool, as Ahab is to look at Pip, Lear discourses on what he sees:

> Poor naked wretches, wheresoe'er you are,
> That bide the pelting of this pitiless storm,
> How shall your houseless heads and unfed sides,
> Your looped and windowed raggedness, defend you
> From seasons such as these?

(III.iv.28–32)

[72]

Melville literalizes these holes, looks not through the clothes but through the body, as if the body had windows, had loops through which he could see. "Take my body, who will," Ishmael brashly proclaims, "take it . . . it is not me" (7:66), and although Melville does not share his bravado, *Moby-Dick* is as if written to provide proof of an invisible self that would come forth, standing in front of the body as its transcendent replacement. "Is man no more than this?" Shakespeare asks, querying man's essence in the midst of inexpressible privation. Melville removes the privation. The rage remains the same. *Moby-Dick* does not undress man; rather, it disembodies him, makes him "threadbare in coat, heart, body and brain" ("Etymology"), much as Ishmael unbuttoning the whale cub probes the animal's essence with his knife. This is the surreal part. In fact, it is the almost psychotic part.

Moby-Dick's relation to *King Lear* is itself one of disembodiment, as if the novel appropriates the play half in order to mutilate it. While lines in both texts are sometimes directly parallel, many novelistic scenes (too many to be accidental) echo the prior text for the explicit purpose of violating it. Thus, for example, at the end of the novel Starbuck says to Stubb: " 'Look through my eyes if thou hast none of thine own'" (119:637). The line recalls—and simultaneously wreaks havoc upon—Lear's words to Gloucester at the crucial point of their meeting: " 'If thou wilt weep my fortunes, take my eyes'" (IV.vi.176). In the earlier text, the challenge cements the bond between the two characters, and we would expect its iteration here to call upon a similar union: Ahab speaking to Pip, or, if not to Pip, then to Starbuck. Melville invokes the line, but he gives it to the wrong character, insisting upon a memory he is simultaneously brutalizing. In fact, in the original text Lear's words mark that hallucinatory moment when the relationship between Gloucester and Lear becomes (metaphorically) an identity. In *Moby-Dick* the line is spoken between two characters who have no (significant) relationship, as if in a macabre joke whose meaning would be as follows. Connections are not identities, cannot even metaphorically so be conceived. Lest we think they can, lest we allow *Lear* to console us with that notion, Melville takes that Shakespearean line—the central line in the play—and crudely makes it trivial. In fact, the relation between the two texts is frequently one of dismemberment. Thus, "Midnight, Forecastle," for example—the first chapter in the novel to be rendered as if it were script—recalls the Shakespearean heath. But while it reminds us of the misery that in Shakespeare's text will have meaning, what it replicates in the sailor's banter is the disassociation of meaning, as if for its own sake. What it replicates is disassociation—

characters from each other, speech from shared context—showing the isolation against which the rest of the novel will level its assault.

On the whole, the novel embodies the play; this is how I understand its struggle with dramatic form. Embodies it in the sense of incorporates it, conceives of it as an inside (material that does not need to be acknowledged because it has already been made integral). At the same time, Melville's relation to Shakespeare's text is akin to Ishmael's relation to the whale. Melville wants to take the text apart to see of what it is made. Yet Ahab has his humanities, and it is of Lear that they are made. This is the central reason that Melville has so little to do to convince us of Ahab's humanity. The completion toward which Melville strains embodies a person made of words, as if—since one cannot fuse real people or characters in one's own text—one might appropriate a mythic double, make him the spirit inside the body, whose presence, though invisible, is so indisputably manifest it need not directly be invoked. It can even be revised and ridiculed. Thus, "'Ahab has his humanities!'" (16:120) not simply because Ahab represents humanity in its incompletion and its grief, but also because in this novel whose central story is the impossibility of transcending incompletion and grief (the impossibility of one character abiding in and as another), Lear *is* Ahab's humanity. That Melville should count on the very psychic completion of which he elsewhere despairs is contradictory and is not. For this idea about the impossibility of embodiment is itself fatal when literalized.

Otherness comes into the body as often as our breathed air, and that image so patently simple, that physiological fact, which rebukes the idea of image by being an actual phenomenon, shows its importance in a passage early in the novel when Ishmael, speaking of essences, goes outside the body, as if suddenly discovering its connection to a genuine externality—an outside that remains outside and is simultaneously conceived as integral: "Oh, Ahab! what shall be grand in thee, it must needs be plucked at from the skies, and dived for in the deep, and featured in the unbodied air!" (33:199). The lines resist the paradox they simultaneously invite. They do not in fact suggest a discrepancy between the body and a larger invisible outside or (to reverse the spatial picture) between the body and a larger invisible inside. Rather, they suggest that to find itself the body must go outside its being, go far outside its being, seek its features not in the human faces that replicate its own, but in what has no features, in what resists imagining, hence in what cannot be desired and therefore cannot be had. There would be more to say about this, but for us, as for Melville, it is deprived of representation. The embodiment Melville desires—like the one desired by his character—is not human and, as these lines acknowledge, resists the confines of human terms. In the crossing of the voices, of the active and the passive, in the appropriation of a language too archaic to be his own, in the direct address itself of author to his subject, Melville momentarily acknowledges the disembodiment of that subject—call it bone dust or call it spirit—from which he, like the carpenter, will make himself a man.

2 The Self in Itself
Hawthorne's Constructions of the Human

It was the spirit of the man that could not walk.
—Nathaniel Hawthorne

Moby-Dick is allegorical, is not the whale about which it
speaks. But it is allegorical in the way in which all novels are
allegorical; it is allegorical in the way in which language
itself is allegorical, because language only refers to objects it
does not embody, because language refers to objects with
which it cannot be equivalent. Yet if *Moby-Dick* is allegorical with respect to actual objects, its primary fiction is one
of literality: to take the whale body apart, as the Pequod
crew does in the central chapters of the novel, or to take the
phantom leg apart, as Ahab does philosophically in his discussions with the carpenter. In distinction, Hawthorne's
tales take *human* bodies apart. They consciously disembody
the man that Melville, in his creation of Ahab, for example
(and as a consequence of the dismemberment of the sacrificial whale), constructs symbolically (within the human
limits of the amputated leg) as a bodily whole. At the same
time, Hawthorne's tales insist that the dismemberments of
its characters, because they are allegorical, do not "count" in
the physical world. That is, while many of Hawthorne's
tales are about parts of the body, or things done to the
body, we are then asked to read the meaning of such actions
in the context of an interpretation that subordinates or
dismisses the corporeality that is its very subject. Thus, in

the critical interpretations, "Rappaccini's Daughter" is not read as a story about a woman whose breath can kill. Rather, it is commonly and correctly read as a tale about the Garden of Eden. "The Birth-mark" is not read as a tale about bodily violation. Rather, it is (also correctly) read as a tale about the perniciousness of a science that does not know its own fatal limits. "Young Goodman Brown" is not read as a tale about pollution of the eyes. Rather, it is correctly read as a tale about temptation and the absence of faith. It is, in fact, only in the name of Goodman Brown's wife ("Faith") that literal and allegorical spheres momentarily intersect. Such stories put a figural meaning in front of a literal or bodily one. They indicate a split between the body of the whole story and the figural interpretation that displaces meaning from the human bodies that are the stories' overt subjects. In fact, while Hawthorne's allegory is most frequently predicated on the severing of one part of the human body from another, this mutilation is accompanied by the implicit directive that we not read mutilation in terms of physical dismemberment, that we not read it by the very terms in which it has predicated itself.

To understand this contradiction, this crossing of directives, we must recall that while Renaissance and classical renditions of allegory emphasize the continuous relationship between the palpable body or emblem and the thing that it signifies, most nineteenth- and post-nineteenth-century interpretations designate allegory as that form of figuration which assumes splitting—of traits or levels of significance—as the mode's most essential feature. To take very different examples, in his *Preface to Chaucer: Studies in Medieval Perspectives*, D. W. Robertson, Jr., writes: "The word *allegory* . . . means . . . 'saying one thing to mean another,' but the thing said in the first place is also true";[1] Paul de Man tells us that "if there is to be allegory, [it is necessary] that the allegorical sign refer to another sign that precedes it";[2] and Angus Fletcher, pointing to the way in which allegory isolates meanings, writes: "A peculiar characteristic of objects that are taken to have daemonic power . . . is that they are capable of existing solely as daemonic objects, almost as if the amulet were not related by nature to any other type of stone or gem."[3] The detachment of the allegorical object from any other *natural* object and the directive to read a phenomenon outside of its immediate context are, in fact, related. Both imperatives predicate a split between the allegorical significance and a representative icon or picture with which we are not allowed to compare it. Hawthorne shows us the problematics of this way of conceiving allegory.[4] Or, rather, he shows us that even when both levels of significance are read as continuous, the word *both* nonetheless implies "two," implies the very doubleness that it may then try to dismiss. One pretense of the assumed split between allegorical levels of significance is that the surface of the allegory, in effect, has no bodily consequences, because, however literal its icon or picture, both the icon and the action that it represents are referred to another (usually doctrinal) level of discourse. Yet notwithstanding this deflection from the physical or corporeal realm—a deflection built into allegorical conventions of interpretation—it is a characteristic of allegorical representations (one that Hawthorne's tales make unmistakable) that their surfaces or icons tell tales of murder and dismemberment, of contagion and violation, of spells cast on the human body, of gross corporeal misappropriation, tell tales of bodily harm. What is complex about Hawthorne's tales is that (like post-nineteenth century interpretations of allegory) their characters try to create a division between their own corporeal essence and the meaning of that corporeality, and (like earlier allegorical renditions, which refuse interpretive separation) they simultaneously register criticism of the meaning that is arrived at by the process of bifurcation between the palpable body and the meaning ascribed to it in some non-bodily sphere. I shall be suggesting that Hawthorne's allegories of the body first attempt to define human identity, and, second, that they recognize that all stable conceptions of identity allegorize the self they ostensibly define. For any attribution of meaning is different from the whole it interprets. Any attribution of meaning is smaller than the whole it interprets. Definition is therefore contingent upon the dismissal of those characteristics that would contradict the particular understanding of the identity in question. In the case of *human* definition, a person is reduced to an "identifying" part. Thus, identity is read as if the part were the whole, the particular characteristic were the person, as in the familiar expression that someone is "all heart."

I should like to suggest that the allegorical mode is, by definition, concerned with identity—its own, that of its subjects—conceived in problematic terms. The allegorical mode is predicated on doubleness not simply because a part is not the whole, nor because allegory has more than one level of significance, but also, as I have been asserting, because allegory often depicts violence done to the human body which we are then implicitly asked not to read in palpable or bodily terms. In Hawthorne's allegories, the case is more extreme, for in the tales an icon (a part of the body) stands not for an abstraction but rather for the whole human body. Thus, for example, of Peter Goldthwaite (the character gutting his house in search of a nonexistent treasure) we are told his action is "an admirable parallel to the feat of the man who jumped down his own throat" (IX:402). This image of self-containment—of a body absorbing itself to depict a body's absorption in itself, its delusion that it could contain itself

[79]

as if its confines were the whole world—is both tautological and character-istic. For here envelopment in the self represents envelopment in the self. Oppositely, for Richard Digby (the man of adamant who retires into a cave and dies "in the attitude of repelling the whole race of mortals—not from Heaven—but from the horrible loneliness of his dark, cold sepulchre" [XI:169]), death does not end but rather makes everlasting the rigidity of a position typified to endure. Rigidity (the man's stony heart) fossilizes his whole body, engraves it in the cave, which represents exemption from the world outside his body—represents exemption from the human community from which he flees, and represents as well, and as fun-damentally, exemption from all that is beyond his own corporeal limits. In these tales as in many others, the unique synecdochic relationship of tenor and vehicle—with part made of the same bodily substance as the cor-poreality for which it stands—throws the double level of allegory into question. In Hawthorne's allegories, what (part of) the human body stands for is the human body.

If the central fiction of *Moby-Dick* is that the dismemberments of which Melville writes are literal and of monster bodies, the central fiction of Hawthorne's tales is that the dismemberments are allegorical and are of human bodies. But precisely because Hawthorne seems to turn conven-tions of allegory back upon themselves, because both surface and second level are elemented of bodily substance, Hawthorne asks about the rela-tion between the fiction of allegory (that form of representation which self-consciously partializes its meanings, separates them from literal bodies) and the fiction of literality (that form of representation which claims to totalize its meanings, insists they be read as integral to the human body). He therefore asks: does the distinction between the allegorical and the literal blur when the subject is not only the human body but the taking of the body apart? In the tales I shall discuss, Hawthorne focuses palpably on the human body, insisting that meaning cannot be written exclusively *on* the body, as, for example, Richard Digby tries to script it, nor exclusively *in* the body, as Peter Goldthwaite (a deconstructive Digby) tries to write it, nor can it be written exclusively *outside* the body, as, I shall suggest, Young Goodman Brown predicates it. The first two ways of schematizing meaning separate the body from its (own) non-corporeal essence, separate the body from itself, and the third way of schematizing meaning separates the body from the outside world. It should be pointed out in passing that these separations are opposite to the fusion desired in *Moby-Dick*. In Melville's novel, characters want to merge with each other. They want to take the world into their bodies. Indeed, they want to make the world's insubstantiality (what lurks behind "the pasteboard mask") *into* a visible body. Hawthorne's characters wish instead to be distilled to a representative essence. Insofar as they want to come into contact with the world, it is not to destroy *its* corporeality but rather to destroy their own.

In *Moby-Dick*, the outside world is conceived of as monstrous; it is conceived of as monstrous *because* it is outside. It must be so conceived so it can be disembodied. It must be disembodied so it can then be incorporated. Thus, for Melville, the outside world is acknowledged in order to be incorporated. It does not exist except in relation to the self, except in the process of being made integral to the self. For Hawthorne, on the other hand, the world is irremediably other. It cannot be incorporated. It cannot be dismissed. Hawthorne harbors no illusion that the world could be sufficiently domesticated ever to be known. The world must be acknowledged at a distance and not in a possession. It cannot be reduced to the size of the human body. In fact, as I have suggested in my introduction, although *Moby-Dick*, with its ostensible double subject—the self and the world— seems to present a more sophisticated consideration of identity and its relations than Hawthorne's concentration on the single subject of a self (with *sophisticated* defined as the ability to imagine two entities rather than one), Melville's ostensible double subject is, as the last chapter has demonstrated, misleading, since the outside world is acknowledged as outside only to be interiorized. For Hawthorne, on the other hand, the world never has anything but the status of an outside. Characters who think otherwise, like Roderick Elliston (about whom I shall have more to say in the following pages), are not simply deluded; their delusions are imagined as monstrous. Of course, Melville's and Ahab's attitudes are no more commensurate than those of Hawthorne and his characters. In this respect, the deformations of the world, as perpetrated by the characters, are similarly rebuked. But there are crucial differences. Insofar as Melville never acknowledges the fact that he is deflecting his subject (of what are human bodies made?) into a secondary question which obfuscates that subject (of what are monster bodies made?), and, deflecting, as well, questions of identity into questions of interpretation, he also never fully relinquishes the motives for the deflection. He never relinquishes the idea that monster or alien bodies might be converted into benign human bodies. He also, and oppositely, never acknowledges, except by indirection and analogy (as the chapter "Brit" makes clear), that human bodies, in their own right, have monstrous characteristics. He thus never fully repudiates the hopes prompting the original deflection. Punishment of his characters notwithstanding, he seems to participate more fully in their confusions than Hawthorne does in the confusions of his characters.

Melville's characters err in believing they can internalize the world, can make it integral to themselves. In the power of so doing, the world must be destroyed. Hawthorne's characters err in imagining they can externalize the self, make it not so much integral to the world as magically commensurate with it. Predicating a world where all must be concrete—since only if phenomena have corporeality can they first be dismembered and then taken into the human body—Melville's novel depends upon fictions of literalization. It depends upon the idea that all meanings have bodies or that meaning can be made integral to one's own body. Thus, *Moby-Dick* swells the world to one engorged self. Contrarily, Hawthorne's allegorical tales splinter the self, try to reduce it to pure essence.

Allegory is the term for the reduction of a thing to a representative emblem, which both stands for the whole object and is then brought into alliance with some other *alien* object, one that lies outside the self. If *allegory* is the "literary" term for the process I have just described, *part-object* is, as I have indicated in the previous chapter, the psychoanalytic term for the same process. Both terms have a philosophical counterpart in the idea of Cartesian dualism, that notion which conceives of the soul as separated from the body. This chapter, like the last one, will ask: what do these terms describe or explain? The experience predicating such terms might account for the feeling—Ahab's feeling—that the self is divided, with *division* here understood as a consequence of ambivalence. In fact, the colloquial expression of ambivalence often assumes bodily expression, as in the wording, "One part of me feels this; another that," suggesting the body could actually be partialized. The terms might speak to the feeling— Ahab's feeling—that something separate from our bodies, and albeit insubstantial, nonetheless defines us more truly than the body does. Alternately, as in Hawthorne's allegories, division would refer not only to the separation of one entity from itself, or of one feeling from another, but also to the correspondence between the self and an imagined correlative in the world. It is in the context of such desired correspondences that I understand Hawthorne's allegorical reductions—Vaughan in "Sylph Etherege" to a miniature, Ethan Brand to a heart, Roderick Elliston to a bosom serpent, the ambitious guest to a monument. The hope of these reductions is that if the self were simplified to a single emblematic thing, it might more easily correspond to the essence of the world (also simplified to a single thing).

Typology is a good comparative model for the desired correspondence, not only because it is the one that Hawthorne in fact used, but also because the implicit assumption of any typological model is that the two things to come into correspondence do so—can only do so—as a consequence of reduction, both self and world reduced to representative (and single) parts. Correspondence requires reduction, requires the phenomena in question to be representatively distilled so that they can—even analogically conceived—have the same metaphysical dimensions. This is crucial, for drawing upon the implicit assumption of the typological model, the winnowing of Hawthorne's characters to a representative bodily part implies the magical idea that the world will imitate this distillation, can be coerced to reduce *itself* to a representative part. Thus, if the fiction of literality is that the world can be taken into the self, the fiction of allegory is that the self, reduced to a single entity, will be allied with the world's essence, suddenly possible to ascertain. Then the self would be accommodated to the world's essence rather than incorporated into its body. For the reduction of the self to a representative bodily part is not simply reduction to a palpable bodily organ. Rather, it is reduction to the centrality for which an organ like the heart stands. Thus, allegory predicates a connection between the self and the world, but this connection is not corporeal. Or rather, it would transcend corporeality as *Moby-Dick* destroyed it.

Tales like "The Artist of the Beautiful" (in which a man constructs a butterfly so real that it flies) or "Drowne's Wooden Image" (about a man who creates the perfect replica of a woman, so close to the true thing that the statue is indistinguishable from flesh) rest content in the illusion that one can make the non-human emblem be—even if only momentarily—in the image of bodily life. These tales aestheticize the body, as Aylmer does in "The Birth-mark" or as Hawthorne himself does in all of the finished novels. Of Fanshawe, the hero of Hawthorne's first novel, all that remains of the man, hardly corporeal in the first place, is a monument. In *The Scarlet Letter*, the novel's explicit subject is the hypocrisy of social forms more pleasing to aesthetics than true to human practicalities or needs. *The House of the Seven Gables* strives to match living persons to portraits in whose molds they only poorly fit. *The Marble Faun*, the one novel that rebels against such aestheticism, turns surrealistically into a nightmare: for Donatello, the novel's hero, not to be a statue is, consequently, to be a murderer. In fact, for Hawthorne, the term *romance*, which figures so prominently in the prefaces, alerts us not simply to unrealistic events but also to that particular absence of realism that makes meanings show, often aesthetically, on its characters' bodies. It is thus no accident that mesmerism plays such a dominant role in *The Blithedale Romance* and *The House of the Seven Gables*. Hawthorne wants to transfix these bodies to the meanings that will make sense of them. In the novels, he thinks he has to do this by artificial means.

[83]

Such a substitution of aesthetic emblem for body might purge the world of human bodies, might memorialize or freeze them, might lock them in rigor mortis and put something presentable in their place. By my use of the word *emblem* I mean to recall the *O.E.D.*'s first definition: "inlaid work, a raised ornament on a vessel." This definition is especially pertinent to the deformations of the body, the price it has to pay when Hawthorne assigns meaning directly to it. Hence, there is a moment in *The Scarlet Letter* when Hester Prynne and Dimmesdale think to run away forever to some never-never God-world where what they have done will make no difference. In exuberance at this idea, Hester removes the letter from her person, freeing her body from its indictment as she thinks to free her spirit. But Pearl, confronting Hester Prynne, does not recognize her mother; the child so unequivocally conceives the letter as part of Hester's body. So Hawthorne's character is forced to retrieve the letter as if it were integral to her corporeal being. Hawthorne explains it thus: "So it ever is, whether thus typified or no, that an evil deed invests itself with the character of doom" (I:211). Indeed, emblematic inevitability is characteristic of a novel in which allegory chisels meanings to irrevocable forms.

Such meanings are often not only immutable, they are also, as in *The Scarlet Letter*, assigned from the outside. In "The Prophetic Pictures," a man and woman sit for portraits they then come to resemble—Hawthorne again insisting that external emblems dictate the fates they seem neutrally to represent. So, too, in "The Minister's Black Veil," in which invisible divisions—between body and soul, one person and another, the mortal world and the inscrutable one—are given impalpable form, as if to imply that since there is no way to rid the world of dichotomies, one must make their existence visible, allowing us to acknowledge because we see separations whose presence has literally been made material. If in "The Prophetic Pictures" the emblem is distanced from the body, and if in "The Minister's Black Veil" the emblem lies directly outside the body, "The Birth-mark" affixes the emblem to the body, making the two inseparable. In the latter story, which is Hawthorne's Faust tale about the man driven to destroy a mark on his wife's face (driven to intercept "the spectral Hand that wrote mortality, where he would fain have worshipped" [X:39]), we see that the birthmark is the mortal mark. Taken away, the woman dies. Hawthorne is here suggesting that emblems of mortality are not mere attributes of life, but in fact comprise its essence. Whether emblems reveal life, whether they are equivalent to life, or whether they are the meanings left in life's wake, in all cases allegory hews meanings out of the body. Because the bodies are mortal, they do not survive the abuse. Although Hawthorne understands this, he nonetheless insists on the sacrifice of the body to the schemata that will make sense of it. Without schemata, without the clarity that brands us with meaning, makes of us its material, we are like Pearl, these stories seem to insist, who cannot recognize what she sees.

The problem with this way of conceiving it, as Hawthorne depicts it in another group of stories—the ones on which this chapter shall focus— may be stated as follows: formal categories are conceptual ones without which life is chaos, a more primitive unviability than that of immortality or evil. But, granted that we depend upon forms to bequeath us distinctions, and that this they are equipped to do, we nonetheless have no trustworthy capacity to perceive them correctly. Thus, we are beholden to the very categorical distinctions we are also likely to misconstrue. In "Young Goodman Brown," for example, the devil says to his assembly that " 'by the sympathy of [their] human hearts' " (X:87), they will scent manifold evil in others. What Brown sees when he looks is that those he has thought most sanctified are most defiled by evil. Such unholy conversions—of Brown's faith to his despair, of those revered to those despised—incriminate us. We are made to see through Brown's eyes and simultaneously to see from outside of them. Since this is a story in which to comprehend is to be culpable, and to fear evil is to know how to project it, we do in our interpretation of Brown what he does to those around him. At that moment we, like Hawthorne, like the devil Hawthorne depicts, make Brown's fate irrevocable. Given the complexity of such moments (akin to the one in which Brown's assumption that others are evil both corrects an earlier naïveté—verifies what cannot but be true—and distorts truth beyond recognition), it is no accident that these moments are depicted surrealistically. Realism is only possible when the world is solid enough to be ascertained clearly. At the moment of intersecting glances—Brown's at those he loves, the devil's at Brown, ours at the characters—we learn we are not separate from what we see, but rather root out of our hearts and externalize the terrors we can no longer bear as internal. "Young Goodman Brown" is the tale of a man in search of an "outside," in search of a world that will give form to what he fears, will extract it from his heart so that he can see wretchedness rather than feel it. The tale does not, of course, end at this moment of catharsis. Rather, it details the predictable consequences. Hawthorne wants to tell us that we do not die of our projections but instead live them through. The story balances between the fatality of Brown's look (the way it makes consequences inevitable) and the tedium of those consequences as they stretch to the duration of a natural life.

In the following pages, I shall discuss tales in which Hawthorne is

[85]

critical of this sort of externalization and of the bodily aestheticism (to which I earlier alluded) that frequently accompanies it. In these tales Hawthorne forbids bodily rearrangements. He forbids externalizations of the non-bodily self (of the sort made by Young Goodman Brown), and he forbids embodiments of the non-corporeal world (of the sort made by Roderick Elliston in "Egotism; or, The Bosom Serpent"). In addition, he equates both externalization and embodiment—and the self-partialization that epitomizes each—with the allegory that is at once his own literary strategy and also the tales' subject. In the first section of the chapter, I shall examine tales that attempt to substitute a part of the body for the whole, or to separate one part of the body from another. In the second section, I shall examine tales in which the hope seems to be that a monument or a manuscript—an inanimate emblem rather than a corporeal entity—could stand not simply for the body but also in its stead. In the final section of the chapter, I shall examine tales that explicitly reject their characters' attempts to allegorize their bodies, to be other than themselves or other to themselves. Throughout these considerations, I shall be suggesting that Hawthorne's investigations of the human—like Melville's disembodiments of the whale—disturb conventional categories in order to ask of what they are truly made. Human beings turn to stone, straw into flesh, sentences are personified, while Hawthorne often uses his motley crowds to teach his *isolatoes* the wider repertoire of humanity. In a world where no category is fixed, where the questions—"what defines the human? what defiles it beyond recognition?"—have no predictable answers, the materials that represent the human (sentences, crowds, straw, or stone) need not have comparable status. Indeed, it is precisely in lieu of these categorical givens that the tales translate their characters precipitously into and out of life, creating a world that is, in the original sense of that word, terrific. Throughout my discussion I shall suggest that Hawthorne both allegorizes his subjects and is simultaneously critical of characters who attempt allegorizations. As I have observed, in the process of the criticism, he queries the meaning of allegory itself. Is meaning in the body? Is it attached to particular parts of the body? Would separating part from the whole (even if only allegorically) violate or dismember the totality of the body? Is allegory an illusion that there is such a thing as a "representative" part? And if one could get at that part (as Ahab in his discussion with the carpenter gets at the leg), would the quintessential reduction of the body to the meaning that stands for it *still* predicate a split, now between the bodily emblem (its flesh and blood essence) and the once again displaced meaning that lies beyond, within, or outside of it?

Thus, the question for Hawthorne, as for Melville, is how literal and figural, part and whole, are to be construed when they are relational rather than equative. "The little word *is* has its tragedies," George Santayana wrote in a clarifying passage Melville and Hawthorne would have taken differently to heart:

> it marries and identifies different things with the greatest innocence; and yet no two are ever identical, and if therein lies the charm of wedding them and calling them one, therein too lies the danger. Whenever I use the word *is*, except in sheer tautology, I deeply misuse it; and when I discover my error, the world seems to fall asunder and the members of my family no longer know one another.[5]

When Hawthorne's characters discover that bodily organs and emblems are not equivalent to the whole body, what falls apart are not members of the family but rather members of the bodily self, for which the "familiar" expression suddenly becomes metaphoric. In the following pages I shall suggest that Hawthorne's concentration on the human body raises questions about what things can be embodied, can show on or in the body. In one of *The American Notebook* entries, Hawthorne writes: "To have ice in one's blood" (VIII:184). Elsewhere he seems only half humorously to suppose that what appears on the body's surface has an origin in the corporeal interior, which could be searched out and found: "Little F. H- used to look into E-'s mouth to see where her smiles came from" (VIII:186). And in the most direct mutilation of the body, which makes an explicit connection between the literal and the figural, embodiment and disembodiment, bodily whole and its parts, Hawthorne writes:

> To make literal pictures of figurative expressions; —for instance, he burst into tears—a man suddenly turned into a shower of briny drops. An explosion of laughter—a man blowing up, and his fragments flying about on all sides. He cast his eyes upon the ground— a man standing eyeless, with his eyes staring up at him in wonderment, &c, &c, &c. (VIII:254)

It is not a coincidence that Hawthorne's three examples of "literal pictures of figurative expressions" are connected to the human body. Hawthorne not only considers the question of identity in human terms; he (as a direct consequence, and as the previous paragraph spells out) asks not how one self is related to another (Melville's implicit question) but rather how the body is related to itself — the totality to its grief and joy, or to the eyes that register either.

In Hawthorne's sketches human beings fully fleshed out are not simply absent, they are also irrelevant. In distinction from the tales, the sketches characteristically locate the world's conflicts as either internal or external, and do not see the way in which such simplifications wrench human or "complete" beings apart. In "Sights from a Steeple," for example, Paul Pry aspires to be outside himself in sights so distanced from the church tower to whose top he has climbed that they are recognizable only in miniature, in unknown corporeal forms. Oppositely, in "Fancy's Show Box," an everyman named Mr. Smith descends to an imaginative church floor, where he kneels to look inward at existence suddenly shrunk to the size of his own soul. If "Fancy's Show Box" characterizes existence by softening corporeality to spirit made momentarily visible, "Sights from a Steeple" steels the self against such revelations by suggesting it is (others') bodies that must be watched. These simplifications (the reduction of the self to other bodies or the reduction of the self to one's own invisible soul) constitute a more frightening enactment of witchcraft than any Hawthorne directly parodies. In both cases the exorcism of the soul from the body — the making of it immaterial — or the soul's domination and possession of the body pivots on a false understanding of the relation between interior and exterior. That relation, correctly seen, would be acknowledged as threefold rather than as dyadic: existing between the body and the soul, between one self and a human other, between all human selves and the non-human world, which cannot be made integral to either human body or soul.

In "Ethan Brand," the opposite impulses of the two sketches to which I have alluded come together in an acknowledgment of the connection between what lies within the body and what lies outside of it. For in distinction to these two sketches, Hawthorne's tales tend to look like mirrors in which divisions within the self are reflected in divisions between selves, and these divisions are further reflected by the separation between the human self and the disembodied natural world. If "Ethan Brand" is fleshed out, is a tale rather than a sketch, this is because it understands that the body's relation to itself and its relation to the outside world are connected, and because it posits the working out of that connection in the context of a human community (as "Fancy's Show Box" does not) without simultaneously repudiating (as "Sights from a Steeple" does) a soul or heart that is both internal and personal. Yet "Ethan Brand" also addresses the question of what would create such separations, as they are illustrated by the two sketches in which the self exists in isolation, a "haunted chamber" or a "desert," or in which the human community goes about its business, its existence documented by a voice that aspires to characteristics of chillness and obscurity, falsely muting the human to a bodied impersonality. I shall be suggesting that in "Ethan Brand," as in Hawthorne's other tales, characters aspire to be "representative men," to be bodies or souls or other, less frequently dichotomized emblematic parts. I thus invoke Emerson's words, not as he originally coined them—as epitomizing central characteristics to which all men should aspire (characteristics, in other words, that would make men *larger* than ordinary life)—but rather contrarily: "representative" in the sense of "emblematic" or "synecdochic." So reversed, the term designates men who would represent themselves by reducing themselves to discrete bodily parts, who—equated with such parts—would be diminished to their size.

In "Ethan Brand," Bartram, the man with no first name, sits with his son late one night tending a kiln that turns the marble of the white hills to valuable lime. We are told this was Ethan Brand's kiln when he deserted it years ago to look for the Unpardonable Sin. The two sitting together are startled by a laugh "like a wind" (XI:83); laughter, mirthless and terrific, echoes throughout the tale, coming from within the human body yet heard from distances away and having the preternatural power (Bartram says in a joke to little Joe) to "blow the roof of the house off": "'Oh, some drunken man . . . who dared not laugh loud enough within doors, lest he should blow the roof of the house off. So here he is, shaking his jolly sides, at the foot of Graylock'" (XI:83). Bartram's explanation is meant to calm by making metaphoric a violence Brand will make literal. The terrible mind-noise Bartram designates as laughter of course turns out to be Brand's, and when he appears, Bartram sends Joe to fetch the villagers to listen to Brand's story. Joe comes back with an array of people—Hawthorne illustrating lives and sins alternative to Brand's. In the midst of this menagerie we are shown a stray dog chasing its own tail, a counterpoint to Brand's story as the village people first ask him to recount it and then are rather distracted by the visualization that duplicates in comic (that is, bearable) terms what they have no mind to hear. It is the narrator who delivers the story in full after the villagers have gone home and Joe and Bartram have retired, for we are compelled to listen to the tale from which the others depart. Brand, sickened by his ruminations as they are revealed in the passage below, climbs into the furnace and is found the next day a skeleton, except for the human heart obtruding between his ribs. The heart is nothing to Bartram, as it was once nothing to Brand, so he pokes at the skeleton and reduces it to ashes.

[89]

The tale is extraordinary on several independent counts. Perhaps the least of these is the explanation to which the townspeople will not listen and which, when we are told it, seems a stylization—like the sketches of Mr. Smith and Paul Pry—inadequately fleshed out:

> When they had gone, Ethan Brand sat listening to the crackling of the kindled wood . . . deep within his mind, he was reviewing the gradual, but marvellous change, that had been wrought upon him by the search to which he had devoted himself. He remembered how the night-dew had fallen upon him—how the dark forest had whispered to him—how the stars had gleamed upon him—a simple and loving man, watching his fire in the years gone by, and ever musing as it burned. He remembered with what tenderness, with what love and sympathy for mankind, and what pity for human guilt and wo, he had first begun to contemplate those ideas which afterwards became the inspiration of his life; with what reverence he had then looked into the heart of man, viewing it as a temple originally divine, and however desecrated, still to be held sacred by a brother; with what awful fear he had deprecated the success of his pursuit, and prayed that the Unpardonable Sin might never be revealed to him. Then ensued that vast intellectual development, which, in its progress, disturbed the counterpoise between his mind and heart. The Idea that possessed his life had operated as a means of education; it had gone on cultivating his powers to the highest point of which they were susceptible; it had raised him from the level of an unlettered laborer, to stand on a star-light eminence, whither the philosophers of the earth, laden with the lore of universities, might vainly strive to clamber after him. So much for the intellect! But where was the heart? That, indeed, had withered—had contracted—had hardened—had perished! It had ceased to partake of the universal throb. . . .
>
> Thus Ethan Brand became a fiend. He began to be so from the moment that his moral nature had ceased to keep the pace of improvement with his intellect. And now, as his highest effort and inevitable development—as the bright and gorgeous flower, and rich, delicious fruit of his life's labor—he had produced the Unpardonable Sin! (XI:98–99)

The moral's relative insufficiency to explain the power of the tale provides an inadvertent demonstration of its own central point. Turn passion for an object into curiosity about its working and you get the sacrifice that is the tale's ostensible subject—the sacrifice of life to the idea that would dissect it. This sacrifice is the one made by Brand. It is the one made *of* Brand, Hawthorne's explanation of what happens to Brand suffering the same didactic reduction. In addition, the moral—that Brand loses his heart in the process of intellectualizing it—is adjacent to aspects of the story (its tableaus and reflections, to which I shall momentarily turn) for which it fails to account; and it also curiously contradicts Brand's *defense* of the crime for which he is ostensibly doing penance. What distinguishes "Ethan Brand" is the way in which the story told by the explicit moral (as it is advanced by the passage above and as it is italicized in the emblem of the heart at the tale's end) comes into relationship with an alternative and contradictory story, for the illustration of the moral seems not simply to deflect from that moral but to offer another story entirely.

We are told Brand loses his heart the moment he conceives it possible to see or study the organ. Yet I would like to suggest that Brand wishes to look at the heart (as Hawthorne makes us look at it, makes us momentarily be like Brand) not because seeing it means understanding it, but rather because seeing it means externalizing it. "'Freely, were it to do again, would I incur the guilt,'" Brand says to the townspeople, "'Unshrinkingly, I accept the retribution'" (XI:90). But one half of the story implies that Brand would incur the guilt so that he could accept the retribution. When Brand climbs into the furnace, he does not do so out of penance. The defiance of his explanation makes this sanguine interpretation implausible. Rather, he subjects himself to fire so that he can make his heart external, so that he can literally be without it. Thus, despite conventional interpretations—the one proffered by Brand and by the narrator—which construe Brand's motives (to study the human heart) as innocent, although the consequences (the losing of the heart) are not, Brand's defiant explanation suggests that the motives desire the consequence. The heart is unbearable. Seeing it or studying it is not an end; it is rather a means for expulsion of the vital organ. These are Brand's last words:

> "Oh, Mother Earth," cried he, "who art no more my Mother, and into whose bosom this frame shall never be resolved! Oh, mankind, whose brotherhood I have cast off, and trampled thy great heart beneath my feet! Oh, stars of Heaven, that shone on me of old, as if to light me onward and upward!—farewell all, and forever! Come, deadly element of Fire—henceforth my familiar friend! Embrace me as I do thee!" (XI:100)

This is Brand turned Ahab, the man who would have no heart, even at that moment when he wishes most succor from the universe. Ahab's appeal in "The Candles" echoes Brand's words:

> "Oh, thou clear spirit, of thy fire thou madest me, and like a true child of fire, I breathe it back to thee. . . . Oh, thou foundling fire . . . again with haughty agony, I read my sire . . . I burn with thee; would fain be welded with thee." (119:642–43)

The desire to be "resolved" into an invisible world bosom, into a "universal throb," and the desire to resolve the self of such a wish by ridding the body of the heart are confused in Brand as they will be confused in Ahab. Brand's description of the stars that are to light him "onward and upward" suggests it is divinity he is after when he embarks upon his search, although if this is a Faust tale, it is personalized by the desire for the "embrace" of the universe as well as by the desire for its power.

Because divinity is unimaginable—because nothing is imaginable—without the body that fleshes thought out, Brand looks for in the world of men what he wishes for from the divine world. Thinking man is made in God's image, Brand knows divinity inheres in man. But when literalizing this idea, when he imagines divinity to have a shape (the shape of the sacred heart) which could first be found in the human body and then separated from it, he is imagining an emblem or a body for what has none. We will be told that "brotherhood," no less than divinity, refuses specific embodiment. Thus, divinity lies outside of the heart as well as within and above it. And while at the beginning of the tale Brand tries to "trample" brotherhood under his feet—this is the tale's verb—at the end of the tale, it is nonetheless visible in the sky: "Stepping from one to another of the clouds that rested on the hills, and thence to the loftier brotherhood that sailed in air, it seemed almost as if a mortal man might thus ascend into the heavenly regions" (XI:101). Brotherhood, like divinity, like all those abstractions in whose name we live, is emphatically dislodged from any specific picture. Yet it is just because he thinks divinity has a body, a shape that could (independently) be known, that Brand imagines particular bodies do not matter. They are containments that must be violated to get to the essence that lies within. Thus, Brand imagines a shape for the divinity that has none, and he simultaneously discounts the shape of the human body as a mere immateriality. For he still cannot understand that the heart can be divine (hence, must not be violated) and that this divinity has no embodiment that can be separated from the human heart. Yet there is no heart outside of the human body or of the world of human selves. The world is too large to be conceived of as an embodiment. It cannot have a heart because it does not have a body. Insofar as Brand *does* understand this, he will have no heart, will—like the world—be an outside with no inside. He will be, as he says, a "frame."

The kiln accommodates this desire. Throughout the tale Brand's contemplation of the fire in the kiln is associated with his search for the human heart. The kiln is personified, and prior to Brand's search it is given daemonic voice: "Ethan Brand," we are told, "had conversed with Satan himself, in the lurid blaze of this very kiln" (XI:89). Such personifications make the kiln into a body. The fire is its heart. In the following comparative (he is here addressing the village people he despises) Brand draws the connection directly: " 'I have looked . . . into many a human heart that was seven times hotter with sinful passions than yonder furnace is with fire' " (XI:90). Brand may in his comparative be acknowledging that his eventual incineration is only a submission of the heart to its own passionate element, which therefore cannot ignite it any more or any differently. At any rate, he is implying that the sight before the eyes (the fire of the kiln) and the sight behind the eyes (the fire of the heart) are identical. In fact, since the Unpardonable Sin is dislodged from any context but that of the human heart, sin and the heart also come into an unspecified equivalence. The search for the Unpardonable Sin is the search for the human heart externalized and made abstract. Brand's central wish, ungratified by the tale, is to abolish the difference between internal and external worlds, to make the fire in the kiln be the fire in the eyes, and this fire a mere reflection of the fire in the human heart. The ultimate goal of this confusion is, as I suggested earlier, to find the world-heart outside the body, which, as Brand specifies in his plea to Mother Earth, will "embrace" him in a literal action we might have mistaken to be a metaphoric one. But since Brand cannot discover the heart outside the body, he will make *his* heart external, and then be consumed by it. Hawthorne describes Brand, an inverted Prometheus, about to leap into the furnace as a "fiend on the verge of plunging into his gulf of intensest torment" (XI:100)—inside and outside effectively confused, forcing the external world to embrace him after all.

The expulsion of the heart from the body is consonant with the other, less palpable expulsion from the body, the ripples of laughter as they echo throughout the tale. We are told that more than anything else laughter "expresse[s] the condition of [Brand's] inward being" (XI:97). We hear the sound initially as it interrupts Bartram's conversation with little Joe. And the same terrible noise that precedes Brand's arrival also ushers him out of the world:

> That night the sound of a fearful peal of laughter rolled heavily through the sleep of the lime-burner and his little son; dim shapes of horror and anguish haunted their dreams, and seemed still present in the rude hovel when they opened their eyes to the daylight. (XI:100)

Laughter is related to the heart first by the way in which the tale makes them coincident, at Brand's appearance and at his death. Second, the two are related as a response is to an idea—in this case Brand's daemonic or

[93]

despairing response to the (false) idea that the heart could exist outside the body. Finally, laughter is the means through which the heart leaves the body. Laughter is an outburst, with that expression literalized. It repels and displaces what in fact belongs within:

> Laughter, when out of place, mistimed, or bursting forth from a disordered state of feeling, may be the most terrible modulation of the human voice. The laughter of one asleep, even if it be a little child—the madman's laugh—the wild, screaming laugh of a born idiot, are sounds that we sometimes tremble to hear, and would always willingly forget. Poets have imagined no utterance of fiends or hobgoblins so fearfully appropriate as a laugh. And even the obtuse lime-burner felt his nerves shaken, as this strange man looked inward at his own heart, and burst into laughter that rolled away into the night, and was indistinctly reverberated among the hills. (XI:87–88)

Insofar as laughter externalizes (by responding to) what is seen from within, it ousts the interior vision, gets it out of the body. Thus, laughter would expel the mind's visions into the world. Or, as the last sentence of the paragraph suggests, it would leave them where they are while vacating the body to look at it. At the tale's end, very much as at the beginning of Brand's search, Brand does not want his heart back. He rather wants to relinquish it. The devil is in his heart. The devil *is* his heart. Fire, he thinks, if not laughter, will blow the roof off his body, will let the terrible thing out. As his name suggests, Brand does not want to cast sin out of his body. He wants instead to cast his heart out of his body in extension of the crime for which he is ostensibly doing penance. Indeed, while most interpretations of the tale see the shape of the heart left within Brand's body as evidence of Hawthorne's giving Brand back the heart he has come to want, it is in fact as consonant with one aspect of the story to read the conclusion—in which we are told that "within the ribs—strange to say—was the shape of a human heart" (XI:102)—not ironically at all, but as a sign of Hawthorne's refusal to take the heart away from Brand, of his insistence that the heart cannot be—not even conceptually, not even in death—situated anywhere but within.

There is, however, another way of reading the story—the one espoused by the tale's didacticism—which implies that Hawthorne agrees with Brand in the latter's assumption that bodies do not matter. This reading would suggest that bodies must be taken apart because they obscure the heart that lies inside of them. Thus, Brand, looking at the townspeople, dismisses what he sees: " 'Years and years ago, I groped into your hearts' " he says, still misapplying physical idioms to non-physical things, and looking now not at their hearts at all but rather at their degenerate bodies, "'and found nothing there for my purpose. Get ye gone!'" (XI:93). But they, on the basis of the same external evidence of the body, falsely dismiss Brand: "Finding nothing . . . very remarkable in his aspect—nothing but a sunburnt wayfarer, in plain garb and dusty shoes, who sat looking into the fire," finding nothing remarkable in the external evidence of the searing going on within, "these young people speedily grew tired of observing him" (XI:94). Because the villagers are no more capable of seeing into Brand's heart (however he testifies to the pain of its existence there) than he is capable of looking into their hearts, the story's conventional explanation suggests that bodies are barriers that stand in the way. They must be dismembered or mutilated to get to the essence that lies inside—an idea exactly contrary to the one (that such dismemberment is sin) the story elsewhere advances.

In line with the didactic reading of the tale, we could say that Brand sacrifices his body when he sees that particular bodies make no difference. Like all hearts, they are the same. Thus, for example, Bartram, left alone with Brand, reads the Master Sin in Brand's heart as a mirror for his own: "They were all of one family; they went to and fro between his breast and Ethan Brand's, and carried dark greetings from one to the other" (XI:88). One could say Brand's body remains alive in the physical visage of Bartram—the man who is all body—and in the visage of the little boy—the child who is all heart, and with whom Brand sees "eye to eye." Mutilation (at least in the reading of the story that follows its own didacticism) does not disfigure man by depriving him of parts of his body. It rather shows his essential connection to what lies outside his body. Mutilation shows man that bodies are immaterial.

In this light, of Giles the lawyer (who argues the case for Hawthorne) we are told he is "but the fragment of a human being, a part of one foot having been chopped off by an axe, and an entire hand torn away by the devilish gripe of a steam-engine" (XI:91). We are also told, however, that although "the corporeal hand was gone, a spiritual member remained." The description, of course, refers to the feeling in and of the phantom limb. But in the context of a tale in which—as one directive of the story suggests—characters need to rid themselves of their corporeal bodies in order to become spiritual members, Giles's mutilation redeems him. And indeed throughout the tale, Hawthorne himself seems intent on taking the body apart, or on showing its parts in relief, as if, severed from the body, they would reveal their shared essence. Thus, Joe, looking through the Jew's diorama, has Brand's eyes "fixed upon him" (XI:95). Joe is not simply seen by Brand, as the idiomatic expression suggests. He also sees with eyes so akin to Brand's that for all practical purposes, there is no difference between them—as at certain moments in *Moby-Dick* there is, for all practical purposes, no difference between Pip and Ahab. In fact, the last look we have of Brand, other than the narrator's, is filtered through Joe's vision of him: "As the boy followed his father into the hut, he looked back to the wayfarer, and the tears came into his eyes; for his tender spirit had an intuition of the bleak and terrible loneliness in which this man had enveloped himself" (XI:98). Emphasizing in other terms the desire for synonymy, the narrator tells us that before Brand set out on his journey he had "thrown his dark thoughts into the intense glow of [the] furnace, and melted them, as it were, into the one thought that took possession of his life" (XI:84). The second explanation suggests that this is a tale in which eyes and limbs, or hearts and thoughts, must be taken out of the body, or synecdochically severed from it, in a dismemberment whose purpose is a "melting" of many into one.

The two explanations I have advanced—that the story advances—are at odds on all significant counts. The didactic explanation insists that Brand has to rid himself of the body in order to discover the heart. The undermining explanation insists that the body cannot be gotten rid of; it is heretical to try to do so. The didactic explanation suggests that Brand thrusts himself into the furnace to pay for his crime. The alternative explanation is that he thrusts himself into the furnace to perpetuate his crime. The didactic explanation suggests that Hawthorne gives Brand back his heart. The subversive explanation suggests that Hawthorne never allows him to relinquish it. Yet both explanations concur in faulting the idea that the heart is invisible *because* it is inside the body. Both agree that not being able to see the heart (or the essence that it symbolizes) is rather a consequence of its not being visible anywhere. The heart is not visible inside the self, because one feels rather than sees it there. Nor is the heart visible inside others' bodies, because one cannot see inside others' bodies, at least one cannot literalize that expression. But the heart is not visible outside the body either, for the idea of looking "outside" the self is equivalent to looking *away* from it. Nor is the heart visible in the outsides of others' bodies, if what one expects to see there is something other than the body. Thus, both readings of the tale suggest dissatisfaction with the idea of seeing and with the idea of a dichotomized outside and inside, conventionally defined, although the first reading would express this dissatisfaction by suggesting that outsides (or bodies) cannot be dismissed, and the second reading by insisting that they must be. For we feel rather than see our connection to other beings, and cannot make emblems of, cannot embody what we feel.

In this respect we are all like Giles, missing the palpable embodiments that would both reify (give external shape to) our meanings and simultaneously make them complete. For Giles, the conventional distinction (that one sees what is outside and visible and feels what is inside and invisible) is exactly reversed. As we also are meant to do, Giles feels what is simultaneously outside ("exterior to" as well as "without" or "missing") and invisible. Thus, the initial distinction between outside and inside, as Brand tries to make it (with "outside" construed as the body, "inside" construed as the heart), is corrected by the tale. The correction would go as follows. It would detach the idea of an "inside" from the figure of a human heart and enlarge it one step further to embrace the totality of a single self. Brand—ironizing the point—throws himself into the furnace and shows us how this is done. He becomes the fiery heart. It would now—going one step further—enlarge the idea of an "outside" so that the designation applied not only to the human flesh but to all that lies exterior to it—whether this exterior be designated by the phantom limb to which Giles nonetheless feels himself connected or whether it be designated by the community of human bodies that lies outside the single self to which it nonetheless ought to feel connected. The tale would then advance a final correction, getting "inside" and "outside" right for the first time. At the end of the tale, the whole human community of corporeal beings is itself shown to be the heart that lies in the body of the world. As if to offer us an image (something too amorphous and large to be codified as an emblem) different from the heart limed within Brand's ribs, Hawthorne depicts the sight of the village as the sun lights it up:

> The early sunshine was already pouring its gold upon the mountain-tops, and though the valleys were still in shadow, they smiled cheerfully in the promise of the bright day that was hastening onward. The village, completely shut in by hills, which swelled away gently about it, looked as if it had rested peacefully in the hollow of the great hand of Providence. (XI:100–101)

The land is like a body in which the human community rests. The land contains the village as the body contains the heart.

If the land is the body and the village is the human heart, then the distinction between inside and outside, as the story has delimited it, is not here corrected; it is actually reversed. Corporeal bodies and palpable dwellings are now conceived of as the land's "inside." The body is the heart. But this heart is the universal one. Hawthorne fleshes the image out:

> Every dwelling was distinctly visible; the little spires of the two churches pointed upward, and caught a fore-glimmering of bright-

[97]

ness from the sun-gilt skies upon their gilded weathercocks. The tavern was astir, and the figure of the old, smoke-dried stage-agent, cigar in mouth, was seen beneath the stoop. Old Graylock was glorified with a golden cloud upon his head. (XI:101)

This is a vision that does not discriminate—between evil men and good men, between churches and taverns, between the man shapes and the mountain shapes, between similitude and the real thing (the image of the heart in the land's body is, after all, only an analogy), for all are part of the universal pulse. I have said this image is the alternative to the one at the end of the tale. The latter emblem reveals Brand's dead heart within his body. The former reveals the collective heart of the human community in the body of the world. The two images come into fused relationship. While the emblem of the heart limed in Brand's ribs is itself isolated and stresses man's isolation, images like that of the village-heart are plural, intermingled, and scattered throughout the tale. Even in the first description of the kiln, before man enters the picture, we see relationships unmutilated by the attempts to pry their respective parts into clarity:

> There are many such lime-kilns in that tract of country, for the purpose of burning the white marble which composes a large part of the substance of the hills. Some of them, built years ago, and long deserted, with weeds growing in the vacant round of the interior, which is open to the sky, and grass and wild flowers rooting themselves into the chinks of stones. (XI:84)

The weeds are inseparable from the interior of the kiln; its vacant enclosures are filled with open sky; the wild flowers are rooted in chinks of stone. All possible discriminations are naturally—by nature—muted out of existence.

Similarly, the alternate readings of the story come into confused relationship. It should already have become clear that they are not easy to tell apart. However the tale offers proximate or alternate clues about Brand's motives (hence, about the meaning of his ending), it is crucial to note that both readings converge in their dismissal of the conventional dichotomy between an outside and an inside: in the one case, as I have suggested, by insisting that the heart is in the body (cannot be expelled from it because it cannot be distinguished from it) and in the other case by suggesting that the heart must be expelled, must be housed in the collective body of mankind. Thus, whether the story be understood as a tale about a man who wants to rid himself of his heart—to brand it on the world—or as a story about a man who wants to find the universal heart and who inadvertently loses his own, either explanation insists this is not a story about simple heartlessness, but rather a story that suggests uncertainty about where the heart resides—on the outside or the inside. The following image would rebuke Ethan Brand, were he alive to see what it represents. It does rebuke the shape of the emblem found between his ribs at the tale's end. In place of that emblem, it acknowledges that the world is larger than morals or emblems, cannot cut itself to human distinction because it will not cut itself to human size:

> Scattered, likewise, over the breasts of the surrounding mountains, there were heaps of hoary mist, in fantastic shapes, some of them far down into the valley, others high up towards the summits, and still others, of the same family of mist or cloud, hovering in the gold radiance of the upper atmosphere. Stepping from one to another of the clouds that rested on the hills, and thence to the loftier brotherhood that sailed in air, it seemed almost as if a mortal man might thus ascend into the heavenly regions. Earth was so mingled with sky that it was a daydream to look at it. (XI:101)

Man cannot fuse with the outside world, cannot become one with it, because the body always intervenes. Yet the natural world embraces the human world. The natural world does to Brand what Brand had wanted to do to *it*. And in encompassing the mortal world, it softens the distinctions it nonetheless insists upon. Brand gives his life, then, for a totality he could have had *in* life but not on human terms. This totality is felt rather than known, seen rather than understood, omnipresent rather than embodied, a mist rather than an emblem. In the specification of the vision as a "daydream" (a word that distills the contradictions of the entire tale) Hawthorne offers us an alternative to the distinctions Brand has tried to make. In fact, the tale offers us alternatives that exactly parallel Brand's: to arrive at a simple meaning by casting out of our minds one half of the story (as Brand tries to cast his heart out of his body), or to acknowledge both sides of the tale and its attendant contradictions, which, like earth and sky, are so mingled as to be inseparable.

The problematic relation between inside and outside (between ostensible oppositions) is insisted upon throughout the tale, mirroring Brand's dilemma. Thus, for example, we are asked to look at the kiln, and at the way in which it casts reflections on the human countenance. But that image is ambiguously complemented by the moonlight in the sky, as it casts reflections on the human countenance. Is this the same light or a different light? What is the relation between the fire in the human heart and the fire in the kiln, or between these and the sky's fire? Hawthorne turns our attention from the story Brand would tell to the stories of the people gathered around him, as the latter stories drown out his words. Do their stories duplicate his own or deviate from it? And what is the relationship between duplication and deviation when it is adjacently conceived? The devil is initially depicted as residing in the furnace, but later he is depicted as residing in the man. Are these conceptions proximate or alternate? Thus, we are made to look within the self for the origin of evil. Brand's story is such a look. But we are alternately asked to look for it in the world, whether that world be depicted by the German Jew's diorama or by the frivolous village people whose lives—compared to Brand's—are as or more pernicious. The displacements to which I refer are made most explicit in the problematic connection between literal ways of understanding the world and metaphoric ways of understanding it. Another way of putting this is to say that Hawthorne's playing off of literality and metaphorization is both at the heart of the tale's conflicts and reveals that heart to insist upon a connection between literality and the outside world, metaphorization and the inside world.

But exterior and literal or interior and metaphoric have neither conventional nor stable associations. We are therefore shown that metaphoric ways of figuring things trivialize what they depict. They distance event from feeling about it by interposing figures of speech between the two, as if hoping that language could empty itself of reality rather than hoping to reflect it. So the German Jew talks about carrying the Unpardonable Sin on his shoulders—the idea of carrying it "on" the body is as close as he wants to come in this debunking of a notion that Brand makes too close for comfort. So Bartram left alone with Brand fears the two will have to deal "heart to heart." But the expression for Bartram's fear wards off the experience unaccommodated by convention by finding the conventional idiom for it. The expression embraces the category to which such dealings would belong. It evades the dealings themselves. In grotesque parody of this subversion, waking the next morning to think that Brand has not tended the fire, Bartram imagines a passion so consuming it could throw a man into the furnace. Hence, Bartram's words do to the thought of Brand what Brand does to himself. But for Bartram, thought bears no relation to the actual world it reflects on. Because he does not understand that words are not literal enactments and yet matter anyway, he also fails to understand how they ever could be literal. Brand's body in the kiln, when Bartram sees it, is as meaningless in reality as the thought that wished to put it there. Bartram's inability to credit his own thought as at all immersed in reality makes him, conversely, unable to let reality—when he sees it— register in thought. In both cases, language intervenes. In the first instance, it takes what we will discover as literal and dismisses it as metaphoric: " 'If I catch the fellow hereabouts again I shall feel like tossing him into the furnace!' " (XI:102). In the second case, Bartram escapes understanding what he has seen by making what is metaphoric literal. " 'Was the fellow's heart made of marble?' " Bartram cries, "perplexed" when he sees that Brand's body, like the marble of the hills has been converted into lime. In each case, experience escapes the meaning that would make sense of it by shifting to another category of discourse, that is, by being displaced. This displacement is analogous to Brand's desire to exteriorize the heart, to shift its location when he cannot bear it to be interior.

Bartram's categorical shifts are possible because he imagines all he thinks and says as a mere manner of speaking. In this respect, we too are like Bartram-Brand. Like Bartram, we normalize the story's violence by categorizing it as an allegory. We then consider allegory as that form of fiction whose literalization has no meaning. Hawthorne will not let us rest long, however, in the satisfactions of such an act, for in the conjunction of the didactic explanation with the explanation that subverts it, he turns a querying of the convention into the tale's subject. At the same time he asks that we examine the alternative to the convention's categorical dismissals. In Ethan Brand's case, the alternative to metaphorizing the world is to understand it literally. Such a reification kills. Metaphorizations of the world, literalizations of the world—these modes of conception, along with the relationship between inside and outside, comprise the tale's subject. Insofar as it enacts a series of displacements about which I have been speaking, these displacements are as if epitomized in the tale's concern with the status of language, or rather its concern with the status of how conception is to "take itself": of whether it is to take itself as embodied in the world (as literal) or as disembodied in the mind (as metaphor). Of course, this way of putting it, which is the tale's way of putting it, is exactly corollary to the problem Ethan Brand ponders. Is the heart "in" the body? Is it in one's own body? Can it be palpably conceived? Would one have to externalize it to so conceive it? Would such externalizations make one heartless? If one looked for the heart outside one's body rather than feeling it within, would this displacement kill? Behind all of these questions is, inescapably, the larger question: why are these alternatives? Hawthorne, like any moralist, answers his own questions. But he answers them indirectly, as he has raised them indirectly. Thus, when Joe and Bartram first hear it, the laugh is "inside" Brand. It sounds "outside," however, "like a wind shaking the boughs of the forest." Even from the first paragraph, inside and outside, literal and metaphoric ways of understanding the world are brought together to be confused. One way of looking at the simile is to see that the laugh does to Brand (to Brand as well as to the listeners) what the wind does to the bough. Forced out of the body, laughter treats the body like a genuine externality, shakes it from outside. The creation of a simile that enacts the spatial displacements that will be the tale's subject cannot be accidental. As if to insist that we question the meaning of what we have heard (is the laugh inside or outside? of what is it made?), Joe, the child whose questions are formed in the image of Brand's, asks, "'Father, what is that?'" (XI:83).

In "Egotism; or, The Bosom-Serpent," Hawthorne answers the question "what is that?" by dismissing the embodied thing as nothing. As Brand is a man who wants to get rid of his heart, Roderick Elliston is a man who would shrink the world to the size of his heart. He harbors an imaginary serpent: self-concern so palpable it is solidified in an actual body. Although his fleshly body is what Roderick sees when he looks at himself, he also sees the (inner) monster image that permeates to the outside and is reflected in his walk. Roderick slithers like the snake that he thinks is housed within him. "Egotism; or, The Bosom-Serpent" is subtitled "From the Unpublished 'Allegories of the Heart.'" Because allegory in its broadest sense refers to a second body of reference different from the entity that stands for it, I take the tale's subtitle to comment on Roderick's reification of the bodily fiction. For Roderick attempts to allegorize (that is, to dichotomize) the idea of a self, to imagine a self within the body (contained there as a separate body, in this case, the body of a serpent). The story asks us to understand that such a fate is "'the commonest thing in the world'" (X:270). The bosom serpent is generic. It defines all human selves. It simultaneously individuates. Although there is some evidence that the snake "'is a family peculiarity,'" Roderick explains, "'to tell you the truth, I have no faith in this idea of the snake's being an heir-loom. He is my own snake and no man's else'" (X:282). Although the self is not fated, what *is* fated is the association of poison and self-regard. "'It gnaws me! It gnaws me!'" (X:269) Roderick says, pleasuring in his pain because pain teaches him particularity. He acts as if affliction, sin, or fate, whose antagonism to his being seems to constitute that being, differentiates his inside from that of any other. Without such differentiation, he perhaps supposes he would be an outside with no (distinguishable) inside.

Yet bodies cannot contain other bodies as the whale contained Jonah. Even in the throes of the fantasy, this fact is acknowledged:

> Horrible love—horrible antipathy—embracing one another in his bosom, and both concentrating themselves upon a being that had crept into his vitals, or been engendered there, and which was nourished with his food, and lived upon his life. (X:279)

The fantasized reduction of the fleshly body to the serpent body upholds the essential truth that one self cannot have two bodies. What nourishes the second body is self-contemplation, and when Roderick's wife appears (she is visible only when he is capable of seeing her), the serpent vanishes, displaced by the body of the outside world. The tale is poised on questions of what constitutes embodiment, of whether " 'the serpent was a physical reptile' " or a " 'symbol' " (X:283) suggested to the fancy by a morbid imagination. In one sense the distinction does not matter, for what the mind has tenacity to conceive, it feels as palpably embodied. In another sense, the fantasmal nature of the construction is crucial, for only if the monster body is genuinely immaterial can it also be dismissed. The discriminations are faultless. The serpent is real when the self gives it credence, when the eyes are rolled backward or inward. When the eyes look outward at the world, the bosom serpent is nothing. In fact, it is just because each man's visions are hidden by the body that each can fancy himself to be alone, the master fiend (Roderick thinks of his snake as a "divinity . . . darkly infernal" [X:274]). The logic, like the loathing, like the concomitant self-aggrandizement, would go as follows: no serpent but a man's own consumes him. Therefore, though he knows that others' breasts contain crimes, since they do not stain (his) life, other bosom serpents must comparably be innocuous. Yet, with a knowledge veering in the other direction (that is, with knowledge, like self-image, comparably dichotomized) Brand and Roderick also know that torture is calibrated to the specifications each defines for himself. Torture cannot but be innocuous except when felt from within. Roderick, as if in an "exercise of ventriloquism" (X:277), makes others turn inside to their own bosom serpents: 'Thus, making his own actual serpent—if a serpent there actually was in his bosom—the type of each man's fatal error . . . or unquiet conscience, and striking his sting so unremorsefully into the sorest spot, we may well imagine that Roderick became the pest of the city" (X:277). The passage's subjunctive is crucial in its distinctions. What is delusive (unembodied) to those outside the private vision is real (embodied) to those who suffer its sting from within.

"Ethan Brand" and "Egotism; or, The Bosom-Serpent" are not the only tales that treat the body as if it could be disassembled. In "The Intelligence Office," men appear in supplication to an official for things lost from "heart, mind, or pocket" (X:327). The scramble of aspirations comprises Hawthorne's parody of human folly that moronically imagines the losses I have alluded to as equivalent. One man inquires after a lock of hair, another after a lost wedding band, a third after his general health, a fourth for cheaper lodgings, a fifth for his missing leg; others want rather to be dispossessed of hearts or sins or lives. The tale first anatomizes human desire in its diversity. Second, it discriminates between what can and cannot be lost, found, or exchanged. Trivial desires can be granted; others are not negotiable. The man with the amputated leg discovers the body will not regenerate itself. Sin cannot be dispelled, even in exchange for a man's whole fortune and "a heart was occasionally brought hither, of such exquisite material, so delicately attempered, and so curiously wrought, that no other heart could be found to match it" (X:325). In the midst of the bedlam a man appears on whom the tale pauses long enough to focus. When the Intelligence Officer inquires about his business, the man says he is in search of a "place." The wish seems simple to gratify. But the occupations held before his eyes (" 'There are many [places] vacant, or soon to be so, some of which will probably suit, since they range from that of a footman up to a seat at the council-board, or in the cabinet, on a throne, or a presidential chair' " [X:322]) are apparently not what the man has in mind:

> In short, he evidently wanted, not in a physical or intellectual sense, but with an urgent moral necessity that is the hardest of all things to satisfy, since it knows not its own object. . . . "Either of the places you mention, indeed, might answer my purpose—or, more probably, none of them. I want my place! —my own place! — my true place in the world! —my proper sphere! —my thing to do, which nature intended me to perform when she fashioned me thus awry, and which I have vainly sought, all my lifetime!" (X:323)

The question posed by the man without a place—it is Bartleby in another guise who appears to us here—is impossible to satisfy. The Intelligence Officer reminds him: " 'Ask for something specific, and it may doubtless be negotiated. . . . But were I to go further, I should have the whole population of the city upon my shoulders; since far the greater proportion of them are, more or less, in your predicament' " (X:323). Notwithstanding the dismissal of the request or the idiosyncracy of the character who poses it, the desire it expresses is fundamental. Human wishes are trivialized to the precise degree that they focus on minute parts—on trinkets or rings or legs—and then mistake those parts for the whole. While the man without a place wishes to know how he fits in the universe outside of him, others in the tale wish to know what will fit in or on them. They do not imagine an "outside" except in the process of making it interior. They do to themselves what allegories do to characters: they dichotomize life by allocating it to representative emblems. The point of the tale is to show us how characters anatomize their lives, how they assume the object of desire to be a bodily part or an equally detached abstraction. Contemplating their lives, they interpret the question "what is that?" as if the body were a pocket in which hearts or minds could fit.

Melville in *Moby-Dick* had answered the question "what is that?" by disembodying a whale. In tale after tale, Hawthorne disembodies a man. Melville knocks his characters bloody against the inscrutability of the whale head. Hawthorne turns his knife cleanly to cut out the inscrutable human heart. *Moby-Dick* is a novel unafraid of continuity because, as I suggested in the first chapter, it raises questions about the body in an ostensible consideration of monsters, which are then dismembered. Although the true subject of *Moby-Dick* is "of what are human bodies made?" the triumph of the novel is that it explores this question while leaving bodies intact. They are killed rather than dismembered. They are killed in order not to be dismembered, or rather the dismemberment takes place analogically as grafting in Pip's discussion with Ahab, or before the novel begins in the emblem of human incompletion — Ahab's amputated leg — an emblem whose meaning is borne out in Ahab's discussion with the carpenter, or in references so brief (the sliced toes of the whale blubber men) they are easy to repress. Hawthorne's tales, on the other hand, focus directly on the questions: What constitutes the human? How does the human escape the body either through transcendence or defilement? What is the relationship between part of the body and the whole? Such a focus dismisses the distinction between "inside" and "outside," at least as Melville conceives it. Because for Hawthorne, as I suggested earlier, the part is both inside the body and equivalent to the body, it — primarily — signifies the body's relation to itself. Thus, unlike Melville, Hawthorne does not ask about the difference between one body and another. Rather, he asks about the relation between a single body and the essence that represents it. Characters who wish to establish their relation to a genuine "outside" (as, for example, Ethan Brand does or, in quite another context, the man without a place) embark futilely on a journey throughout the world for what (like the dog chasing his own tail) they could have found within. Here Hawthorne is advocating not the solipsism of Roderick Elliston but the consciousness of little Joe in "Ethan Brand" — the being who has plumbed the depths of his own heart without being drowned in them and who hence knows he has room in his heart for those outside his bodily person.

For Melville the world that will not sanction fusion between persons is monstrous. In *Moby-Dick* the relish for disembodiment is directly related to the rage that there is no literal (that is, bodily) connection between one man and another. The hope of mutilation is that if the self could be disinterred, taken out of its skin (an idea Melville plays with as early as *White-Jacket*),[6] it would be shown to have the same "parts" as all other men; all might exist within an identical corporeal body. Insofar as narrative in *Moby-Dick* is encyclopedic, its central illusion is that it contains all the body's parts. It is a dictionary, a catalog, a sum, a whole that hymns the totality (between one man and another, between one man and the world) that the world denies. In *Moby-Dick* parts of the body (the whale's or man's) *never* seem emblematic. They do not epitomize a single man. Instead, they epitomize his separation from other men. Oppositely, when Melville's narrative does focus on one bodily entity—the doubloon as navel, the leg Ahab and Pip might share—this bodily entity contains symbolic glue. It is no longer a part, but rather becomes, as the mind magically dreams it, an image of the universal body in which selves will be "squeeze[d] . . . into each other."

Contrarily, Hawthorne's disembodiments do not enlarge the self. They rather distill it to an essence. They reveal outsides without insides or insides without outsides. In "Feathertop: A Moralized Legend," the central character is an unintentional parody of the bodily incompletions on which so many of Hawthorne's characters try to make good. He is a hollow man made of witchcraft and straw, a man with a paltry wit and a "counterfeit of an ear," who plays the human part to perfection (X:234–36) and has breath made of smoke. But although in this tale, a witch, Mother Rigby, apes the human form in a simulation so vulgar it is mistaken for the real thing, the man of straw betrays her by sensing what he—and most humans together—lacks. When a real woman is about to fall in love with him, he gazes in the mirror and sees, as he later tells the witch: "'myself, mother—I've seen myself for the wretched, ragged, empty thing I am!'" (X:245). By this revulsion at the self when it sees that it is nothing without a human soul, Feathertop threatens to acquire one. Like many of Hawthorne's characters, he catches himself in the act of being allegorized and falls apart in the discovery that he is a man missing vital parts, that he is a body without a soul, as Ethan Brand tried to be a heart without a body. Feathertop is created as an inhuman or monstrous body (a body without an inside) as Roderick creates an inhuman or monstrous body (thinks that his body can house another body, can internalize and so *contain* dichotomy as if it were one of the body's parts).

In these tales, then, the attempt to treat a body part as if it were a synecdoche (whether substitution is achieved by bodily addition or subtraction) enacts the desire it does not specifically state: the wish not to have a whole human body, to be an outside or an inside, a part that becomes a whole because it has no reference to anything external to it. I take this desire to be the subject of "The Intelligence Office," whose characters are dismissed by the narrator. They are metaphysically diminished to the size of the thing for which they search. Hawthorne thereby rebukes characters who conceive of the body synecdochically. The tales' endings enact the rebuke by forcing bodily emblems back into the body—back into their proper place, as we have seen in "Ethan Brand." Insofar as Brand attempts to cast his heart out of his body, whether symbolically (by substituting the mind for the heart) or synecdochically (by his terrible laughter) or bodily (by climbing into the kiln), we see Hawthorne legislating against the partializations. We see the prohibition against bodily division in the insistence that even in death the shape of the heart lies "within . . . strange to say." We see it in the alternatives to the visible shape of the emblematic heart, images in which shapes cannot be discerned because they are multiple and fused, whether these be images of the village in the palm of providence or of earth mingled with sky, or the mirrored depictions of furnace and heart, as one seems not so much an image of the other as an extension of the other. As a consequence, it is impossible to say whether Brand is consumed by his heart or whether Brand's heart is consumed by the furnace. The distinctions no longer make a difference. We see Hawthorne's negation of Brand's desired dichotomy finally in the relationship between the tale's didactic or explicit moral and its shadowy subliminal one as both are offered up by different aspects of the same story. Precisely because the evidence arises from different aspects of the tale (however that evidence seems to contradict itself), one interpretation cannot be used to dismiss the other, since each in itself cannot account for the whole tale. Both interpretations are forced into relationship.

In "The Hall of Fantasy," Hawthorne had spoken of a place where we can "prefigure to ourselves" a "state, in which the Idea shall be all in all" (X:185). This Idea would not be equivalent to the reductive bodily emblems about which I have thus far been speaking, nor would it be equivalent to the inanimate memorials of the body to which I shall momentarily turn. Rather, the emblem (bodily organ or inanimate thing) would be the means through which a "prefiguring Idea" and the human body could come into correspondence, the single space where the two could meet. The "prefiguring Idea," like man's "proper place," evades definition. It is, in fact, craved to the precise degree that it will not pin itself on anything reductive or specific, although, as I am suggesting, it utilizes both reduction of the human body and specificity (the sacrifice of the whole body to a particular part) as a means to an imagined end. The end, could it be specified, might be the attainment of being without consciousness or consciousness without being—the terms are reversible precisely because in the purity of the impossible state equations no longer exist;

there is only *one* term—the generating term. Allegory is enlisted in the attainment of this state because allegory is that strategy that partializes what it represents. The hope that invests itself in allegorical construction might be stated as follows: if one could only get the body small enough, winnow it to a representative part, one might then coerce the essence of the "prefiguring Idea" first to the same reduction and then to the same thing. Hawthorne's characters therefore tear through bodily entities with encyclopedic fervor, whether these be things inside their own bodies, as in "The Intelligence Office" and "Egotism; or, The Bosom-Serpent," or things outside their bodies, as in "Ethan Brand" or "Earth's Holocaust" (X:381–404) (in which all of the world's evils are tossed into a huge bonfire). In the last tale, however, we are shown the discrepancy between the totality of the sacrifice and its ultimate meaninglessness. Although the embodiments of man's folly are eagerly fed to the fire, the heart that has confected them lies untouched. It is by definition untouchable, if to touch it means to purify it. Since the earthly embodiments are merely types, the heart will replicate them again. Still, the hope in "Earth's Holocaust," as in the other tales, is that if one could dispense with corporeality, it would then be possible to fuse self and prefiguring Idea.

In "The Old Manse," looking at the Concord River, Hawthorne gives us an image for the desired typological reduction:

> All the sky glows downward at our feet; the rich clouds float through the unruffled bosom of the stream, like heavenly thoughts through a peaceful heart. We will not, then, malign our river as gross and impure, while it can glorify itself with so adequate a picture of the heaven that broods above it . . . Yes; the river sleeps along its course, and dreams of the sky, and of the clustering foliage, amid which fall showers of broken sunlight, imparting specks of vivid cheerfulness, in contrast with the quiet depth of the prevailing tint. Of all this scene, the slumbering river has a dream-picture in its bosom. Which, after all, was the most real—the picture, or the original?—the objects palpable to our grosser senses, or their apotheosis in the stream beneath? Surely, the disembodied images stand in closer relation to the soul. But, both the original and the reflection had here an ideal charm; and, had it been a thought more wild, I could have fancied that this river had strayed forth out of the rich scenery of my companion's inner world. (X:7–8, 22)

The picture first shows us how a typological correspondence looks when sky is on the earth, when sky is in the water. Second, it attributes to the natural world a heart-enabling correspondence—it suggests that natural and human worlds beat with the same bodily part. Third, it insists on the fusion of the picture in the river's bosom and the picture in the man's. For Hawthorne what is crucial is not the fact that the world reflects the mind (with emphasis on duplication or doubling, as we have seen it in *Moby-Dick*) but rather the fact that when the mind shucks off corporeality, it finds itself *in* the world. As the passage's last sentence indicates, only out of the self, in some "disembodied" state, can an "original" or "prefiguring Idea" and the human representation of it stray into each other.

Yet everywhere in Hawthorne's tales the idea and the embodiment remain at a terrible remove. "She looked redundant with life" (X:97), we are told of Rappaccini's daughter. But *is* she? the tale asks. In what way does how she looks accord with how she is? Although in "The Antique Ring" a character explaining the meaning of a narrative he has spun out coyly remarks, " 'You know that I can never separate the idea from the symbol in which it manifests itself' " (XI:352), in most of Hawthorne's tales, such separation is appalling. People fall apart, their centers will not hold, for they can never be matched to the "prefiguring Idea" that either lies inside their bodies or is displaced from their bodies—as Beatrice's poison is not of her own agency but is rather from a source outside of her, is her father's. In "Sylph Etherege," the story in which discrepancy has other fatal consequences, a woman is betrothed to a man of whose portrait she has become enamored. But when Sylph meets Edgar Vaughan, her ostensible beloved, she finds him monstrous by comparison. He, justifying the discrepancy between his appearance and that of the portrait he has sent her, says, " 'Well, my conscience is clear. I did but look into this delicate creature's heart; and with the pure fantasies that I found there, I made what seemed a man' " (XI:118). Vaughan's statement, jolting enough in its implications that one could see into the heart (as Brand tried to grope into it), could see through the bodily walls, even at a distance, is more astonishing still when we recall that what is being looked at is not itself corporeal. Hawthorne credits Vaughan's idea, if credit lies in confirmation of the consequences. For Vaughan has looked into or at *something* and, according to its specifications, has made the portrait of what he "looks like" different from what he "is." Sylph disappears in the too-wide chasm between the image and the embodiment. She becomes "gossamer," ridding herself of a body, since bodies betray images with which they refuse to coincide. Explaining her ethereal nature, Vaughan tells us Sylph is perhaps going to heaven " 'to seek the original of the miniature' " (XI:119). The original evades the body—hers as well as his. It is, by definition, what the mortal body cannot be or have.

When, as in "Sylph Etherege," the "original" is outside the body, is "Idea all in all," even the body taken apart will not yield the sought-for essence, because it exists in some unearthly sphere. Hawthorne seems here to be insisting that the essence of the self is not simply invisible, it is also (to contradict the assumption of a tale like "Earth's Holocaust") not interior. We see, not only in "Sylph Etherege" but in other tales as well, that the true image of the body lies emphatically outside of it. " 'Oh, friend,' " Monsieur du Miroir says to his own reflection, " 'Break down the barrier between us! Grasp my hand! Speak! . . . A few words, perhaps, might satisfy the feverish yearning of my soul for some master-thought, that should guide me through this labyrinth of life, teaching wherefore I was born, and how to do my task on earth, and what is death' " (X:171). In still other tales, characters flee their bodies, seeking escape from an inhabiting essence that wrongly defines them. So of Catharine in "The Gentle Boy," we are told she is "so white from head to foot with the drifted snow that it seemed like Winter's self, come in human shape to seek refuge from its own desolation" (IX:100). Though the personification would take refuge in some other form or state, Catharine's mind does not know how to abandon itself to anything but severity. In other tales, refuge is to be found not connected to the self (albeit in a mirror image) nor in escape from the self (in some other form or state) but rather in the scrutiny of others' minds and behaviors. We are told in "Peter Goldthwaite's Treasure": "It is one great advantage of a gregarious mode of life, that each person rectifies his mind by other minds, and squares his conduct to that of his neighbours, so as seldom to be lost in eccentricity" (IX:400). Yet whether the body is ransacked for its essence, whether it abandons its corporeality to seek essence elsewhere, or whether it strives to find that proper essence by aligning itself with others, the results are unsatisfactory. Even assuming the heart is "found," as the body obscured its heart, so the heart will obscure its meaning. The object of the search is apprehended only to *become* the physical barrier that had obstructed it. The displacements I am describing explain the maze-like experience that haunts Hawthorne's characters' searches. The moment a thing is found, is conceived of as a thing, is the moment it becomes a barrier to the Idea now at another remove from it. The problem is not that bodies contain other bodies (which are inaccessible because hidden) nor that these representations exist outside of human bodies (which are inaccessible because absent), but rather that some things have no bodies, are, like the Concord River, pure reflection. In the tales to which I shall turn, the self gives up the desire to be one with itself or one with multiple images of another self. In rage at the recognition that the self cannot be completed either in itself or out of itself by the world, characters instead sacrifice life to a whole *conception* of it. They thus no longer wish to be representative men, or to make parts of their bodies representative. Rather, they wish to abandon bodily representations entirely, to vacate the body, to be immortalized or dead.

[110]

Although many of Hawthorne's characters are obsessed with birthmarks and veils, with stone faces and paintings, the other side of the obsession focuses on the desire to force into visible form those phenomena that have none. If the self could find something both inhuman and exterior to it that would represent it as an essence, this object would eliminate the various schisms about which I have been speaking—whether the split inheres between the body and the heart or between the body and another body (the monster body inside it), or whether it exists between a self and its outside reflection in an external thing. If, in the tales about which I have thus far spoken, Hawthorne takes his characters apart, makes them disembodied images, in other tales he replaces the human self entirely. It is toward the replication of life—life divorced from bodily person and from even representative corporeal essence—after which the artist of the beautiful and Drowne with his wooden image so arduously strain. In "Drowne's Wooden Image," we are told of the figure who walks the seacoast town:

> On the whole, there was something so airy and yet so real in the figure, and withal so perfectly did it represent Drowne's image, that people knew not whether to suppose the magic wood etherealized into a spirit, or warmed and softened into an actual woman. (X:317)

For a moment the wood is the woman, or the other way around. " 'But is it alive?' " (X:471), Annie, in "The Artist of the Beautiful," asks of the butterfly Owen Warland has made. And Robert Danforth, the ultimate man of sense (with sense also understood as flesh), pays the image the ultimate compliment and criticism solidified into a single statement: " 'Well, that does beat all nature!' " (X:472). The theme of non-corporeal form imbued with life wholly self-sufficient will never again be as delicately rendered as it is in "The Artist of the Beautiful" and "Drowne's Wooden Image." Behind all of these tales, however, and behind the novels that take aesthetic image as symbol for the magical wedding of body and spirit, are tales that directly address the question of why man should want life in his image—in his image rather than in himself.

The substitution of image for self is made explicit in "The Ambitious Guest." In this tale a young man traveling through the Notch of the White Hills on his way to Vermont stops to rest for the night in a cottage located at the slope of a mountain so steep that "the stones would often rumble down its sides, and startle [the inhabitants] at midnight" (IX:324). The secret of the young man's life, as he reveals it to the family that houses him for the night, is his yearning not to be forgotten. He tells us that he could bear to live an unacknowledged life; he could not bear the thought of dying without commemoration. The problem with this ambition, and in fact its very essence, is that it has yet to find an object. "'Were I to vanish from the earth to-morrow,'" he confesses, "'none would know so much of me as you . . . But, I cannot die till I have achieved my destiny. Then, let Death come! I shall have built my monument!'" (IX:328). Monuments thus conceived are to memorialize the self—by what means is immaterial, and in fact it is no accident that the young man focuses on the certainty of the monument rather than on what it is to represent or on how it is to be achieved. In this respect, without an object, the monument has a status comparable to that of the Idea which, unfleshed out, will nonetheless prefigure all. A monument is displaced from life. It is not made of life's accomplishments but rather stands outside of them, freezing them into static form. The young man himself acknowledges the discrepancy between desire for such a monument as it materializes in his mind and the way in which his desire parodies, by rendering contentless as well as frozen, the life it is memorializing:

> "You think my ambition as nonsensical as if I were to freeze myself to death on the top of Mount Washington, only that people might spy at me from the country roundabout. And truly, that would be a noble pedestal for a man's statue!" (IX:328)

As the young man talks, others confess to comparable dreams. The father imagines owning a house at the bottom of the mountain, imagines how his tombstone would be situated in the open for all to pass and see. The children wish to take a drink from "the basin of the Flume" (IX:330)—which is nearly impossible, since the Flume tumbles over a precipice deep inside the mountains. The grandmother wishes that when she dies a mirror could be held to her face, for she explains that there is an old legend insisting that the dead will never rest in peace "'if anything were amiss with a corpse, if only the ruff were not smooth, or the cap did not set right'" (IX:332). The daughter entertains wishes that issue from "lonesomeness" (IX:330), whose remedy, though unspecified, would probably have as its object this, or some similar, young man. But when he tries to prod her to speak ("'Shall I put these feelings into words?'" [IX:331], he provocatively asks) she rebukes him: "'They would not be a girl's feelings any longer, if they could be put into words.'"

The ideas of putting feeling into words, of moving the cottage to a visible place, of arriving at a mountain stream rumored to be inaccessible, of imagining that death itself will immobilize the body while leaving the corpse's eyes open and still able to ascertain the bodily world are hopes that, however different, harp on the same theme. In each case they translate life into material, that is, into visible form. Thus, in the minds of others, as in the mind of the ambitious guest, the desire for being is replaced by the desire for its palpability—for existence outside the body, yet (much as the grandmother depicts it) accessible to its scrutiny. Life from within its vital boundaries is not so much paltry—something wanting in achievement—as it is excruciatingly unclear, that which is felt rather than seen, intuited but lacking the coherent shape a monument would bequeath to it. Although the young man claims that he does not mind whether he is known in his lifetime as long as a monument stands for him after his death, the unspoken part of the wish is that he cannot be known in life, since life, by definition, does not clarify itself accordingly. In this connection, the young girl's refusal to allow the guest to articulate her dreams ("'They would not be a girl's feelings any longer, if they could be put into words'") lies at the heart of the tale. Translate feeling into form (whether of words or of monuments) and you replace it by externalizing it. The tale focuses on the desire for such externalization, and plays upon the knowledge the reader has from the beginning [7] that in death the body is destroyed rather than made either visible or complete. As the young man muses on the fact that "Old and young, we dream of graves and monuments" (IX:332), his dream—their communal dream—instantly comes true. The tale's focus, however, is not on the irony implicit in the instant gratification of the wish, nor on the fact that the guest who most passionately desires the monument not only fails to receive it but has his very existence called into question ("Others denied that there were sufficient grounds . . . to suppose that a stranger had been received into the cottage [that] night" [IX:333]), but rather on the human desire to exchange life itself for an embodied meaning, on what prompts the desire for such an exchange when it is not simply construed as "vanity" or ordinary ambition.

The feared mountain slide rumbles above the characters' heads and begins its descent toward the cottage. As the initial instinct of each was to convert life to commemorative emblem, so the communal instinct now is to run outside the cottage and seek safety in "a sort of barrier [that has] been reared" without. "Alas!" we are told by the narrator, "they had quitted their security, and fled right into the pathway of destruction" (IX:333). The house remains intact. Had they stayed inside, they would have been preserved. For to be, by definition, is to reside within, to feel rather than see the forms our lives have taken. "'As yet, I have done nothing'" (IX:328), the youth initially claimed, unabashed by the discrepancy between the monument and the undone, as well as unspecified, thing for which it will some day stand. As I suggested earlier, however, this discrepancy is not accidental. Rather, it defines the difference between a monument and a life. If we dream of graves and monuments, of images of ourselves hewn in marble or other stone, this is not so much a consequence of vanity as it is of despair that we cannot see our lives, will not know them from without, as, for example, the grandmother wishes to do. She wishes to have the mirror held to her dead face to ascertain that all is in order, that all *has* an order she could in life, at best, plan. "'I want one of you,'" she says to her children, "'when your mother is drest, and in the coffin . . . to hold a looking-glass over my face. Who knows but I may take a glimpse at myself, and see whether all's right?'" (IX:332). If the monument could *be* the body (the idea of the statues frozen on Mount Washington), or if the monument could be *in* the bodily apparel (as the grandmother hopes the death garments will clothe the body-monument inside of them), we might embody, as well as dream, the palpable shape for which the idea of a monument stands. In many of these tales, then, Hawthorne's characters want to put some thing into their bodies, want to put themselves into their bodies (but a self made visible and complete, made solid as marble or slate), as earlier we saw Melville's characters wish to put (other) characters inside their bodies. 'Their bodies were never found" (IX:333), Hawthorne tells us of the whole crew. What does survive is the house from which they fled—a vacated body of sorts. They could have survived in their bodies, but that survival would have been cluttered by what Hawthorne calls "tokens," those things in fact left 'by which those, who had known the family, were made to shed a tear for each" (IX:333). Even in death what represents the self are things fragmented from life, made in its piecemeal image.

The desire to translate life into the inhuman monuments that will complete and replace it is differently frustrated in "The Devil in Manuscript," about a man named Oberon, who burns a pile of his own manuscripts because he claims the devil is "in" them.[8] Oberon's tales are about the devil. They are also tales incited by evil thoughts. The story enacts a series of displacements. The initial displacement—Oberon's refusal to acknowledge that he plans to destroy the work because no one will publish it—causes another displacement: the private act of incineration, which comes to have public consequences. As the manuscripts go up the chimney, they start a larger fire on the roof, which threatens the town. Oberon's response—pleasure overtaking panic—is itself a displacement of the alarm we might suppose him to feel. Since the manuscripts would not set the town on fire metaphorically, he will see that they do so literally in an act that avenges a public consensus (that they are worthless) with which it ostensibly concurs. In addition, Oberon, putting the pages into the fire, says he would thereby rid himself of the "horror . . . created in my own brain" (XI:171). While the narrator-friend who witnesses the destruction ridicules the idea of the papers actually embodying the idea of a fiend, Oberon is incapable of any irony toward these papers that are, as it were, still fervently part of him. He will, in fact, prove the existence of the devil by showing that the fire has a palpable substance to consume. He will make the devil material in flame since he cannot prove its materiality in print.

The interest of the tale lies finally in the question of how the devil is to be taken. While Oberon invokes him metaphorically ("'the devil of the business is . . . [t]hese people have put me . . . out of conceit with the tales'" [XI:173]), the issue of publication aside, he is trying to give the devil substance on and of paper, and thereby to exorcise the fiend from his heart, his life, his mind. Perhaps the point of the unsuccessful repudiations is that anything that occasions complexity of response cannot easily be exorcised—whether the exorcism be from the image in the mind onto the paper or from the paper into the fire. As if to prove that what is substantial resists conversion to nothing, the fire to which Oberon feeds the manuscripts simply gives his thoughts body. Although he bitterly remarks, "'What is more potent than fire! . . . Even thought, invisible and incorporeal as it is, cannot escape it'" (XI:177) as the roof begins to burn, bitterness gives way to the dimensions of another size as we are ecstatically told, "'The Fiend has gone forth by night'" (XI:178). The devil is *in* the manuscripts as the devil was *in* the human mind. Trivialize this fact by relegating it to metaphor and it takes retaliatory measures—makes itself visible, shows the external form spirit can take when, to be acknowledged by the world, it must *consume* that world. The displacements and separations that the tale has attempted (the friend's attitude from the author's, the devil in the mind from the devil in the manuscript, the devil in the manuscript from the embodied devil in the fire, the fire of composition from the fire in the chimney) are forced into alignment by the tale's conclusion. While "The Devil in Manuscript" is customarily dismissed as a sketch that has little but biographical interest, it is a sophisticated demonstration of the fact that monuments, whether of paper or fire, will not stand *for* the things they represent if this idea means not simply to represent them but also to replace them. As in "The Ambitious Guest," the attempt to reify the self apart from the body comes to nothing. In "The Devil in Manuscript," life will not be displaced. It will not be expelled from the mind onto paper;

having it *on* the paper does not take it *out* of the mind. Nor will it be converted from paper into nothing. The dislocations do not rid the mind of the devil, nor the town of the devil. They rather reify him everywhere.

As in Melville's "I and My Chimney," a tale in which a monument or edifice (here a chimney) represents a self and is simultaneously part of it, in "The Devil in Manuscript," the manuscript stands for the devil in the mind and for the devil in the town and is simultaneously part of both. Melville's "I and My Chimney" in fact offers us a lesson on how to read Hawthorne's tales about monuments. Melville's story is about a man who looks upon his chimney "less as a pile of masonry than as a personage,"⁹ it is "king of the house" (333). It is the "backbone" (341) of the house. Tapping it to perceive whether it contains any hidden closets is akin to physicians "of life insurance companies tap[ping] a man's chest" (352). There is no point in asking: What does this tale mean apart from what it says? since the only "external" meaning we would want to supply is rendered interpretively gratuitous by the narrator himself. Frustrated by his wife's attempt to tear the thing down, to find its meaning out, he brushes her aside thus:

> "here for once I must say my say. Infinite sad mischief has resulted from the profane bursting open of secret recesses. Though standing in the heart of this house, though hitherto we have all nestled about it, unsuspicious of aught hidden within, this chimney may or may not have a secret closet. But if it have, it is my kinsman's. To break into that wall would be to break into his breast. And that wall-breaking wish of Momus I account the wish of a church-robbing gossip and knave." (352–53)

The wall-breaking wish to tear the chimney down, to discover its secret closet and to find what the latter hides (whether such a wish issue from the wife, from the architect-demolition expert, or the textual critic, all implicitly portrayed as one), is chastised in the narrator's combination of exasperation and scorn. Although we see the relationship between narrator and chimney specified in litany-like insistence and bounded by assonance ("I and my chimney," "my chimney and me"), we know the fact of the relationship but cannot crack its meaning. It is just Melville's point that the relationship *has* no meaning, if meaning depends upon the severance implicit in allegorization—of man from chimney, house from its "backbone," body from soul. "'This chimney may or may not have a secret closet,'" the narrator crossly says (*himself* not in possession of what he defends, and of what the reader wishes to know), "'But if it have, it is my kinsman's.'" If Melville goes on for over thirty pages daring us with a relationship whose meaning is immaterial severed from an external context, it is to prove that we, like the man's wife, like the insurance inspector and the carpenter, like the numerous outsiders who aggravate "the chimney and me," cannot get at the thing except by demolition, which Melville will not let us do. So, in the 1851 "Preface" to the tales, Hawthorne is to say of his stories, "They never need translation" (IX:6). They forbid translation, forbid the very severance of life from its palpable embodiment that the ambitious guest and Oberon alike conceive of as deliverance.

The desire to memorialize life in stone (which would make it permanent and visible) or to destroy it by fire (which would reduce it to visible ashes) or to knock the chimney down (and discover its secret recesses) is prompted by the same wish to displace meaning from the body, to give it a separate body, whose significance would be clear. The very construction of the problem as one of a separable "inside" (in the case of the chimney) or "outside" (in the case of Oberon and the ambitious guest) predicates an impossible severance, a displacement of the thing from itself. In "I and My Chimney," the critic, like the architect, is patient at first; both want access badly enough to tolerate the narrator's apparently fatuous explanation: "Going through the house, you seem to be forever going somewhere, and getting nowhere" (340), we are told, and we hang on that word *seem*. But it will not give way. Melville will not allow the "picturesque" to yield to what he calls the "pocketesque" (332). This tantalization ultimately rebuked is also characteristic of Hawthorne, as he equates houses and bodies, implies that he is leading us "in" to the equivalent of "being" only to turn around and chide us with our expectations.

In "The Old Manse," we are stopped short at the door:

> Has the reader gone wandering, hand in hand with me, through the inner passages of my being, and have we groped together into all its chambers, and examined their treasures or their rubbish? Not so. We have been standing on the green sward, but just within the cavern's mouth, where the common sunshine is free to penetrate, and where every footstep is therefore free to come. I have appealed to no sentiment or sensibilities, save such as are diffused among us all. So far as I am a man of really individual attributes, I veil my face. (X:32–33)

And in "Main-Street," talking now about that particular house sanctified as a church, he questions the very desire that would *want* to make us go inside:

> A meaner temple was never consecrated to the worship of the Deity. With the alternative of kneeling beneath the awful vault of the firmament, it is strange that men should creep into this pent-up nook, and expect God's presence there. (XI:57–58)

For Hawthorne, as for Melville, houses are not just dwellings, they are bodies of sorts—hence the explicit confusion of the two when Hawthorne tells us in "The Old Manse" that we have not entered his being. In "The Ambitious Guest," to abandon them is to die. But if from one point of view there is no "out," from another point of view there is also no access. So Hawthorne bars the door of his own habitation, or in "Main-Street" suggests that if we do indeed get in the house-body of God, no Presence will be found there. Insofar as the family in "The Ambitious Guest" lets the stranger into house and heart, hospitality itself seems connected to annihilation. In fact, we are told that every family should "still keep a holy place, where no stranger may intrude." Although there is an immediate disclaimer to this dictum ("Is not the kindred of a common fate a closer tie than that of birth" [IX:327]), given the consequences, the initial assertion still stands as a warning that ought not to have been qualified. It therefore appears that the body-house cannot be entered. When the idea of bodily entrance is literally conceived, it is dismissed as an absurdity (as in "Main-Street") or else as a violation the narrator explicitly wards off (as in "The Old Manse").

Others can be admitted to the self if the terms of bodily relationship take the dictional form of "to see" rather than "to enter." In "The Old Apple-Dealer," the spectator-narrator, looking at a virtual stranger, domesticates the image, houses the man in contemplation, and renders him in the process a "naturalized citizen of my inner world." In fact, the spectator-narrator of "The Old Apple-Dealer" so familiarizes the stranger, the unkempt, unknown man, that—construing an attack of which the apple dealer is the object—he answers in the latter's behalf, answers as if in his stead:

> Many would say, that you have hardly individuality enough to be the object of your own self-love. . . . Yet could I read but a tithe of what is written there, it would be a volume of deeper and more comprehensive import than all that the wisest mortals have given to the world; for the soundless depths of the human soul, and of eternity, have an opening through your breast. (X:446)

In Hawthorne's tales bodies appear to have openings (though not doors), while houses do not. This is, in fact, logical, for since houses stand for bodies that contain the human soul, they cannot have literal openings from which people can come and go. Could people do so, the metaphor of the house would falsify what it represents. It is by dint of such falsification that Hepzibah and Clifford imagine they are imprisoned in the House of the Seven Gables (that something external to them is keeping them within it) or that they can escape from the house (when they take the ride on the train). The idea of escape, like the idea of imprisonment, is one that must be relinquished. Both verbs when applied to the body-house falsify the place where people are to live.

Since the body in Hawthorne's tales cannot be entered and will not tolerate violation, the idea of access to another is different from dismemberment as we have seen it in *Moby-Dick*. The Hawthorne character set straight does not attempt to tear through bodily walls, but he does hope to see through them, hopes to make them transparent, and in the process to match the self's essence with that of the outside world. Thus, in "The Old Apple-Dealer" and "The Old Manse," the body is a house through which the spectator can look. The spectator or outsider cannot enter the body, but he can look into the soul. For if there is a difference between one body and another, there is also a presumed, second difference between a body and its non-corporeal substance. It is just because the self is *not* all body (because there is a posited difference between body and soul) that the soul can be seen without the body's being entered. The spectator's glance both acknowledges the division between one body and another (acknowledges the difference by admitting that what he sees, he sees from outside) and simultaneously heals the division by showing it has no consequences. The soul can be seen, can, as it were, be possessed, although the body is left intact. "I have appealed to no . . . sensibilities, save such as are diffused among us," Hawthorne staunchly says in "The Old Manse." The soul is among us. Hence, the opening in the breast does not cut into the body. Rather, it cuts a cross-section through the communal bodies of the world.

Hawthorne's representation of "outsides," which may not be entered or which, entered, are found empty—whether these be represented by houses, churches, or monuments—and his representation of "insides" (the latter shining through the body, existing as if in a general body)—whether represented by the old manse or the old apple-dealer—exactly reverse the conventional notion that the soul is interior, private, and inaccessible and that bodies, houses, or monuments are exterior or public and therefore open to entry. Rather, it mystifies these distinctions, suggests they are more complex, as I shall discuss in greater detail when, in the next section, I turn directly to examine the connection between Hawthorne's reversal of these ideas and his assumptions about allegory. For the devil is in the mind, but it is also in the town. Only on paper—in the manuscript—is it nothing at all.

"Alice Doane's Appeal" accentuates the confusions between body and soul, inside and outside, private and public, human entities and stone ones. If we have seen a tale exist in and through a manuscript, in "Alice

Doane's Appeal," we shall see the narrator try to depict the devil's release—again in an uncustomary manner: through a tale's "performance" (XI:269) rather than through its print. An aspiring author takes two young ladies on a walk to Gallows Hill, telling them that although others do not "obey the summons of the shadowy past" he has often courted "the historic influence of the spot" (XI:267). There is talk of witches and martyrs and a half-enraged despair that most people do not remember the "date of the witchcraft delusion" although it happened less than a century ago (XI:267). Here, as in "Main-Street," that tale in which the same stretch of land continually changes its looks by contact with people who traverse it at different historical moments, the narrator's tale runs time backward. Since he is reading from a manuscript he wrote long ago and since the story he reads is set in 1692, since, in addition, he has violently told us his feelings of the importance of the past, we think he will deliver an historical narrative. In fact, though, "Alice Doane's Appeal" has no discernible marker between what is historical and what is personal. It has *no* "markers" or distinctions where we would conventionally expect them to be. Many of its confusions arise from the difficulty in knowing whether its various statements are to be attributed to the frame story or its interstices, whether it designates a fate private or public, what border exists between characters in the narrator's story and characters who are outside of it. The dream-like aspect that haunts the whole arises from the difficulty of making the conventional separations between inside and outside on which meaning depends. Baffling the distinction between the past and the present in a syntax that tortures one into the shape of the other, the narrator says of the two listeners: "I made them sit down on a moss-grown rock, close by the spot where we chose to believe that the death-tree had stood" (XI:269).[10]

Then we have the interior story proper. We are told about Walter Brome, who was found murdered a hundred years ago, left where he was killed with his face covered with snow. Brome was murdered by his lover's brother, Leonard Doane. But in yet another collapsed distinction Doane and Brome are, it turns out, twins.[11] Moreover, as Leonard Doane looks down at the body of the man he has murdered, the corpse suddenly assumes his father's appearance. This story, as I have thus far recapitulated it, is itself (in the narrator's tale) a story told by Leonard to a wizard, as Leonard tries first to understand why his sister loves Walter Brome (because he is made in her brother's image) and, second, to discover why he must kill Walter Brome (they are "joint possessors of an individual nature, which could not become wholly the property of one, unless by the extinction of the other" [XI:272]). As Doane tells the story to the wizard

[120]

(who himself bears a relationship to the narrator of the story since the latter works his narrative black magic on the two women), he, like the narrator in his mindfulness of the past, is smitten by remorse. But he is alternately filled with the desire to murder Alice, whose honor he has just defended. To stave off Doane's accusation, Alice and her brother wander through a graveyard, where Alice appeals to Walter Brome to absolve her of any sin—this after she realizes that both her sexual guilt and Doane's murder of Brome were instigated by the wizard. While the two walk, the surrounding graves suddenly give up their bodies, and we are told all the dead are there. Yet as in Young Goodman Brown's vision, all the dead turn out to be all the damned. Hawthorne, envisioning the form damnation will take, shows us that those who went to the grave as lovers now throw glances of hatred upon each other; those thought to be saved are now dressed as devils. Even an innocent woman sees "her little son among the accusers" (XI:279).

In the context of these conversions of the dead into the live, of the innocent into the guilty, we see that the women listening to the tale are implicated—by their association with the wizard—in the crimes to which we had first assumed they merely listened. We are initially told that the wizard issued from the "blush" of the wood-wax that grows all over Gallows Hill. But some pages later, the same word is used to indicate the color on the women's cheeks. If this is guilt by verbal association, it is no less insinuating for being once or twice removed from direct connection. The "blush" in the initial description is a verb directly conjoined to "history" (XI:267) and, in the second description, ostensibly to the "crimson west" (XI:277). But as the passages below indicate, color is, in both cases, a suffusion that moves illogically though inevitably from the natural to the supernatural, from the historical to the personal—specifically to those persons of wizard and women. Hawthorne is here insisting on connections between all those personae we would be most likely to want to keep apart. Of the wood-wax (from which the wizard springs) we are told:

> the curious wanderer on the hill will perceive that all the grass, and every thing that should nourish man or beast, has been destroyed by this vile and ineradicable weed: its tufted roots make the soil their own, and permit nothing else to vegetate among them; so that a physical curse may be said to have blasted the spot, where guilt and phrenzy consummated the most execrable scene, that our history blushes to record. (XI:267)

And of the ladies, after the narrator has finished his story:

> Not a word was spoken, till I added, that the wizard's grave was close beside us, and that the wood-wax had sprouted originally

> from his unhallowed bones. The ladies started; perhaps their cheeks
> might have grown pale, had not the crimson west been blushing on
> them. (XI:277)

In line with the tale's other reversals and confusions, in which the murder
of a brother is really a murder of a father, in which guilt and innocence are
mortally indistinguishable, in which in story if not in the world, in death if
not in life, we must be forced to acknowledge connections between people
ostensibly opposite, to acknowledge the fact that sexual passion and
righteous passion alike result in murder. It is appropriate that even the
identity of the women outside the frame of the story be additionally
associated with the identity of the twins (Leonard Doane and Walter
Brome, hard to tell apart because their names uncannily rhyme) as well as
with that of the wizard, appropriate that innocent and guilty, the natural
and the supernatural, be colored with the same "blush."

When the narrator has accomplished his task of confusing his
characters outside of the tale as well as within it—when he has made what
he calls "unseen spirits" (XI:277) fill the bodies of all—he takes pleasure in
that confusion. Speaking of the two innocents, he says: "sweeter victory
still, I had reached the seldom trodden places of their hearts and found the
well-spring of their tears" (XI:280). The tale's central insistence is that divisions are arbitrary, whether these divisions apply to the "inside" or the
"outside" of the story, to the past or the present, to the crimes within a
family or to the larger American family of the new world. Yet despite this
contextual blurring, or perhaps as a consequence of it, it is not incidental
that the narrator should lament the very absence of monuments, with their
hard and fast distinctions (which it has worked so hard to destroy) that
separate selves from each other—as Melville would have understood
it—or selves from themselves—as Hawthorne understands it. Thus, the
narrator, standing on Gallows Hill, from where he tells the story, wishes
some commemorative, some embodied thing, to clarify the meaning of his
story.

> Yet ere we left the hill, we could not but regret, that there is nothing
> on its barren summit, no relic of old, nor lettered stone of later
> days, to assist the imagination in appealing to the heart. We build
> the memorial column on the height which our fathers made sacred
> with their blood, poured out in a holy cause. And here in dark,
> funereal stone, should rise another monument, sadly com-
> memorative of the errors of an earlier race, and not to be cast
> down, while the human heart has one infirmity that may result in
> crime. (XI:280)

Monuments (or references to them) appear at either end of the story, as
if standing sentinel over its chaos, trying to contain the tale's insides. If my

[122]

own metaphor utilizes the metaphor of a body (the monuments standing for the flesh, the story for its disembodied innards), that is because this figure is suggested by the tale's own concern with bodies. We see the concern first in the way in which one body turns into another and second in the multiple bodies that rise from the grave. Finally, we see it in the fact that although the narrator in the frame story says he yearns for monuments, because they would commemorate "the errors of an earlier race," he actually yearns for them because, could they exist, they would clearly designate a single and clear object of commemoration. Monuments would designate the human body as an object having external integrity—separate from all other bodies—and as an object having internal integrity, with lust, for example, wholly unrelated to the desire to avenge it. Monuments would make of man a coherent piece, would make of man a marble faun. They would make him innocent as Donatello, whose experience, when not protean, cannot be complex. Insofar as contradictions and transformations characterize a single life, and characterize life itself, no monuments can be. If they exist, their meaning is incoherent. So we are told: "Every fifth of November, [young men gather] in commemoration of they know not what" (XI:267).

"Blessed are all simple emotions, be they dark or bright!" Hawthorne wrote in "Rappaccini's Daughter." "It is the lurid intermixture of the two that produces the illuminating blaze of the infernal regions" (X:105). All separable states—personal or historical, past or present, the three characters inside the story, the three characters in the frame, those who are damned, those who are saved, the natural and the human—are consistently forced into a relationship conjunctive rather than alternative. The narrator's power over his listeners—reducing them to tears and terror—seems commensurate with the wizard's power over the characters in the story proper. The compulsive accusations—Leonard's of Walter Brome, the narrator's of Cotton Mather and of the Puritans for whom he stands, the child's of his mother—have the ring of a single accusation. Repeated actions or patterns take precedence over individual identities and it is consonant with the conversion of single characters into mythic figures that the tale should end, very much as Flannery O'Connor's "Revelation" later will, depicting rowdy crowds that march both hierarchically and in confusion through the sky. All are indicted in the accusation against which the tale's title makes its rebuked appeal. No one is innocent. Any single action—indeed, any single being—has its counterpart in an antithetical being, or an antithetical feeling and action.

The tale's dogged insistence upon "counterparts" may be seen in its most memorable scenes. The first "objectively" depicts Walter Brome's body as we see it unburied in the snow directly after the murder. The second records the same scene but now through Doane's eyes, as he confesses his guilt to the wizard. The third shows the surreal landscape, which intervenes and makes the connection between the public story and the private one. The first reads as follows:

> A hundred years, and nearly half that time, have elapsed since the body of a murdered man was found, at about the distance of three miles, on the old road to Boston. He lay in a solitary spot, on the bank of a small lake, which the severe frost of December had covered with a sheet of ice. Beneath this, it seemed to have been the intention of the murderer to conceal his victim in a chill and watery grave, the ice being deeply hacked, perhaps with the weapon that had slain him, though its solidity was too stubborn for the patience of a man with blood upon his hand. The corpse therefore reclined on the earth, but was separated from the road by a thick growth of dwarf pines. There had been a slight fall of snow during the night, and as if Nature were shocked at the deed, and strove to hide it with her frozen tears, a little drifted heap had partly buried the body, and lay deepest over the pale dead face. An early traveller, whose dog had led him to the spot, ventured to uncover the features, but was affrighted by their expression. A look of evil and scornful triumph had hardened on them, and made death so lifelike and so terrible, that the beholder at once took flight, as swiftly as if the stiffened corpse would rise up and follow. (XI:269–70)

The scene that precedes this one in the story's chronology (though not in the narrative retelling of it) is rendered through Leonard Doane's eyes:

> "I trod out his accursed soul, and knew that he was dead; for my spirit bounded as if a chain had fallen from it and left me free. But the burst of exulting certainty soon fled, and was succeeded by a torpor over my brain and a dimness before my eyes, with the sensation of one who struggles through a dream. So I bent down over the body of Walter Brome, gazing into his face, and striving to make my soul glad with the thought, that he, in very truth, lay dead before me. I know not what space of time I had thus stood, nor how the vision came. But it seemed to me that the irrevocable years, since childhood had rolled back, and a scene, that had long been confused and broken in my memory, arrayed itself with all its first distinctness. Methought I stood a weeping infant by my father's hearth; by the cold and blood-stained hearth where he lay dead. I heard the childish wail of Alice, and my own cry arose with hers, as we beheld the features of our parent, fierce with the strife and distorted with the pain, in which his spirit had passed away. As I gazed, a cold wind whistled by, and waved my father's hair. Immediately, I stood again in the lonesome road, no more a sinless child, but a man of blood, whose tears were falling fast over the face of

his dead enemy. But the delusion was not wholly gone; that face still wore a likeness of my father; and because my soul shrank from the fixed glare of the eyes, I bore the body to the lake, and would have buried it there. But before his icy sepulchre was hewn, I heard the voices of two travellers and fled." (XI:273)

Although Leonard Doane tries to bury his victim, he, like so many of Hawthorne's characters, is caught in the uncompleted act, frozen in the act. In this case, however, the freezing attaches itself to the object of Leonard Doane's action, to Brome's face, or, rather, to the snow that covers it. The snow covers the man on the ground, as he should otherwise have been covered by the decency of human hands. Yet despite the indications that nature compensates for the burial that man fails to complete, there are contrary indications that the identity of the human face is both inadequately covered *and* inadequately revealed. We are thus made to think: had Doane seen whom he was killing, the murder would not have taken place. Alternately, we are made to think that it is because Doane sees whom he is killing that the murder *does* take place. I have suggested that in both of these two scenes (dead man seen by the stranger and dead man seen by the son) the natural world does for the victim what the human world should have done for him. In the first scene it recognizes the violation. It therefore buries the man—tries to cover his visage. In the second scene, in which Leonard recognizes that the man is his father without being moved by the suspicion, response is again displaced—this time to a literal and external "movement," the wind's waving of the dead man's hair. Although Leonard Doane weeps, his tears are displaced. They do not recognize the man as a father; they rather shrink from him as an enemy. Insofar as Doane does recognize the man as a father, he feels fear rather than grief. Because the impulse to bury the father arises out of discomfort rather than grief, feeling is more alien for being amiss that it would have been for being absent. Since Doane's feelings remain "frozen," the compensatory "natural" response makes them properly fluid in the literal movement of the man's hair. For what is not felt inside must apparently be shown from outside. These alternating rhythms of freezing the body to a clarity that in fact *hides* from the person who ought to recognize it the identity in question, and the freeing it to a particular image whose details simultaneously blur in a recognition both indistinct and perceptible—these alternating rhythms of freezing and freeing (and their concomitant intimations of the dead man's identity and the *absence* of that recognition) are what give the tale its power.

What is interesting about the three scenes is the way in which they progressively clarify the identity of the buried face. The tale can be regarded as a series of unveilings—first by the stranger, then by the murderer, finally by the narrator—which reveal the shifting identity of the person who is again and again unsuccessfully buried. When looked at by the stranger, the face appears anonymous. When looked at by the murderer-son, the face appears as kin. And when looked at by the narrator and his audience (the girls and readers alike) in the final scenes when the dead are not only unburied but in fact rise from their graves, the face becomes plural and uncannily pervasive, assuming an anonymity that implicates us all. In the transitional scene that turns the tale from a story of private guilt into a story of public guilt, the diamond hardness of the world is ruffled by stirrings of culpability as characters begin to recognize that what lies beneath the frozen visage of self and of world is a body that is their own:

> The trees were hung with diamonds and many-colored gems; the houses were overlaid with silver, and the streets paved with slippery brightness; a frigid glory was flung over all familiar things, from the cottage chimney to the steeple of the meeting house, that gleamed upward to the sky. This living world, where we sit by our firesides, or go forth to meet beings like ourselves, seemed rather the creation of wizard power, with so much of resemblance to known objects, that a man might shudder at the ghostly shape of his old beloved dwelling, and the shadow of a ghostly tree before his door. One looked to behold inhabitants suited to such a town, glittering in icy garments, with motionless features, cold, sparkling eyes, and just sensation enough in their frozen hearts to shiver at each other's presence. (XI:274)

It is only in the final scene that the ice melts for good. The identity of the faces as "each tomb gives up its ghost" is suddenly then pluralized. In that final vision, in which the town is "no longer arrayed in . . . icy splendor" that hides the identity of its inhabitants, what we see through the "indistinctness" is "the universal heart" (XI:278), faceless, indeed bodiless, or rather existing in all bodies, impossible to separate or to allocate to only a few damned, though in the hierarchical last scene, where the guilty and the innocent ascend separately to heaven (or at any rate to the sky), Hawthorne again seems to distinguish between those *deemed* guilty (as the child accuses the mother of being guilty) and those who are in fact guilty. Such distinctions collapse, however, under the tale's consistent pattern of shuttling back and forth in a motion that cancels distinctions and makes all universally culpable. In the clarity of this pattern (although nothing else about the tale is clear) we see the tenuous relationship between kin and anonymous face, between the acknowledgment of guilt and the ability to repress it, between the attribution of evil to those scapegoats who are sacrificed and the acknowledgment that our fate is a common one, one incorporated into the "universal heart." It is precisely this wavering motion that makes identity impossible to fix—that either of murderers or of murdered. It is impossible to establish a monument in memory of a given event or person, for what is memorialized will shift.

In "The Ambitious Guest" we saw the characters' desire to separate the self from itself, to stand outside their own lives, which, memorialized in monuments, would be both visible and whole. Hawthorne rebukes that desire. In "The Devil in Manuscript" we saw a man attempt to purge the devil first from his mind onto paper and then from paper into ashes. Here the self would not be amplified, existing outside the mind or in external embodiment. It would rather be diminished. Evil would be thrust outside the mind in external *dis*embodiment. Hawthorne rebukes that desire. In "Alice Doane's Appeal" we see a more strenuous effort to oust the self from itself, to separate inside from outside, as if, like the two women who listen to the tale, or like the narrator who writes it, the self could be a spectator listening to its own story—could stand outside its life and see it, memorialized in monument or reified in print. In "Alice Doane's Appeal," then, "inside" and "outside," which Hawthorne again forces into alignment, are connected to a larger set of oppositions—public and private, familial and historical, innocent and guilty. Hawthorne similarly forbids the separation of these terms, insisting they are related. Hence, the appeal for innocence—Alice Doane's or ours—cannot be granted. Like the monument that would memorialize the self by standing in its place (clearly delineated) because separated from the human character, innocence does not exist except severed from the human character. In "Alice Doane's Appeal," the past does not lie outside the self. The past is part of the self, is the self's genesis. It is the self's identity, when identity is unburied and shows its true face.

The idea of identity predicated "outside" the self, as in "Alice Doane's Appeal," forbids literalization. Although the self must acknowledge that it is related to an exterior, related to an "outside" it would repudiate as other, it must also understand that it has real corporeal limits that define, restrict, and only in a certain sense allow access to the world. For Hawthorne, as for Melville, if the body is a house, this idea is a metaphoric one forbidding an actual "out." One may have commerce with the world by its entry through the eyes, but one may not forsake the body, as if it were only a residence, as, I shall suggest in a moment, Wakefield tries to do. Only housed within the body may one safely look outside of it. When, in *The House of the Seven Gables*, Clifford (too amorphous to seem to have a body) inhabits his self, this is the precise moment he can also look outside of it. Thus, Clifford muses directly after he looks through the window at "the extremity of the street" (as Peter Goldthwaite before him had momentarily looked), "had I taken that plunge, and survived it, methinks it would have made me another man!" (II:166). The narrator reiterates: "He needed a shock; or perhaps he required to take a deep, deep plunge into the ocean of human life, and to sink down and be covered by its profoundness, and then to emerge, sobered, invigorated, restored to the world and to himself" (II:166). The self's immersion in itself turns it naturally to the outside. The identification of dwelling in the house with habitation in the world is the way in which I understand the ostensible paradoxes that have been implicit in my discussion of the stories. For although Hawthorne says one cannot leave the self (if this means to exist elsewhere), he simultaneously insists that, as with Clifford and Peter Goldthwaite, to be *in* the self is to have *access* to the outside world. In fact, it is just because we are trapped in separate bodies, because we cannot exist outside of our flesh, because we are not bodies within bodies or bodies outside of other bodies, are *not* synecdoches (though we may choose to so represent ourselves, as, for example, we do when we dichotomize body and mind), that we *are* separated from each other and, simultaneously, have need of that image which would overcome without violating (as the narrator, talking about the old apple-dealer, does) the terms of separation, whether it be expressed as the "universal heart," as "disembodied image" diffused among us all, or as a heart in the palm of providence.

In "Wakefield," a man, for apparently no reason, vacates his life to look at it. This tale epitomizes the self-abandonment against whose literality the tales about which I have been speaking warn us, for in the process of looking at his life, Wakefield loses it. Unlike the characters in "The Ambitious Guest," however, Wakefield remains alive. We are told he is one of the living dead. In this tale Hawthorne is showing us the consequences when characters receive the absention from their lives they think they have wanted and simultaneously remain alive to appreciate the consequence. We are told: "The man, under pretence of going a journey, took lodgings in the next street to his own house . . . and without the shadow of a reason for such self-banishment, dwelt upwards of twenty years" (IX:130). His house, his life, and his wife are attachments to his being which he delusively thinks he can regard from the outside while he still retains possession of them. What is curious about the tale is Wakefield's motivation for the action. We are told that when he leaves Mrs. Wakefield one morning after ten years of matrimony, he himself does not know that he is "destined" not to return. Wakefield has no motivations, "no suspicion of what is before him" (IX:132); he is unconscious of the action in which he shrouds himself. Thus, motivation, while it comes from within the self—because the self is detached from it—seems nonetheless alien to it. So the split within the man generates the secondary split between the man and his life. Yet Wakefield's action is not aberrant. The narrator tells us: "We know, each for himself, that none of us would perpetrate such a folly, yet feel as if some other might" (IX:131). If this is a tale that dramatizes the imp of the perverse, then it does so by suggesting that human nature itself is imbued with perversity. It is something done by an other or which we attribute to an other, because it comes so naturally to our own minds that it does not seem improbable. In thought if not in deed, that other is ourselves. And this is exactly what Wakefield attempts to make of his own life—an other that is yet himself. Wakefield's action cannot be explained in terms of character, since, except for "a peculiar sort of vanity" (IX:132) and "a little strangeness" (epithets amorphous enough to define us all), Wakefield has no character. He is a man almost deprived of a life before he determines to dispense with it further. We are told by the narrator, who has turned his attention momentarily (and, he maintains, digressively) to the more self-conscious wife, that "we must hurry after him, along the street, ere he lose his individuality, and melt into the great mass of London life" (IX:133).

It is Hawthorne's crowds—and the disembodied heart that beats as if in their one anonymous body—that legislate against the terrors of an individual frozen in emblematic rigidity. In this respect, crowds are redemptive. It is not incidental that anonymous crowds appear in so many of Hawthorne's tales—the people outside of Oberon's house, the villagers rummaging through the body-house at the end of "The Ambitious Guest," the hordes of the dead in "Alice Doane's Appeal"—for these crowds mediate the rigidity of the individual life that would in judgment or pride memorialize its solitude, would disavow connection to all other beings. They rescue the self from its isolation by incorporating it—whether this incorporation be conceived as a throng of bodies that move around the single self and absorb it into their mass, or whether incorporation be conceived in bodily terms of absorption into an actual living organ, into the universal human heart. Hawthorne's distinctions are faultless. Despite the narrator's initial concern, Wakefield cannot get lost in the crowd. To be one of the crowd is first to know how to inhabit one's own separate body. Of Wakefield, who would surrender his life, we are told "the crowd swept by, and saw him not" (IX:138). It is his fate to be as isolated from the mass of humanity as he is from his own life. Wakefield is a character who would become Poe's man in the crowd. But he would simultaneously also be Poe's narrator, who *follows* the man in the crowd. In this respect,

Wakefield and Hawthorne's narrator seem much like splits of a single person: the narrator, like Wakefield, telling of a life as he sees it from outside. Yet the tale transforms its focus from the question Wakefield would ask—can one watch one's life from outside of it?—to the question Hawthorne would make him ask—if one *is* outside one's life is there anything left to watch?

After the first night away, when Wakefield has executed his plan, has not returned home, we are told "It is accomplished. Wakefield is another man" (IX:135). And as he ruminates on Mrs. Wakefield, who, as much as himself, is the object of the capricious experiment, he determines, "He will not go back until she be frightened half to death" (IX:136). Will not go back until her existence records the estrangement of his. What excites Wakefield from his customary torpor is feeling (whether of grief or anguish) felt on his account. He wants feeling to be outside of him, to be felt for rather than by him. Such an insistent wish to be "another man," to "[step] aside for a moment" (when that expression refers to one's life), and so to expose oneself "to a fearful risk of losing [one's] place forever" to "dissever [the self] from the world," to vanish, to give up one's place "without being admitted among dead" is the predicament of the man who would exchange life for memorialization. As Wakefield leaves, he smiles at his wife, an expression incidental and momentary.

> But, long afterwards, when she has been more years a widow than a wife, that smile recurs, and flickers across all her reminiscences of Wakefield's visage. In her many musings, she surrounds the original smile with a multitude of fantasies, which make it strange and awful; as, for instance, if she imagines him in a coffin, that parting look is frozen on his pale features; or, if she dreams of him in Heaven, still his blessed spirit wears a quiet and crafty smile. Yet, for its sake, when all others have given him up for dead, she sometimes doubts whether she is a widow. (IX:132–33)

Images taken from life but frozen into the mind's interpretation of them replace life itself. The smile replaces the man, as the man has replaced himself. Or, rather, the displacement that more accurately describes Wakefield's departure from his life turns into a conversion of the man into a synecdoche, a memorial that signifies the human totality that was. In fact, when, after a ten-year separation, Wakefield bumps into his wife and they stand "face to face, staring into each other's eyes" he has the anonymity he thought he wanted: she does not recognize him. No longer lover or husband, he is in fact another man.

After Wakefield's first night away, the narrator addresses him:

> Poor Wakefield! Little knowest thou thine own insignificance in

this great world! No mortal eye but mine has traced thee. Go quietly to thy bed, foolish man; and, on the morrow, if thou wilt be wise, get thee home to good Mrs. Wakefield, and tell her the truth. Remove not thyself, even for a little week, from thy place in her chaste bosom. Were she, for a single moment, to deem thee dead, or lost, or lastingly divided from her, thou wouldst be woefully conscious of a change in thy true wife, forever after. It is perilous to make a chasm in human affections; not that they gape so long and wide—but so quickly close again! (IX:133)

What makes "Wakefield" a tale of terror is that the exemption from the self of which Hawthorne's characters so frequently dream is not difficult to achieve. It is, in fact, easy to achieve. We achieve it all the time: Hawthorne insists Wakefield is an ordinary man. He is called "feeble-minded" and "insignificant"; we are told he is not "perplexed with originality" (IX:131). Being "other" to ourselves—as if dead to ourselves—we are simultaneously dead to those around us. We do not matter in this world. We have no designated "place" outside the bodies that are our lives. Unless we keep the ground we walk on we will be converted from life into static image. This is what Hawthorne's characters dream they want—the grandmother in "The Ambitious Guest" able to see her appearance in the world, to see the smile on the coffined face.

Habiliments of Flesh and Blood

Allegory, as we generally understand it, implies a split, whether between an icon and what it represents, between the story and some other level of significance, or between a particular emblem posited by a story and the meaning of that emblem recoverable in some detached sphere. I should like to suggest that for Hawthorne the split, as his allegorical representations enact it, *externalizes* divisions otherwise felt from within. As my discussion has thus far illustrated, one crucial difference between all non-literal language and allegory in particular is that the latter not only renders the object in question non-bodily—as, for example, metaphor would—it also partializes that object. In addition, at least for Hawthorne, the "object" in question is a *bodily* human self. Allegory partializes the self for the explicit purpose of exteriorizing or making visible divisions that would be internal or otherwise disembodied. I do not wish to imply that all allegory has the same goal as Hawthorne's allegory does, although I would imagine that most allegory often has the same effect—that of displacing discrepancy from within the self to an exterior realm. This is the case in "Young Goodman Brown," a tale about the way in which the self rids itself of conflict by projecting it outside. It is the case in "The Minister's Black Veil," which takes the split between the body and soul (between what is material and what is not) and makes the split external. It is the case in "The Hollow of the Three Hills," in which a woman, kneeling on the ground with her forehead resting on a witch's knees, elicits the voices of those she has wronged. As she listens to their recriminations, the voices slay her. One moral of the tale is that, could we hear, in their own voices, what we have done to others, it would instantly kill us. Another moral is that recognition of our guilt is contingent upon hearing others tell what our own imagination too charitably constructs. Only if heard from outside (as the woman in the tale is literally outside, in the hollow of the three hills, on the outskirts of the supernatural) can meaning be known.

Hawthorne's repertoire on the subject of relations between the internal and the external is as various as these examples illustrate. But, as I have suggested, in a significant portion of the tales allegory is a consequence of an unacknowledged split that, existing first within the self, is then made exterior to it. That Wakefield "has no suspicion of what is before him" (IX:132), that he does not know why or that he will not return home, is the internal manifestation of his separation from himself. The separation within the "self-banished Wakefield" (IX:136)—within the man banished from himself and banished by himself—will be externalized in his actual departure from his residence. The latter separation allegorizes the former. Externalization is the theme of which that story is made. Thus, allegory projects internal divisions to the outside world. I take projection to explain the meaning of Ethan Brand's heart outside the body, of the devil first outside the mind and then outside the house, of the characters in "Alice Doane's Appeal" outside the frame of the story or of the dead outside their graves. I take projection to explain the meaning of the body outside the life in "Wakefield" and of the life outside the body in "The Ambitious Guest."

The split *within* the body, were it to be acknowledged internally, as allegorical modes of representation choose *not* to acknowledge it, would focus, as Descartes in the *Meditations* does, on the unmendable difference between corporeal body and incorporeal mind or soul. "I here say, in the first place, that there is a great difference," Descartes writes,

> between mind and body, inasmuch as body is by nature always divisible, and the mind is entirely indivisible. For, as a matter of fact, when I consider the mind, that is to say, myself inasmuch as I

[132]

am only a thinking thing, I cannot distinguish in myself any parts, but apprehend myself to be clearly one and entire; and although the whole mind seems to be united to the whole body, yet if a foot, or an arm, or some other part, is separated from my body, I am aware that nothing has been taken away from my mind.[12]

Notwithstanding the remove of the philosopher from the fiction writer, both are concerned with what is alien to our being and with what is integral to our being; with the way in which the alien and the integral constitute identity; with how much (what part of) identity can be lost to being while leaving something still intact; with the nature of that "something" and the problem of how to specify it, respectively, impalpable and unclear. For Hawthorne, as for Descartes, the proof of the difference between the mind and bodily substance is that while the body can be separated, part from the whole, such separations are unthinkable when applied to soul, mind, or heart.[13] Yet despite the fact that body and soul are different from each other, the soul is nonetheless tied to the very body from which (because of this difference) Hawthorne's characters imagine it could be detached. Although the parts of the body may be severed from each other, the non-physical image on which one pins the idea of the self cannot be severed from the body. Melville puts it thus: "Our souls belong to our bodies, not our bodies to our souls. For which has the care of the other? which keeps house? . . . Simpletons show us, that a body can get along almost without a soul; but of a soul getting along without a body, we have no tangible and indisputable proof" (*Mardi;* p. 505). One knows one's body *is* one's own because one cannot be separated from it as one can from other bodies.

Allegory's solution is to externalize the split between body and soul, which can be neither wholly united nor wholly pried apart. Thus, one consequence of allegorical projection is that it unites *outside* the body what will not be wholly united or separated *within* it. A second consequence is that meaning is not lost in the separation of body from mind or self from world. Indeed, allegory insists that it is precisely in the spaces made by these separations that meaning is *found.* Allegory, like life, promises a meaning it simultaneously withholds. But unlike life, it delivers its meanings. It does this first by displacing the split within the self to the outside world. It alternately delivers meaning by displacing the split between the self and the world to a sphere inside the self. This we have seen in "Egotism," in which Roderick Elliston tries to incarnate the bosom serpent, tries to make the difference between the world and the self integral to the self. Allegory internalizes what is naturally other or alien to the self (the man who, in "The Intelligence Office," wants to *feel* his "proper place"). It then externalizes what is properly integral to the self (the man who goes looking for his proper place as if it could be found in the office of a magistrate). Through such displacements, allegory creates correspondences out of the very severances—body from mind, self from world—of which the self despairs.

The first question we ask of an allegorical construction is: "what is its meaning?" I take the insistence upon the fact that a thing (split from itself and projected to an outside) *has* meaning to be the primary goal of allegorical construction. Allegorical correspondences not only totalize the self, they also give significance to separate human actions whose meaninglessness is predicated on their partiality. Melville says in *Mardi*: "Though many of my actions seem to have objects, and all of them somehow run into each other; yet, where is the grand result? To what final purpose, do I walk about, eat, think, dream?" (459). A final purpose, additively conceived, must come from "outside," "beyond," or "above"—whether the externality be conceived as outside the human body, outside the human realm, or outside of the embodied emblem—must come from the essence or Idea with which any of these strives to correspond. In "Night Sketches," Hawthorne insists meaning cannot come from within. To the man walking alone at night, the problem is represented in the following terms:

> The wet sidewalks gleam with a broad sheet of red light. . . . Methinks the scene is an emblem of the deceptive glare, which mortals throw around their footsteps in the moral world, thus bedazzling themselves, till they forget the impenetrable obscurity that hems them in, and that can be dispelled only by radiance from above. (IX:429)

The hope of externalization is that if dichotomy were *outside* the body, it would be visible. If it were visible, it would be palpable. If it were palpable (that is, if body and mind alike had substance), the division between the two could be healed. Division itself would then have a representational body, one that could conceptually join body and mind because both would now be made of the same "identical" substance. We see meaning given its own body in Sylph Etherege's portrait of Vaughan—a miniature that bears no relation to the man or to an accurate conception of the man. For Sylph, as for the rest of us, knowledge or meaning cannot have a direct object if it does not have a body. I take the absence of a body to be the source of Donne's cry in *Devotions upon Emergent Occasions*, invoking as it implicitly does the connection between literality and the body, the body's absence and the consequent need for figural correspondence: "My

God, My God, thou art a direct God, may I not say a literal God . . . but thou art also . . . a figurative, a metaphorical God."[14]

To give body to what has none is what Hawthorne's allegorical constructions characteristically do. They then, however, create the illusion that meaning could exist without reference to a *particular* body, that to draw upon the terms of the last chapter, meaning could be read in the context of human bodies all identical to each other. For although the point of the projection is both to unify the split between palpable and impalpable essence and to provide an icon for it, this icon no longer refers to the particular body that generated it, since it is precisely the point of the projection to liberate the image from that body. The icon rather refers to bodies all alike. There is an apparent contradiction, then, between the initial impulse (to give the self's division its own body) and the final consequence in which the projected icon has material substance all its own, disassociated, as it were, from the boundaries of the self that predicated it. But the inevitability of this consequence suggests that one function of the projection—to make the image refer to all bodies alike; hence, indirectly, to unite all bodies—cannot be incidental to the motives that generated the allegorical representation in the first place. Thus, although Hawthorne's tales do not portray the self in realistic terms of individuated character, we do not dismiss these representations because we cannot recognize or identify them. Instead, we recognize them differently; we identify them with ourselves. If meaning exists only divorced from particular bodies, then it applies to us all. So Hawthorne stubbornly insists at the door to the Old Manse. Particular bodies exist, but, as Puritan typology would have taught Hawthorne, they are irrelevant.[15] Indeed, while Hawthorne's characters have names, the names individuate and differentiate as they do in the real world—not at all. For when our names duplicate each other, duplication is of no consequence, replicated as names are in those to whom we have no other (real) relation. When names differ one from the other, that difference fails to matter, for names do not issue from our lives but rather are assigned to them, and are, moreover, given to us in the metaphorical prefaces to those lives.

We see the truth of identic duplication in tales like "The Wedding-Knell," in which Hawthorne subjects his characters to double and triple exposures. In this tale a character comes into relation with another as if he were initially an image made in the mind, then a reflection of all previous embodiments of that image, and, finally, the last in a series of composite others. In "The Wedding-Knell," Mrs. Dabney, who gave her heart in her youth to a man she did not marry, has been wed twice before: first to a man who forced "the dislocation of [her] heart's principles," second to an unkind Southern gentleman who "had inevitably driven her to connect the idea of his death with that of her comfort." The bridegroom, Mr. Ellenwood, similarly aged sixty-five, is oppositely virginal. We are told that he will come to Mrs. Dabney with a legacy of "forty years of celibacy," a man whose feelings "preyed upon themselves, for want of other food." Yet the wedding turns into a wake, as Mr. Ellenwood, dressed in funeral garb, bids his bride: " 'Come, my bride! . . . Let us be married; and then to our coffins!' " (IX:34). While Mrs. Dabney shrinks from the viciousness, Ellenwood insists the cruelty is her own:

> "Cruel!" repeated he; then losing his death-like composure in a wild bitterness, — "Heaven judge, which of us has been cruel to the other! In youth, you deprived me of my happiness, my hopes, my aims; you took away all the substance of my life, and made it a dream, without reality enough even to grieve at—with only a pervading gloom, through which I walked wearily, and cared not whither. But after forty years, when I have built my tomb, and would not give up the thought of resting there—no, not for such a life as we once pictured—you call me to the altar. At your summons, I am here. But other husbands have enjoyed your youth, your beauty, your warmth of heart, and all that could be termed your life. What is there for me but your decay and death? And therefore I have bidden these funeral friends, and bespoken the sexton's deepest knell, and am come, in my shroud, to wed you, as with a burial service, that we may join our hands at the door of the sepulchre, and enter it together." (IX:35)

In truth, Mrs. Dabney is guilty of all that Ellenwood accuses her. For the "she" and the "he" in this tale hark back to a history only half their own. It was Mrs. Dabney or a woman like her who failed to be the person whom Ellenwood could love. It is Mrs. Dabney who deprived Ellenwood of an object for his affections. But it is also (a man like) Ellenwood, a stereotypical woman of a man, who gave Mrs. Dabney a coldness akin to celibacy. In their acceptance of each other's accusations (albeit the proper object of each accusation is "another" person) Mrs. Dabney and Mr. Ellenwood acknowledge their connections to others they never knew. To the extent that both did to others what each accuses the other of, they are one with the person they also only represent. All Mr. Ellenwood's hopes have been riveted on (a) Mrs. Dabney, as all Mrs. Dabney's early aborted love has been diverted to (a) Mr. Ellenwood. Insofar as neither has satisfied his or her original desire because of the cruelty of the other, the two do not meet for the first time, but rather are brought back together as those whom "adverse circumstances have separated through life" (IX:36). It is in a tale like "The Wedding-Knell" that we see Hawthorne's mastery in depicting characters who *contain* as well as epitomize other versions of themselves. If the tales I have spoken of earlier disembody the human image, tales like "The Wedding-Knell" make the human image delusively multiple, make it "representative," now more closely in Emerson's use of the word.

There are liabilities to a representational mode whose consequence is a fusion in which all men are the same man, representative, and where the idea prefigures all. In the 1851 "Preface" to the *Twice-Told Tales*, Hawthorne, scrutinizing what he has done, complains of the adequacy of the representation: "we have allegory, not always so warmly dressed in its habiliments of flesh and blood, as to be taken into the reader's mind without a shiver" (IX:5). Allegory, like typology, attempts to give body to what has none, to give the "inside" an attire. One problem with the endeavor is that it must substitute for flesh and blood (not themselves separable from the human body) the habiliments that will stand in lieu of flesh and blood, and which falsely claim equivalence with them. Another problem with the allegorical endeavor is that allegory falsely historicizes the self's present by suggesting that it has the fixture of a past. Alternately, in its memorialization of the past, it suggests that the past has a "finished" relation to the present. It is no accident that Hawthorne variously calls his tales "Allegories of the Heart" and "psychological romance." Hawthorne's tales attempt to decipher the complicated relation between history or the past and psychology or the self's present. I shall conclude with Hawthorne's criticism of his characters' attempts to allegorize their lives—of the way in which allegorizations deny the unique moments of history, on the one hand, and our connection to those histories, on the other—for it is in this criticism that the paradoxes, as we have seen them in the tales discussed thus far, are finally made explicit.

"Roger Malvin's Burial" and "My Kinsman, Major Molineux," written at the same time, begin with historical prefaces. "Roger Malvin's Burial" occurs in the year 1725, after Lovell's Fight, one of many defenses against the Indian attacks. "My Kinsman, Major Molineux" occurs in the year when the "kings of Great Britain had assumed the right of appointing the colonial governors" (XI:208) to the provinces. The prefaces, taking their information as they actually do from historical sources,[16] are important, for they locate both action and meaning within the framework of particular circumstance. "My Kinsman, Major Molineux" is the tale of a man who does not realize that New Englanders loathe rather than revere those who lord their power over others. He thus wishes to be such a man. In this tale false relations exist between Robin and his worldly cousin.

In "Roger Malvin's Burial," the tale of a man who will not bury his father-in-law because he wants to keep his distance from the mortal man lest he be contaminated by fatality, false relations exist between Reuben Bourne and Roger Malvin—hence, between Bourne and his family, Bourne and himself. Relatives are people who are related but other. History is a past that has a present bearing on our lives. The subject of both tales is the allegorical falsification of relations. As I am suggesting, the tales are schematic opposites. One takes place in the city, the other in the town. The subject of one is the denial of relations. The subject of the other is the wish to have one's relations become one's identity. Although both tales take place outside, as if directly under the divine eye, the externality in these tales is different from that I have previously associated with allegorical constructions. In these two tales the world "outside" the self is not the sphere where the self can magically be redefined; it is merely the world of natural history. In both tales, the story Hawthorne tells is of the self's proper relation to another when, notwithstanding the respective characters' attempts, relations cannot be allegorized. In both stories, allegorical conception would transport Roger Malvin and Major Molineux to an ahistorical place (where death does not exist and tyranny has no consequences) with Reuben and Robin (names scarily proximate) tagging along after them. In the historical world, there is no transport. There is neither complete disassociation nor complete identification. In the historical world human beings are different. The difference is at first the source of Robin's despair when he cannot find his kinsman. It will become the source of his relief when he sees Molineux debased. Contrarily, the connection between lives, however differentiated they may be, is the source of Reuben's repulsion when he must leave Roger Malvin dying in the wilderness. It will become the source of his hope, when he can return to acknowledge the relation between his father and his son, between the world of generation and himself. Robin will discover that we are not the same person. Reuben will discover that the proper understanding of the discrepancy is not to shrink from the separation between the self and the other, but rather to behave toward the other as if he were one's self, with analogy understood as such.

In "Roger Malvin's Burial," two men wounded in an Indian skirmish stop to rest in the wilderness as they make their way home. "'Nor would it avail me anything, if the smoke of my own chimney were but on the other side of that swell of land,'" Roger Malvin tells Reuben Bourne, the younger man. "'The Indian bullet was deadlier than I thought'" (X:339).

The fact is important, for although Reuben, his future son-in-law, would stay with the dying man, Malvin repetitively tells him that such a gratuitous sacrifice would, in addition, ensure Reuben's own death. Throughout the agonized debate in which Malvin tells Bourne he should continue on, we are struck by Malvin's generosity to the man he regards as a son and by the sacrificial impulses of Bourne himself. We are explicitly told: "No merely selfish motive . . . could have induced him to desert his companion, at such a moment. But his wishes seized upon the thought, that Malvin's life might be preserved, and his sanguine nature heightened, almost to certainty, the remote possibility of procuring human aid" (X:342). Therefore, we are assured that Reuben's culpability is not in leaving Roger Malvin. Rather, it is in what happens to the heart when, against its will, it must abandon a human other.

The one promise the dying man exacts is that when Reuben is healed he " 'return to this wild rock, and lay my bones in the grave, and say a prayer over them'" (X:344). This Reuben promises to do. But when Dorcas (Roger Malvin's daughter and Reuben Bourne's wife to be) assumes that Roger Malvin is both dead and buried, Reuben does not contradict her. Hence, Roger Malvin's bones lie unburied in the wilderness. Reuben and Dorcas marry and have a son, Cyrus. Like all Hawthorne's characters tormented by deeds they have wrongly done, Reuben fails to prosper. Some fifteen years later (when Cyrus is grown to Reuben's age at the tale's beginning), in search of a better livelihood, the three set off into the wilderness, led half-wittingly in the direction of Roger Malvin's bones. Reuben embarks on the journey thinking it is "Heaven's intent to afford him an opportunity of expiating his sin" and that "find[ing] the bones . . . and . . . having laid the earth over them, peace would throw its sunlight into the sepulchre of his heart" (X:356). Inadvertently we hear that it is in Reuben's heart Roger Malvin has been buried, in the heart rather than in the ground. One night, at a distance from the place where the family has set up camp, Reuben shoots what he thinks to be a deer. In fact, it is Cyrus, whom, we have been told, is dearer to Reuben Bourne than his own life—killed on the very spot where Roger Malvin's bones "lie so long unburied." The story is filled with unarticulated puns akin to that of "dear" and "deer." Reuben Bourne's name itself brings disjointedly together the idea of burying the dead and bearing the dead in a delayed past tense. Such implicit or near puns command our attention, for they mistakenly draw into relation objects or persons whom the characters confuse. Although the objects these words name are not in fact the same, the averted puns, lingering just below the tale's surface, show us in linguistic terms the source of the terror out of which Reuben Bourne shrinks from the dead. He will not go near the dead man, for to near him is to be him.

What is Reuben's confusion, father-in-law with self, son with father-in-law? What is Reuben's sin? What is the tale's subject? As if to raise this last question, at the point in the story which relates Reuben's marriage to Dorcas, the narrator simultaneously chastises our interest in the event. "As my tale is not of love," we are grimly told, "it shall suffice to say, that, in the space of a few months, Reuben became the husband of Dorcas Malvin" (X:348). Indeed, this tale is not of love. Rather, it is of the expectations we have of ourselves, and of the lies we tell in lament for those expectations when we find their fulfillment impossible. Should Reuben bury the dead man or become the dead man?[17] This is a question the tale had seemed to answer for us. Had Reuben stayed with Roger Malvin he would have died. Yet in a more harrowing sense to return to bury Malvin is to bury in oneself the knowledge one *will* die, that no retreat can escape it—will die as or in oneself, and not analogically as or in one's father or one's son. Instead, Reuben buries Malvin's image (not his body), Malvin's image (not, conceptually, his own) in the heart become a sepulchre.

Although the sacrifice of Cyrus Bourne is terrible in the present, as the sacrifice of Roger Malvin was terrible in the past, Reuben does not feel grief (he instructs Dorcas to feel it for him) because he thinks of the death as if it were his own. Reuben's tears, when he sees he has shot Cyrus, are of gratitude rather that grief: "His sin was expiated . . . [and] a prayer, the first for years, went up to Heaven from the lips of Reuben Bourne" (X:360). Reuben, we have been told, loves only in his own image, for only in that confine can the self guard against the atrocities it might otherwise perpetrate against the other, who is now thought safe precisely because his image is undifferentiated from the mind that conceives it. Yet not to know the difference between one's self and another for fear one will be contaminated by the object of one's connection (in the case of Roger Malvin) or for fear one will oneself contaminate the object of one's connection (in the case of Cyrus Bourne) is not to afford protection for the other. It is, oppositely, to make him the victim of one's murder. In the case of Cyrus, it is to give life illegitimately because one treats the life one bears as if it were one's own. Not to know the difference between one's self and another is to have to kill one's son, not made properly "other," too much loved, as Roger Malvin was loved too little. Or, to reverse the notion, as the story itself does, it is to have to kill one's son because, like the self, he is loved too little, as Roger Malvin—who had so awfully to be abandoned—is loved impotently and hence too much.

" 'How shall I dare to meet her eye?' " (X:341), Reuben asks Roger Malvin as he contemplates telling Dorcas he has left her father to lie unburied in "'this howling wilderness'" (X:355). The problem of how to meet another's eye is where the trouble begins. As Reuben turns to leave Roger Malvin, having promised the one thing Malvin asks—the one thing he will not get (that Reuben return to bury his bones)—Roger Malvin's voice recalls him:

> "Reuben, Reuben," said he, faintly; and Reuben returned and knelt down by the dying man.
> "Raise me, and let me lean against the rock," was his last request. "My face will be turned towards home, and I shall see you a moment longer, as you pass among the trees." (X:345)

What matters when nothing in fact matters is human connection. But it is the human connection that Reuben Bourne breaks:

> Reuben, having made the desired alteration in his companion's posture . . . walked more hastily at first, than was consistent with his strength; for a sort of guilty feeling, which sometimes torments men in their most justifiable acts, caused him to seek concealment from Malvin's eyes. But, after he had trodden far upon the rustling forest-leaves, he crept back, impelled by a wild and painful curiosity, and, sheltered by the earthy roots of an uptorn tree, gazed earnestly at the desolate man. . . . Roger Malvin's hands were uplifted in a fervent prayer, some of the words of which stole through the stillness of the woods, and entered Reuben's heart, torturing it with an unutterable pang. They were the broken accents of a petition for his own happiness and that of Dorcas; and, as the youth listened, conscience, or something in its similitude, pleaded strongly with him to return, and lie down again by the rock. (X:345–46)

Bourne can love Roger Malvin when he knows the man will live, will recover to be himself—with the understood play on the literal meaning of that expression. But when Malvin's death seems certain, when Bourne's leaving makes it certain, Reuben cannot look at the man. Rather, Reuben cannot look at him directly, although it was of looking Dorcas in the eye that he had originally expressed concern. Reuben, first in evading Roger Malvin's eyes and second in returning to look at the man covertly, is breaking the human connection. He is asking: what does the other look like when we have disassociated him from ourselves, when he has become inhuman? For if Roger Malvin is dead, Reuben will not be leaving a man to die, he will instead be leaving a corpse. Once converted from a spirit to a body, Roger Malvin *must* be looked at covertly because bodies no longer know how to look back. They cannot make human connections. Of course, it is really Reuben who no longer knows how to make human connection. And this inability is occasioned not simply by the fact that he is leaving Roger Malvin to die, but by the more excruciating fact that he is doing it against his will, against all he once held sacred, all that in his mind defined *his* connection to the human. Thus, it is Reuben Bourne's connection to himself that is broken in the evasion of Roger Malvin's eyes. At the moment of willed abandonment, the self is made unrecognizable, is made other to itself.

The tragedy of this story, then, is the tragedy of a world whose tale is not of love. It is the tragedy of choices we feel compelled to make, feel are forced upon us, but which we must acknowledge as our own since they are not anyone else's. It is the tragedy of man's inhumanity to man in a context understood as chosen *and* coerced. In short, it is the tragedy of being human, with all that this entails. For Roger Malvin and Reuben Bourne what being human entails is profound affection that does not make a difference. Affection cannot save Malvin's life. It could have killed Reuben Bourne in a gratuitous sacrifice. While Hawthorne does not mean to depict a Biblical eye for an eye, he does mean to insist that for Bourne to save his own life, he must leave Roger Malvin alone. It is on this hard fact that the tale's savagery focuses. For it is just the exchange (that his life should cost him the abandonment of another's) that Bourne cannot accept. Hawthorne, in disregard of what Bourne does and does not find tolerable, scripts a world that enacts human violence as a given. As the family later tracks through the wilderness, we are defiantly told that the three walk "into a region, of which savage beasts and savage men were as yet the sole possessors" [X:353]. He scripts a world whose savagery we must accede to as human by definition. Bourne cannot bear the definition. He cannot recognize in the definition what he considers human. He cannot recognize himself. So he renounces humanity, if this is what humanity means. He will not look Roger Malvin in the eye. He kills off the other as he has killed off part of the self, since the acceptance of the human self, as Hawthorne lays it out for him, implicates him in a crime more devastating than murder.

What is terrible about Reuben Bourne's position is that he has only an incidental part in Roger Malvin's fate. What is intolerable about the human position is that its part is more often than not incidental, is inadvertent rather than planned. In addition, and further degrading that part, Reuben's promise, though hardly trivial, matters to the *dead* man. There is no way, any longer, it can matter to the *live* one. What Hawthorne would have Bourne do is to look Roger Malvin in the eye—to look at him as he is leaving him; to accede to the sacrifice and to his part in the sacrifice; to accede to the way in which one life, not equivalent to another, sometimes has to sacrifice that other in order to save itself. Bourne cannot do it. Most of us cannot do it. Instead, we look away. We make part of the self other. We make the other dead. Then we marry and breed, as if in a yet more passionate pull away from the averted human connection, with its tangled sorrow and savagery an integral part of its love.

We have been told in the historical preface to the tale: "The open bravery displayed by both parties was in accordance with civilized ideas of valor, and chivalry itself might not blush to record the deeds of one or two individuals" (X:337). Such a statement and the "heroism" to which it a sentence earlier explicitly alludes take on terrible bitterness in the context of the narrated events that follow. Thus, we could say that the real conflict is displaced from the battle between the white settlers and the Indians. It takes place at the moment Bourne leaves Roger Malvin. Not before in the Indian battle, and not after in Bourne's lie to Dorcas. Indeed, even prior to the moment when Bourne assents to Dorcas's false understanding that her father is dead and buried, we see Bourne's discomfort at the mention of Roger Malvin's name: "His first impulse was to cover his face . . . against an imaginary accusation" (X:347). The lie to Dorcas (which Bourne and critics after him assume to be the act of which he is culpable) is itself a displacement, a making of the terrible moment other than the truly terrible moment in order to be able to bear it.

Thinking the problem through, Bourne conceives it in the following terms: "He felt, that, for leaving Roger Malvin, he deserved no censure. . . . But concealment had imparted to a justifiable act, much of the secret effect of guilt. . . . He at times almost imagined himself a murderer" (X:349). What is concealed is not Bourne's crime, however, if this crime refers to what he hides from Dorcas. What is concealed is Roger Malvin's face, when Reuben refuses to look at it. Thus, the crime is one of concealment differently defined: the evasion of his eyes when Roger Malvin tries to meet them, and a looking at Malvin in a way that first obscures and then denies the latter's life and pain. Not being able to look at Roger Malvin at the time, and not being able to look at him in recollection (the covering of the eyes when Dorcas mentions her father's name), Bourne cannot return to bury the man, cannot return to see the rot death makes of man. "It is the cause, it is the cause," Othello says, "let me not name it to you" (V.ii.1–2), invoking a pronoun for which there is intentionally no antecedent. In Hawthorne's different context, it is better to be a murderer than a helpless mortal being. Or, rather, mortality involves murder in ways too commonplace to name. The story is thus about the intolerability of the difference between one self and another when this difference exacts death of which one is both innocent and in which one is implicated. Reuben cannot bear the difference between the dead man and himself. Therefore, he makes Roger Malvin inhuman so that the dead man may be left. He then makes himself unrecognizable so that he can live with himself. The lie to Dorcas simultaneously conceals and socializes both of these transformations. For while Roger Malvin would not have Bourne stay with him, "'would not have your blood upon my soul'" (X:341) what Bourne gets for leaving is Roger Malvin's soul upon and in his heart. What Reuben cannot bear is that all men are mortal, and that mortality manifests itself not simply in the rotting of the body but also in the rotting of our ideas about the human spirit. Before this decay, "civilized ideas of valor" so touted in the preface are themselves lies. So false battles hide real ones, although the heroics alluded to at the beginning—at all conceptual beginnings—as in the case of Reuben Bourne, for what it is worth, enable us to go on.

To make the self "other" is what allegory hopes to do, either, as in "Roger Malvin's Burial," by disassociating the self from the foreign body that would contaminate it or, as in "My Kinsman, Major Molineux" (now, in a reversal of the meaning of the phrase "to make the self other," to make the self *into* another rather than to be disassociated from him), by incorporating the other, as Robin wishes to do in his identification with Major Molineux. As Reuben has wanted no connection with his kinsman, Robin will want connection between himself and his kinsman to become an identity. In "My Kinsman, Major Molineux," Robin, a country boy, comes to the world of the relatively big city (a small New England town) to find his kinsman, Major Molineux, whom he hopes will take him in, will help him make his way in the world: "'Well, Sir,'" Robin says, explaining himself to a gentleman whom he meets on the street, "'being nearly eighteen years old, and well grown, as you see . . . I thought it high time to begin the world'" (XI:225). Of course, Robin means it is time to begin his task in the world, but his speech betrays his pretensions. At the end of the tale, when he would flee from the spectacle he has seen—"'Will you show me the way to the ferry?'"—the request is rebuked: "'No, my good friend Robin, not to-night, at least,'" says the gentleman. "'Some few days hence, if you continue to wish it, I will speed you on your journey. Or, if you prefer to remain with us, perhaps, as you are a shrewd youth, you may rise in the world, without the help of your kinsman, Major Molineux'" (XI:231). Resonating against the conventional expression, and also against Robin's earlier misunderstanding of it, the gentleman's words tell Robin he may rise in the world, may rise in rather than start it. If Reuben Bourne's pretensions have to do with endings and our relations to endings, Robin's pretensions have to do with beginnings and our relations to beginnings.

Robin had wanted Molineux to be a great and lordly man, a man who, by virtue of their contact, could make Robin great and lordly, too. This, as I have suggested, is a form of contagious magic exactly opposite to what we saw in Reuben's aversion to Roger Malvin. Robin has allegorized Major Molineux—created an image discrepant with the man—so as to allegorize himself. To pin one's hopes on transformation—on the missing, magic relation who when found will confer power (as, for example, Sylph Etherege does)—is at the heart of the allegorical impulse. History would tell Robin that the aristocracy he reveres is abhorred by the town, that "the people looked with most jealous scrutiny to the exercise of power, which did not emanate from themselves" (XI:208). On the night Robin arrives in the little New England town, the famed kinsman is to be tarred and feathered, majestic if at all only in his agony. But in this story of great expectations, Robin does not know of his cousin's fallen stature, and the people whom, upon encountering, he asks to help locate his relation, do not tell him. Rather, they show him how to see for himself the fantasy in his mind punished and corrected in the process of being externalized. This is the historical response, the non-magical response, the response that would ground power in the limitations of one's own body or in one's own body politic. The tale teaches Robin to be terrified of any source of power not his own. It makes him scrutinize the image he has cherished, makes him see it so that he can laugh at it, with that expression literalized. In fact, the story's most hallucinatory moment occurs when Robin (first shocked at the sight of the ridiculed Molineux) joins in the crowd's raucous laughter—himself laughs at the spectacle he had thought he wanted to be.

As Robin waits for the procession that will bring Molineux before his eyes, we see the townspeople issue from their houses to keep the vigil with him. They empty from their houses as Robin's false image will be emptied from his mind. The rhetoric of the passage below brings the two expulsions together. The people themselves (like Robin's relation to his kinsman) seem inadequately individuated and also inadequately joined. We are told that "scattered individuals, and then denser bodies, began to appear." "Shapes without [allegorical] model[s]" comprise Hawthorne's world of the real. The people, in addition, participate in Robin's confusion. While they have presumably helped plan the midnight spectacle, they seem ignorant of its meaning: "Eager voices hailed each other from house to house, all demanding the explanation, which not a soul could give" (XI:227). Like Robin, they want an explanation for the bedlam that comprises the activity of the historical world. Therefore, the question put to Robin is crucial: "'Will you recognize your kinsman . . . if he passes in this crowd?'" In the midst of the bedlam:

A mighty stream of people now emptied into the street, and came rolling slowly towards the church. A single horseman wheeled the corner in the midst of them, and close behind him came a band of fearful wind-instruments, sending forth a fresher discord, now that no intervening buildings kept it from the ear. Then a redder light disturbed the moonbeams, and a dense multitude of torches shone along the street, concealing by their glare whatever object they illuminated. The single horseman, clad in a military dress, and bearing a drawn sword, rode onward as the leader, and, by his fierce and variegated countenance, appeared like war personified; the red of one cheek was an emblem of fire and sword; the blackness of the other betokened the mourning which attends them. In his train, were wild figures in the Indian dress, and many fantastic shapes without a model, giving the whole march a visionary air, as if a dream had broken forth from some feverish brain, and were sweeping visibly through the midnight streets. (XI:227–28)

The image of a dream "broken from some feverish brain" is echoed in the tale's multiple references to sleep: the people look out their windows in "the attire of the pillow, and confused by sleep suddenly broken" (XI:227); as Robin waits for his kinsman to pass, he hears a "low, dull, dreamy sound, compounded of many noises . . . a sleep-inspiring sound" (XI:221); even before the crowd begins to gather, we hear "the sound of drowsy laughter stealing along the solitary street" (XI:218). But if the world in which Robin will have to rise, as if from the confusions of sleep, is a world of nightmare, then this way of putting it is euphemistic or metaphoric. Hawthorne's repeated insistence on the hallucinatory aspects of Robin's experience—the aimless waiting, the shabby treatment at the hands of strangers, the jostled expectations—suggests this is the stuff of which *waking* life is made. Although images of a dream haunt the story, when we examine them closely, we see they are images of a dream that is interrupted or broken.

For Robin, who, at our first sight of him, is banking on privileges he does not have (promising the ferryman an extra fare for his delivery late at night), human impotence at first does seem dream-like. Robin carries a "heavy cudgel, formed of an oak sapling" (XI:209). But the "idea" (that like a scepter/sword it would wield authority) does not "prefigure all"; it does not prefigure anything. Robin, stopping at the tavern, imagining that on credit of his relation to Major Molineux he will be advanced a dinner, is instead sent back to the streets with a Dickensian parting: "'Better trudge, boy, better trudge!'" About to brandish his oak cudgel, he is stopped because "a strange hostility in every countenance, induce[s] him to relinquish his purpose of breaking the courteous innkeeper's head" (XI:214). In a world where a look rebukes a stick, it strikes us if it does not strike Robin that impotence and incoherence go together in this town, and that the meaning of both if they have one must be put together piecemeal.

As Robin walks down the New England street, the first passerby he encounters carries a long and polished cane, which, unlike Robin's, is actually vested with power. We are told that the man, in further distinction from Robin, is on "in years, with a full periwig of grey hair, a wide-skirted coat of dark cloth, and silk stockings rolled about his knees." At regular intervals "he utter[s] two successive hems, of a peculiarly solemn and sepulchral intonation" (XI:210). While the hems refer to the clearing of the voice, confusion sets in a moment later. Standing before the barbershop, Robin, grabbing hold of the man's coat to ask about Major Molineux, is shaken off as follows: "'Let go my garment, fellow! I tell you, I know not the man you speak of. What! I have authority, I have—hem, hem—authority; and if this be the respect you show your betters, your feet shall be brought acquainted with the stocks.'" Just when we think the word has changed its reference from the man's voice to his garment, explanation becomes metaphoric: "His two sepulchral hems . . . broke into the very centre of his rebuke, with most singular effect, like a thought of the cold grave obtruding among wrathful passions" (XI:211). The word's connotation wavers between an image and a sound, between the clearing of the voice and the bottom of the dress, seeming to settle on neither.

These hems will be further mystified by their association with a prostitute who tries to lure Robin inside her house by telling him it is Major Molineux's. At first, all Robin can discern of her is "a strip of scarlet petticoat, and the occasional sparkle of an eye" (XI:216). The cloth of the man before the barbershop, the clearing of the voice, the edge of the scarlet petticoat—these are the remnants of meaning, not the whole thing. We think we are approaching the whole thing—the "prefiguring Idea" behind the massive confusion—when at the beginning of the processional that will annunciate Major Molineux's humiliation and Robin's initiation into the world, we are told: "A mass of people, inactive, except as applauding spectators, hemmed the procession in, and several women ran along the sidewalks, piercing the confusion . . . with their shrill voices of mirth or terror" (XI:228). Here the narrator toys with a connotation psychologically closer to the near-suffocating events that follow. But the confusion of connotations, like the confusion of sounds (like the confusion of meanings for which this disarray stands), is finally collective, signaling mirth and terror alike. As if to hammer in the point that there is no single meaning, no single or stable sense, no Idea, the narrator, in a deranged half-step (or full letter) away from the repetition of his own pun, blurs the connotations introduced thus far to a worse parody of silence:

> A moment more, and the leader thundered a command to halt; the trumpets vomited a horrid breath, and held their peace; the shouts and laughter of the people died away, and there remained only a universal hum, nearly allied to silence. Right before Robin's eyes was an uncovered cart. There the torches blazed the brightest, there the moon shone out like day, and there, in tar-and-feathery dignity, sate his kinsman, Major Molineux! (XI:228).

In these terrible transformations of the voice to the garment (first the man's, then the whore's), of the garment to the metaphor of suffocation in which all meanings are as if "hemmed in," of all these released and blurred in hallucinatory mirth and terror to the hum "allied to silence," Major Molineux arrives, the conversion of his state dramatized by the linguistic conversions the tale has been at pains to make both Robin and reader suffer:

> He was an elderly man, of large and majestic person, and strong, square features, betokening a steady soul; but steady as it was, his enemies had found the means to shake it. His face was pale as death, and far more ghastly; the broad forehead was contracted in his agony, so that his eyebrows formed one grizzled line; his eyes were red and wild, and the foam hung white upon his quivering lip. His whole frame was agitated by a quick, and continual tremor, which his pride strove to quell, even in those circumstances of overwhelming humiliation. (XI:228–29)

As Robin catches Molineux's eye—in a stare of recognition (to which I shall return) having its obvious counterpart in Reuben Bourne's aversion from Roger Malvin's eye—he is himself affected by a kind of mental inebriety:

> he heard a peal of laughter like the ringing of silvery bells; a woman twitched his arm, a saucy eye met his, and he saw the lady of the scarlet petticoat. A sharp, dry cachinnation appealed to his memory, and, standing on tiptoe in the crowd, with his white apron over his head, he beheld the courteous little innkeeper. And lastly, there sailed over the heads of the multitude a great, broad laugh, broken in the midst by two sepulchral hems; thus—"Haw, haw, haw—hem, hem—haw, haw, haw, haw!" (XI:229)

These are sounds with no meaning, the parody of a laugh, the way it would be written rather than the way that it would sound. The perpetual dislocation—reference shifted again and again, throughout the whole tale only to come to this—is the verbal enactment of the tale's subject. As if to taunt us with the burial of meaning, we see, one last time, the man with the "polished cane in a fit of convulsive merriment, which manifested itself on his solemn old features, like a funny inscription on a tomb-stone" (XI:229–30).

How in the world is meaning to be made? How is it to be made out? How is it to be figured if it cannot be made out? Following the tale's linguistic tracks as I have traced them thus far, we note they are attended by Robin's corollary attempt to see what he is experiencing. From the moment he arrives, his wandering through the town is attended by a Joycean half-light. The only figure depicted clearly is, in fact, Robin's. We see him by "the newly risen moon" and by the aid of the ferryman's lantern. The conjunctive lights give us, in distinction to what follows, "a very accurate survey of the stranger's figure" (XI:209). They show us his naïveté, his youth, his pathetic self-assurance compounded into one. As Robin sits on the church steps trying to make out where or who he is, we see moonlight fall on the rooftops, "'creating,'" we are told, "'like the imaginative power'"—like *Robin's* imaginative power—a "'beautiful strangeness in familiar objects'" (XI:221). This is the language of romance before romance is chastised by its own vulgar mistakes. In the throes of the enchantment, however, the vision looks like this:

> The irregular, and often quaint architecture of the houses, some of whose roofs were broken into numerous little peaks; while others ascended, steep and narrow, into a single point; and others again were square; the pure milk-white of some of their complexions, the aged darkness of others, and the thousand sparklings, reflected from bright substances in the plastered walls of many; these matters engaged Robin's attention for awhile. (XI:221)

The geometrics of form, not organized into discrete meaning, duplicate in visual terms a confusion that the "hum" or the "hem" render in aural ones. When Robin does make out a configuration it is of the church on whose steps he is sitting. "'Perhaps this is the very house I have been seeking,' thought Robin" (XI:221). Yet, proffering the opposite of platitudinous comfort, Hawthorne is not, in fact, intimating that all would be well if the mansion Robin wished to enter were the one in the sky. If, outside the church, the world is cluttered with unclear objects, the inside of the church, seen as Robin looks in the windows, is stripped bare. The church is a holy place, then, not because its emptiness points to the existence of a Father above but, rather, because its emptiness leaves man room to contemplate the insignificance of any relations in a world sorrowed by the double facts of his isolation and the world's incoherence. God is not exactly

[149]

absent to witness this chastening, but He is not present either, if *present* means clear or embodied. "Oh, that any breathing thing were here" (XI:222), Robin will say when, in grief, he looks away from the following vision:

> Robin arose, and climbed a window-frame, that he might view the interior of the church. There the moonbeams came trembling in, and fell down upon the deserted pews, and extended along the quiet aisles. A fainter, yet more awful radiance, was hovering round the pulpit, and one solitary ray had dared to rest upon the opened page of the great Bible. Had Nature, in that deep hour, become a worshipper in the house, which man had builded? Or was that heavenly light the visible sanctity of the place, visible because no earthly and impure feet were within the walls? The scene made Robin's heart shiver with a sensation of loneliness, stronger than he had ever felt in the remotest depths of his native woods; so he turned away, and sat down again before the door. There were graves around the church, and now an uneasy thought obtruded into Robin's breast. What if the object of his search, which had been so often and so strangely thwarted, were all the time mouldering in his shroud? What if his kinsman should glide through yonder gate, and nod and smile to him in passing dimly by? (XI:221–22)

Robin's fantasies about his kinsman are shortly to be invaded. The light enters the church as the truth will invade his mind, leaving mind and "builded house" evacuated. But if the passage illuminates by glossing ahead of time what cannot be glossed at the time (because at the time Robin's experience is too overwhelming to be rendered coherently), it shows the supernatural ray of light incomprehensible as well as bright. The real power of the light lies in the discrepancy between the sharpness of its focus and its unclear meaning. Yet we see, as Robin does before he turns away, that meaning is to be read not in the holy house nor in the holy writ, but rather in the light as it comes into one and lays itself upon the other—"one solitary ray" advancing to the pulpit, to the Bible itself, to illuminate directly what man has not a prayer of comprehending. Even this way of putting it anthropomorphizes what it explains, for nature in its own service is paying devotions here. In the multiple displacements—the mortal place of worship from the natural place of worship, the ostensibly empty church from the church invaded by light, light's bequeathal of meaning from Robin's inability to comprehend it—Robin turns in his mind's eye to a more hospitable dwelling, for the church-house seems to be one where we confront the terror of separation—from each other, from God—unsolaced by saving relations:

Recalling his thoughts from this uncomfortable track, he sent them over forest, hill, and stream, and attempted to imagine how that evening of ambiguity and weariness, had been spent by his father's household. He pictured them assembled at the door, beneath the tree, the great old tree, which had been spared for its huge twisted trunk. . . . There, at the going down of the summer sun, it was his father's custom to perform domestic worship. . . . Robin distinguished the seat of every individual of the little audience; he saw the good man in the midst, holding the Scriptures in the golden light that shone from the western clouds . . . He perceived the slight inequality of his father's voice when he came to speak of the Absent One; he noted how his mother turned her face to the broad and knotted trunk; how his elder brother scorned, because the beard was rough upon his upper lip, to permit his features to be moved; how his younger sister drew down a low hanging branch before her eyes; and how the little one of all . . . burst into clamorous grief. Then he saw them go in at the door; and when Robin would have entered also, the latch tinkled into its place, and he was excluded from his home. (XI:222–23)

The two passages noting worship in the church and domestic worship outside are crucially juxtaposed. The first tells of being alone in God's presence, in the house built by man, the second of communal worship that takes place under the sky. The first tells of a light whose coldness inspires awe, the second of a light that naturally ends the common day. The first tells of solitude so awful it evades expression, the second of grief that shows itself freely on the face. The first tells of a pulpit, the second of a central tree, which by the rhetoric of (man's) salvation (we are told it had been spared) is associated with the crucifixion. Given these differences, it would seem that Robin's home has been unnaturally abandoned for the perversions of the city. And it is true that in the city devotion is a mystery, something Robin wants to flee. But the comparisons are not simple. For the door *does* close behind Robin, and not simply because he is away. It closes behind him, as it closes behind us all when we leave the familial house to find our own place in the world.

What *is* a place in the world? The story will not allow us to fathom the question simply. The "deep hour" of Robin's watch, when he is spellbound and bewildered, tortured by who he is, by who he metaphysically is, does not propose a question that admits of an answer either familial or communal. The wrong way to see Robin is as a fool who ought to have stayed in the natural fold with his brothers and sisters. To stay where one is, is to be given one's place, to be *given* rather than to find it, and still by virtue of (other) human relations. That one has a place in the world is an idea the story rebukes. This is true because one's place in the world changes. It is true because man's place is not properly in the world, nor is it in the church where Robin is not fit to stay. Like the hem-hum-haw (the word that will not retain any stable relations), like the light shining on the Bible, with the relation between light and Bible indecipherable, man's place in the world both shifts and is unclear. Place cannot be assigned, as, for example, the British government wishes to assign it—to make arbitrary designations of power govern—or as allegory wishes to assign it, with its similar governance of meanings external to the object in question. Both allegorical assignations and foreign assignations, attributing meaning from outside, intersect in Hawthorne's criticism of them. Assigned meanings are static, and exterior to the objects and persons to which they attach. They are also single. Conversely, meanings in the temporal world are ambiguous and multiple. While allegory depends, moreover, first upon splits and second upon these splits straddling meaning between one body and a separate other, in this tale divisions are shown to be *internal* to the self in question. Robin is shown (twice) the man with the double complexion (one side painted black, the other red). As the rioters approach, we are told "'a thousand voices went to make up that one shout.'" And when Robin fails to understand this he is catechized as follows: "'May not one man have several voices, Robin, as well as two complexions?'" (XI:226). The statement about several voices is not meant to suggest that people are duplicitous. It *is* meant to suggest that division is inside the self. While in this tale allegory tries to cure the real split between the self and the outside world by bringing the self into alignment with a second body whose identity it could assume (as Robin wishes to assume the characteristics of Major Molineux), the world of temporality and history rejects the solution. When Robin's eyes meet Major Molineux's, Robin looks away. We are told: "They stared at each other in silence, and Robin's knees shook, and his hair bristled, with a mixture of pity and terror" (XI:229). Robin has made a mistake about who Major Molineux is and about who he, Robin, is. Laughter is an attempt to expel pity for the man and terror that he will be the man. The laughter does for Robin what looking away had done for Reuben. If Reuben had looked away from Roger Malvin because he feared Malvin would impose upon his body an image of the mortal self, Robin looks away from Major Molineux because he fears he has externalized his own vision of himself—the spectacle of the boy with no worldly power.

Although Hawthorne's models—in Puritan American typology, in various Renaissance and classical texts—conventionally enlist allegory to accomplish providential history, Hawthorne in these two tales seems to find the allegorical model dangerous. In the clear disjunctions they

[152]

enact—between one self and another, between allegory and history, between the tales' prefaces and their bodies—"Roger Malvin's Burial" and "My Kinsman, Major Molineux" differ from the other tales I have discussed that do not consider the historical world at all, and they differ from other tales (like "Endicott and the Red Cross" or "Main-Street") that conflate history and allegory. "Roger Malvin's Burial" juxtaposes the historical preface (the battle between Indians and white men) to the battle in the tale between one man and another. Hawthorne seems to be suggesting that while the historical battle is possible to win, it is disastrous to win the allegorical battle. In "My Kinsman, Major Molineux," the preface and the body of the tale bear the relation of elaboration rather than of opposition. Nonetheless, the clarity of the preface is contrasted to the allegorical confusion that follows. Hawthorne's criticism of allegory when he articulates it unambiguously is that allegory mistakes the conflict within the self for the conflict between the self and the outside world. Hence, Reuben Bourne thinks he is guilty of a lie to Dorcas. In fact, he is guilty of his failure to acknowledge his proper relations—to Roger Malvin and to himself. The failure to acknowledge the conflict within—in Robin's case, the desire to transform the conflict within to a realm outside, to find his kinsman rather than himself—leads to the inability to see conflict outside the self where it genuinely exists (it leads to Robin's inability to see that the New Englanders loathe Major Molineux). Allegory thus distorts the self's relation to itself and to the outside world. It falsely implies that one person could be another or, alternately, need have no relation to any other. Such ideas falsify the complexity of relations in the historical world. I take the puns in "My Kinsman, Major Molineux," with their unspoken emphasis on the "mayhem" of relations, to point to this complexity.

If allegory is clear, history is incomprehensible. Its meanings are not neat, and the loyalties it inspires, properly understood, are divided. Insofar as Major Molineux participates in the tyranny of foreign rule, he is to be abhorred. But the rancor of the people's vengeance perpetuates the very tyranny that has repelled them. Their brutality makes them one with the power in whose name Molineux is reviled. Major Molineux's degradation is not simply cruel, it also has no (specific) meaning. Or, rather, what meaning it does have—the people's rage at Tory rule—seems an inconsequential part of a more inexplicable violence that first enlists a cause and then subsumes it: "On they went, like fiends that throng in mockery round some dead potentate, mighty no more, but majestic still in his agony. On they went, in counterfeited pomp, in senseless uproar, in frenzied merriment, trampling all on an old man's heart. On swept the tumult, and left a silent street behind" (XI:230). Whatever he has done, Molineux has not deserved the desecration by which he is here swept up. In the wake of the procession, Hawthorne intimates that such causes as we invoke—the Tory's or the revolutionary's—are mere shields for the unleashing of a more general rage at human impotence too overwhelming to be contained adequately by any single cause. The explanation is not meant to dismiss the rebellion or the brutality that occasioned it. Rather, it is meant to suggest what invests historical events with power. Any event is the peg on which to hang a mortal grievance. The nature of the grievance, however, is as dimly spelled out as are Major Molineux's sins. The reverence paid to the Bible in the tale's other central processional is similarly inexplicable: "There the moonbeams came trembling in, and fell down upon the deserted pews, and extended along the quiet aisles. A fainter, yet more awful radiance, was hovering round the pulpit, and one solitary ray had dared to rest upon the opened page of the great Bible" (XI:222).

Both revilement and worship must, it seems, be witnessed without comprehension, and also must be witnessed without being either repelled or internalized. In addition, not understood, the experiences must be endured without being subjected to outside (allegorical) interpretation, must be understood on their own terms—with the simultaneous understanding that they have none, or none that are stable. Revilement and worship cannot themselves be kept separate. As the language describing Major Molineux ("majestic in his agony") and the language describing the devotions (the "awful radiance") suggest—each description appropriating adjectives we would associate with the opposite context—revilement and worship are integral to one body.[18] Although Molineux has done wrong, or although wrong has been done through him, the story implies a connection between the desecration of the man and the desecration of the deity. Molineux is crucified (with that expression undiminished for being metaphoric), and part of the tale's power, in fact, lies in the implicit connection between the processional in the church and the processional in the street, between the search for the man and the search for the God. Its power lies in the confusion between man and God, in the apparent inability to recognize either properly. Robin cannot *be* God; that is the only kinsman whose power would truly give him the stature he has wanted. But the correct understanding of not being God, of not being omnipotent and immortal—of, instead, being like Roger Malvin—is not to revile the image. Instead, it is to accept the "sensation of loneliness, stronger than he had ever felt." Loneliness is strong because it ushers in the recognition that no connection to human others and no palpable connection to a divine Other can lift one out of one's body, can rescue one from the destiny of having a separate body. Because, as I have suggested, the tale denies not the existence but rather the presence of God (with the latter understood as possible to embody), in lieu of that embodiment, all we have are signs, and, as Puritan typology or the unlearned world itself would have taught Hawthorne, more often than not, signs are false.

In "Roger Malvin's Burial," Reuben ties a handkerchief to the branch of the tree against which he leaves Roger Malvin sitting:

> The handkerchief had been the bandage of a wound upon Reuben's arm; and, as he bound it to the tree, he vowed, by the blood that stained it, that he would return, either to save his companion's life, or to lay his body in the grave. (X:344)
>
> As he gave a parting look, a breeze waved the little banner upon the sapling-oak, and reminded Reuben of his vow. (X:346)

At the end of the tale, we see that the branch on which the handkerchief has been tied has withered and died. The moment Cyrus is sacrificed, however, "the withered topmost bough of the oak loosened itself, in the stilly air, and fell in soft, light fragments upon the rock" (X:360). This is allegory with a vengeance. It is the reliance on signs to give things significance, and by means external to the self, which can then easily interpret them. In "My Kinsman, Major Molineux," the oak branch becomes an oak cudgel, and we see early on that it is powerless to mean or do. In the historical world, objects are assigned meanings. Since these assignations are human, they can be both false and arbitrary. The world is going to have to stand—Hawthorne seems to insist, in "My Kinsman, Major Molineux"—on the confusions allegorical meanings rectify by their imposed assignations. Robin must rise without his kinsman's help. He must rise in a world where bodies cannot be partialized, where meanings are not external. He must rise in a world where significance once figured—or where impossible to figure—must simply be endured. He must rise in a world where no branch falls.

"He says NO! in thunder,"[19] Melville wrote of Hawthorne. Since Hawthorne's work does not negate, indeed, says nothing in thunder in any conventional sense, it is difficult to understand the meaning of such a remark. This particular remark of Melville's is not, in fact, anchored to a context. Let us suppose, however, that what attracted Melville to Hawthorne is the latter's making the body immaterial as well as Hawthorne's simultaneously vehement criticism of this same immateriality. It is in their respective nay-saying—Hawthorne's to the immateriality of the human body, Melville's to the destruction of the world's body—to the making of *it* immaterial that the concerns of the two authors most uncannily intersect.

While Melville was at work completing *Moby-Dick*, Hawthorne published "Ethan Brand," then under the title of "The Unpardonable Sin." Ahab seems made half in Brand's image (the image of intellectual pride), half in his antithesis, for Brand annihilates himself, not the world of others. Critics like Edwin Haviland Miller[20] suggest it was Melville's friendship with Hawthorne that transformed *Moby-Dick* from a simple whaling story to the symbolic novel we now have; at the very least, this statement ignores the traces of *Moby-Dick* as we see them, for example, in a novel like *Mardi*. Nonetheless, the scenes most obsessed with the problematics of relationship—the scenes between Pip and Ahab—were presumably written during the year the friendship between the two men took on, at least for Melville, life-transforming importance. Brand is the prototypical example of Hawthorne's allegorical heroes, for the desire to thrust the heart out of the body, to have it be in the world, has as its object that magical correspondence in which heart and world beat with the same pulse. The world does have a heart. This Hawthorne acknowledges, in the image of the village lying in the palm of providence. But the heart is not Brand's. The heart cannot exist wholly outside the body, as Brand has wished, any more than it can exist wholly inside the body, as Ahab has wished. Thus, only metaphorically is Pip woven of Ahab's heartstrings. Yet Melville, writing to Hawthorne, who had (also in a letter) recently praised the newly completed *Moby-Dick*, expresses his gratitude in the following terms: "Your heart beat in my ribs and mine in yours, and both in God's. A sense of unspeakable security is in me this moment, on account of your having understood the book." As the letter continues, the images of fusion, one heart into another's body, shift, as if to realign themselves with the central fiction of Hawthorne's work: "Whence come you, Hawthorne? By what right do you drink from my flagon of life? And when I put it to my lips—lo, they are yours and not mine. I feel that the Godhead is broken up like the bread at the Supper, and that we are the pieces."[21] These are images of persons and images between persons in a context unsanctioned by literary pretext. Two months later Hawthorne moved unexpectedly from Lenox back to Concord in what could be interpreted as his attempt to escape an intensity outside of the protective fiction of disembodied personae. He moved far enough away to impose sufficient distance between himself and these unremorseful representations of a relationship impossible by human definition. For the heart cannot exist in someone else's body any more than the body can be broken up into representative pieces. The power of *Moby-Dick*, however, like the power of the tales, rests in the wish and the despair associated with these opposite ideas. Seduced by the thought that there really could be a bodily exchange or, alternately, that the self could be uncaged from its fleshly person, could lie like the village in the palm of providence, Ahab sacrifices the Pequod-world and Brand his own body. In the wake of the sacrifices, Ahab's of the world, Brand's of his own body, in the wake of the hope in whose name the sacrifices are made, the self is thrown back on the trial of human relations.

Notes

Introduction

1. Henry David Thoreau, "Ktaadn," in *The Maine Woods*, ed. Joseph J. Moldenhauer, in *The Writings of Henry David Thoreau* (Princeton: Princeton University Press, 1972), p. 71.

2. Our modern conception of personal identity as dualistic relies primarily on Descartes's *Meditations*, although it should be noted that other sixteenth-century philosophers are differently cognizant of the issue, and that later philosophers from Locke and Hume to the present offer important restatements of the problem, with their own attendant distinctions. For a good introduction to the history of the philosophic issue, see the collection of essays *Personal Identity*, ed. John Perry (Berkeley and Los Angeles: University of California Press, 1975), and *The Identities of Persons*, ed. Amélie Oksenberg Rorty (Berkeley and Los Angeles: University of California Press, 1976).

3. All references to Hawthorne's works are from *The Centenary Edition of the Works of Nathaniel Hawthorne* (Columbus: Ohio State University Press, 1974). The first number indicates volume; the second, page. For the reader's convenience, I list here the titles that correspond to the relevant volume numbers: I, *The Scarlet Letter*; II, *The House of the Seven Gables*; III, *The Blithedale Romance*; IV, *The Marble Faun*; VIII, *The American Notebooks*; IX, *Twice-Told Tales*; X, *Mosses from an Old Manse*; XI, *The Snow-Image* and *Uncollected Tales*; and XIII, *The Elixir of Life Manuscripts*.

4. All references to *Moby-Dick; Or, The Whale* are from the text edited by Charles Feidelson, Jr. (Indianapolis: Bobbs-Merrill, 1976). The first number indicates chapter; the second, page.

5. Ralph Waldo Emerson, *Nature*, in *The Complete Works*, centenary ed., 12 vols. (Boston and New York: Houghton, Mifflin & Co., 1903), 1:74.

6. Idem, "The American Scholar," in *Complete Works*, I:83.

7. Edgar Allan Poe, *The Narrative of Arthur Gordon Pym*, ed. James A. Harrison, 17 vols. (New York: Thomas Y. Crowell, 1902), 3:140.

8. In the context of these philosophic concerns, Stanley Cavell's work is crucial, and I shall have more to say about it in my chapter on *Moby-Dick* where it becomes directly relevant. On distinctly literary grounds, I wish to mention Leslie

Fiedler's discussion of *Moby-Dick* in *Love and Death in the American Novel* (1960; rev. ed. New York: Stein & Day, 1975) and Frederick Crews's discussion of Hawthorne's tales in *The Sins of the Fathers: Hawthorne's Psychological Themes* (Oxford: Oxford University Press, 1966), to which I see my own study as both proximate and indebted. My work diverges from Fiedler's and Crews's in the following opposite directions. While Fiedler posits the crucial importance of characterological splits—between Ishmael and Ahab, men and women, Fedallah and Starbuck, white men and black men—my discussion imagines such splits as existing *within* characters rather than between them. I thus psychologize or internalize the divisions Fiedler construes in discrete, albeit oppositional, characterological terms. Put differently, my discussion implies that characters are genuinely "parts" of one another. They do not respect the fictional boundaries of persons, as these boundaries are advanced by the social and literary conventions that posit an idea like that of "character." Alternately, in his brilliant examination of Hawthorne's tales, Crews eschews literary conventions of allegory, rather endorsing psychoanalytic conventions to explain the dynamic of the tales. In my discussion of the tales, I suggest that allegory and psychology are not alternative ways of reading the tales, but that allegory (that literary convention predicated on splits in and of meaning) is itself a psychological strategy for exemplifying or externalizing psychological or philosophical issues. Thus, if my reading of *Moby-Dick* psychologizes or *internalizes* splits of the self, thereby rejecting literary conventions (in this case of discrete character), my reading of Hawthorne points to the way in which literary conventions (in this case of allegory) are not opposed to philosophical and psychological imperatives and the conflicts that they generate, but rather *externalize* them.

9. My comment glosses the subject of Jean Piaget's whole book (trans. Eleanor Duckworth) (New York: Columbia University Press, 1970).

10. *Mardi and a Voyage Thither* in *The Writings of Herman Melville*, ed. Harrison Hayford, Hershel Parker, and G. Thomas Tanselle, Northwestern Newberry ed. (Evanston, Ill.: Northwestern University Press, 1957–), vol. 3 (1970), p. 78.

11. *Nature's Work of Art: The Human Body as Image of the World* (New Haven: Yale University Press, 1975), p. 6. The concern with the body, in the palpable terms in which I am speaking, is not absent in English literature, but it is characteristically confined to the gothic.

12. Vladimir Nabokov, *Lolita* (New York: Berkley Publishing Corp., 1955), p. 100.

13. *Religious Affections*, ed. John E. Smith, in *The Works of Jonathan Edwards* (New Haven: Yale University Press, 1957–), vol. 2 (1959), p. 211.

14. "The Mind," in *Scientific and Philosophical Writings*, ed. Wallace E. Anderson, in *Works of Jonathan Edwards*, vol. 6 (1980), p. 350.

Chapter 1

1. See especially the discussions by F. O. Matthiessen in *American Renaissance: Art and Expression in the Age of Emerson and Whitman* (New York: Oxford University Press, 1941); R. P. Blackmur, "The Craft of Herman Melville: A Putative Statement," in Blackmur, *The Lion and the Honeycomb* (New York: Harcourt, Brace, & World, 1955); the full-length studies of Melville by Newton Arvin

(*Herman Melville* [New York: William Sloane Associates, 1950]) and Warner Berthoff (*The Example of Melville* [Princeton: Princeton University Press, 1962]); and Richard H. Brodhead's first chapter in *Hawthorne, Melville, and the Novel* (Chicago: University of Chicago Press, 1976).

2. The three alternatives, respectively, are advanced by Henry Nash Smith, in "The Image of Society in *Moby-Dick*," in *Moby-Dick Centennial Essays*, ed. Tyrus Hillway and Luther S. Mansfield (Dallas: Southern Methodist University Press, 1953); Leo Marx, in *The Machine in the Garden: Technology and the Pastoral Ideal in America* (New York: Oxford University Press, 1964); and D. H. Lawrence, in *Studies in Classic American Literature* (New York: T. Seltzer, 1923).

3. The first idea is dominant in studies as diverse as R. W. B. Lewis's *The American Adam: Innocence, Tragedy, and Tradition in the Nineteenth Century* (Chicago: University of Chicago Press, 1955) and Lewis Mumford's *Herman Melville: A Study of His Life and Vision*, rev. ed. (New York: Harcourt, Brace & World, 1962); the second in Leslie Fiedler's *Love and Death in the American Novel* (1960; rev. ed. New York: Stein & Day, 1975); the third in Alfred Kazin's "Introduction" to *Moby-Dick* in the Riverside ed. (Boston: Houghton Mifflin, 1950); and the fourth in studies like Lawrance Thompson's *Melville's Quarrel with God* (Princeton: Princeton University Press, 1952).

4. See, for example, Robert Zoellner's *The Salt-Sea Mastodon: A Reading of Moby-Dick* (Berkeley and Los Angeles: University of California Press, 1973) and Paul Brodtkorb's *Ishmael's White World: A Phenomenological Reading* (New Haven: Yale University Press, 1965).

5. I would like here to acknowledge my indebtedness to Stanley Cavell. While this book was conceived and half completed before I had read *The Claim of Reason: Skepticism, Morality, and Tragedy* (Oxford: at the Clarendon Press, 1979), it was not written before I had read the earlier "The Avoidance of Love: A Reading of *King Lear*" (in *Must We Mean What We Say? A Book of Essays* [New York: Scribners, 1969], pp. 267–353), that essay which anticipates Cavell's later work and which deals with the play in whose issues *Moby-Dick* is mired in a directly imitative way. I take the recurrence in my discussion of *Moby-Dick* of certain Cavellian topics that announced themselves in connection with *King Lear* to be a partial consequence of the relation of the two primary texts. But although claims of indebtedness can be overstated, it is not an exaggeration to say that Cavell taught me the importance of prepositions for indicating our attitudes toward our bodies and our minds, that how we speak of our bodies and minds is revelatory of our ideas about them. In *Moby-Dick*, that novel so excruciated by the question of proper relationship, of inner to outer, prepositions and what they signify matter in a crucial way. Thus, it could be said that Cavell taught me a vocabulary for the subject I consider.

6. While *The Dictionary of American Slang* supports the suggestion that this pun would be contingent upon twentieth-century meanings, the *O.E.D.* notes that as early as 1820 "screwy" was used as slang to mean "unbalanced by alcohol." Melville may or may not have had the current colloquialism, detached from its original metaphoric context, available to him. I would argue that he did—that he invented such a meaning if it were not already accessible—precisely because the consequence to which Pip here alludes is not simply that of perishing, but of doing so by going crazy.

7. See John D. Seelye, "The Golden Navel: The Cabalism of Ahab's Doubloon," *Nineteenth Century Fiction* 14, no. 4 (1960):350–55.

8. Benjamin writes: "The novel is significant . . . not because it presents someone else's fate to us . . . but because this stranger's fate by virtue of the flame which consumes it yields us the warmth which we never draw from our own fate. What draws the reader to the novel is the hope of warming his shivering life with a death he reads about" ("The Storyteller," in *Illuminations*, trans. Harry Zohn, ed. Hannah Arendt [New York: Schocken Books, 1973], p. 101).

9. See, for example, John Seelye, "*Moby-Dick*: Line and Circle," in Seelye, *Melville: The Ironic Diagram* (Evanston: Northwestern University Press, 1970), pp. 60–73, which discusses Ahab's thinking as linear, Ishmael's as circular.

10. The major discussions of the relationship between the two texts are in Matthiessen's *American Renaissance* and Charles Olson's *Call Me Ishmael: A Study of Melville* (New York: Reynal & Hitchcock, 1947). While these studies acknowledge *Moby-Dick's* imitative sight imagery and the connection between the characters and the respective texts, they do not discuss why and in what ways Melville transforms the earlier text.

11. Ludwig Wittgenstein, *Tractatus Logico-Philosophicus* (London: Routledge & Kegan Paul, 1951), p. 139.

12. See, for example, *Symbolism and American Literature* (Chicago: University of Chicago Press, 1953), by Charles Feidelson, Jr., who regards Melville's impulse for symbolism as an impulse for paradox, for a merging of opposite points of view.

13. "Melville and His Critics," in *Moby-Dick as Doubloon*, ed. Hershel Parker and Harrison Hayford (New York: W. W. Norton, 1970), p. 232.

14. *Love and Death*, p. 387. The words between the two halves of the quotation are my own and of my own construction, though the interpretation is consonant with ideas Fiedler espouses throughout his discussion of the novel.

15. In *Love and Death in the American Novel*, Fiedler describes the American dream of love as exemplified by "an archetypal relationship which . . . haunts the American psyche: two lonely men, one dark-skinned, one white [who] have forsaken all others for the sake of the austere, almost inarticulate, but unquestioned love which binds them to each other and to the world of nature which they have preferred to civilization" (p. 192).

16. Henry A. Murray is therefore right to speak of "Ahab's last suicidal lunge" as "the hero's umbilical fixation to the Whale," in *"In Nomine Diaboli," New England Quarterly* 24 (December 1951): 452.

17. For discussions that read the novel as essentially Ishmael's narrative, see Paul Brodtkorb *(Ishmael's White World)*, who analyzes the ways in which Ishmael incorporates the characters he also presents; Walter Bezanson ("*Moby-Dick*: Work of Art," in *Moby-Dick Centennial Essays*), who talks of two Ishmaels, the narrator and the character; and Thomas Woodson ("Ahab's Greatness: Prometheus as Narcissus," *ELH* [September 1966]), who discusses Ishmael's task in fashioning Ahab.

18. "Invitation to Form," in *The Image in Form: Selected Writings of Adrian Stokes*, ed. Richard Wollheim (New York: Harper & Row, 1972), pp. 104–5.

19. The *O.E.D.* connects the Old English and Old German words for "body," and speculates their common derivation from a foreign source, namely, from the words for "cask" in Greek and medieval Latin.

20. Charles Cook, in "Ahab's 'Intolerable Allegory,'" in *Discussions of Moby-Dick*, ed. Milton R. Stern (Boston: D. C. Heath, 1960), points out that Ahab has

projected all evil onto the whale, and attributes this to an "ignorance of the mortal entanglement of good and evil" (p. 64). What needs to be stressed, however, is evil's intolerability, not because it is not good but rather because it is not single, because it must come into complicated internal relationship with attributes that contradict it.

21. In *The Enchafèd Flood: or The Romantic Iconography of the Sea* (New York: Vintage, 1950), W. H. Auden speaks of Ahab's "fantasy of being a self-originating god . . . begetting itself on the self" (p. 136). Although the conclusion is mine rather than Auden's, incest so understood would shed its ordinary sexual connotations to reveal primitive identic ones.

22. See Jonathan Edwards's *Images and Shadows of Divine Things*, ed. Perry Miller (1948; reprint ed. Conn.: Greenwood Press, 1977). Incorporating both notions, of nature analogizing man and of earth analogizing heaven, Edwards writes: "Why is it not rational to suppose that the corporeal and visible world should be designedly made and constituted in analogy to the more spiritual, noble, and real world?" (p. 65). For a general discussion of the expanded typological sense in American literature, see also Stephen Manning's "Spiritual Exegesis and the Literary Critic," in *Typology and Early American Literature*, ed. Sacvan Bercovitch (Amherst: University of Massachusetts Press, 1972).

23. Frank Kermode, in *The Genesis of Secrecy: On the Interpretation of Narrative* (Cambridge, Mass.: Harvard University Press, 1979), writing about the relationship between interpretation and secrecy, suggests that the power of narrative lies in its promise of entry to the meaning of a given work from which our lack of comprehension exiles us. Kermode's metaphor is interesting, for it intimates that a text has palpable dimensions that could enclose or exclude. And the idea about a narrative's having two sides (something we perceive as an otherness but experience from within as comprehension) is linked to Stokes's notion about the way in which paintings and artifacts draw us into their frames.

24. *A World Elsewhere: The Place of Style in American Literature* (New York: Oxford University Press, 1966), p. 237. For other studies that discuss the existence of American fiction outside of a social confine, see Marius Bewley's *Eccentric Design: Form in the Classic American Novel* (New York: Columbia University Press, 1957), Richard Chase's *American Novel and Its Tradition* (New York: Doubleday Anchor, 1957), Joel Porte's *Romance in America* (Middletown, Conn.: Wesleyan University Press, 1969), and, of course, Lawrence's *Studies in Classic American Literature*. See also Hawthorne's discussions of "romance" in the prefaces to his novels.

25. In *Frontier: American Literature and the American West* (Princeton: Princeton University Press, 1965), p. 13.

26. Ibid., p. 21.

27. See Annette Kolodny, *The Lay of the Land: Metaphor as Experience and History in American Life* (Chapel Hill: University of North Carolina Press, 1975), for the equation of the land and lover in America.

28. *American Renaissance*, p. 286.

29. Herman Melville, *Pierre; Or, The Ambiguities*, in *The Writings of Herman Melville*, ed. Harrison Hayford, Hershel Parker, and G. Thomas Tanselle, Northwestern Newberry ed. (Evanston, Ill.: Northwestern University Press, 1957-), vol. 7 (1971), p. 119.

30. Ibid., p. 131.

31. *The Confidence Man: His Masquerade*, ed. Hershel Parker, Norton Critical ed. (New York: W. W. Norton, 1971), p. 191.

32. *Pierre*, p. 149.

33. William Faulkner, *The Sound and the Fury* (New York: Random House, 1946), p. 132.

34. Henry D. Thoreau, *Journal*, ed. Bradford Torrey and Francis H. Allen, 2 vols. (1906; reprint ed. New York: Dover, 1962), 2:249.

35. Ibid., 2:219.

36. Vladimir Nabokov, *Lolita* (New York: Berkley Publishing Corp., 1955), p. 160.

37. See the last chapter of Cavell's *Claim of Reason*, to which, though in a proximate context, the expression of these particular ideas is indebted.

38. Michael Polanyi and Harry Prosch, *Meaning* (Chicago: University of Chicago Press, 1975), p. 35.

39. Ibid., p. 36.

40. *Psychology* (New York: Henry Holt, 1892), p. 218.

41. (New York: Doubleday, 1978), p. 71.

42. "Of Being," ed. John E. Smith, in *The Works of Jonathan Edwards* (New Haven: Yale University Press, 1957–), vol. 6 (1980), p. 206.

Chapter 2

1. (Princeton: Princeton University Press, 1962), p. 291.

2. "The Rhetoric of Temporality," in *Interpretation: Theory and Practice*, ed. Charles S. Singleton (Baltimore: Johns Hopkins University Press, 1969), p. 190.

3. *Allegory: The Theory of a Symbolic Mode* (Cornell: Cornell University Press, 1964), pp. 87–88.

4. While the critical literature on Hawthorne's tales has dealt amply with the subject of allegory, it has spoken of allegorical problems almost exclusively in formal terms. Thus, it has attempted to discriminate Hawthorne's use of allegory from his use of the symbol (see, for example, Hyatt Waggoner's *Nathaniel Hawthorne: A Critical Study*, rev. ed. [Cambridge, Mass.: Harvard University Press, 1963]), or it has focused on Hawthorne's conversion of historical events to symbolic ones (see, for example, Roy Harvey Pearce's "Romance and the Study of History," in *Hawthorne Centenary Essays*, ed. Roy Harvey Pearce [Columbus: Ohio State University Press, 1964], pp. 221–44]). Alternately, criticism has turned its attention to the relationship between psychological states and their public counterparts (see, for example, Larzer Ziff's "The Artist and Puritanism," in *Hawthorne Centenary Essays*, ed. Pearce, pp. 245–69), or it has documented the relationship between the tales and their sources (see Frank Neal Doubleday's *Hawthorne's Early Tales: A Critical Study* [Durham, N.C.: Duke University Press, 1972], and Lea Newman's *Reader's Guide to the Short Stories of Nathaniel Hawthorne* [Boston: G. K. Hall, 1979]). Where criticism has spoken about the psychological implications—as, for example, in Frederick Crews's *Sins of the Fathers: Hawthorne's Psychological Themes* (Oxford: Oxford University Press, 1966) or Terence Martin's "Method of Hawthorne's Tales," in *Hawthorne Centenary Essays*, ed. Pearce, pp. 7–30—these discussions have stopped just short of exploring the way in which literary strategies

exploit, exaggerate, and finally become the identic subject that they problematically act out.

5. George Santayana, *Scepticism and Animal Faith: Introduction to a System of Philosophy* (New York: Dover Publications, 1955), p. 71.

6. Herman Melville, *White-Jacket; Or, The World in a Man-of-War*, in *The Writings of Herman Melville*, ed. Harrison Hayford, Hershel Parker, and G. Thomas Tanselle, Northwestern Newberry ed. (Evanston, Ill.: Northwestern University Press, 1957–), vol. 5 (1970). See chapters 1, 9, 19, 29, 47, and 92 for the way in which the jacket is not a mere garment but is spoken of as part of the body itself.

7. As Frank Neal Doubleday points out (*Hawthorne's Early Tales*, pp. 141–45), Hawthorne was working with a plot—the death of a particular family in a mountainslide—that his audience would have known. Hence, the outcome of the wish and its attendant irony are implicit from the tale's beginning. But they are implicit before the end in the tale's *internal* evidence, too. When the young man tells the family that he would like to be frozen to a statue on the summit of Mount Washington, the young girl chides him: "It is better to sit here, by this fire . . . though nobody thinks about us" (IX:328)—better to be alive in our bodies than dead out of them.

8. Hawthorne tacitly acknowledges the autobiographical link between his protagonist and himself; in "Preface" to the 1851 edition of the tales, he says that the author burned his own tales and marveled "that such . . . dull stuff . . . yet . . . possessed inflammability enough to set the chimney on fire!" (IX:4). In "Alice Doane's Appeal," another story about a young man who wants to make the devil literal, there is reference to the same fire.

9. *Great Short Works of Herman Melville*, ed. Warner Berthoff (New York: Harper & Row, 1969), p. 333.

10. Perhaps the tenses are tortured because Hawthorne is bringing together what Frederick Crews, in the tale's most interesting interpretation, in *The Sins of the Fathers* has called the connections between "ancestry [and] incestry" (p. 58).

11. This is an eerier retelling of the William Wilson fable, or, to cast back to earlier roots, it is a tale that bears relation to Brockden Brown's *Edgar Huntly; or, Memoirs of a Sleepwalker*, ed. David Stineback (New Haven: College and University Press, 1973). "Alice Doane's Appeal," with its surreal glaze of events, has more than passing connection to Brown's novel—a novel that confuses the lives of two ostensibly independent families, confuses the narrator and his subject, the pursued and the pursuing, the sleepwalker and the man awake. In *Edgar Huntly* blurred distinctions are specifically advocated by Waldegrave (the character whose death is to be avenged), who leaves, before his death, a treatise espousing the collapse of all bodily distinctions: "His earliest creeds," we are told, "tended . . . to deify necessity and universalize matter; to destroy the popular distinctions between soul and body, and to dissolve the supposed connection between the moral condition of man anterior and subsequent to death" (p. 132).

12. "Meditation VI," in *The Philosophical Works of Descartes*, trans. Elizabeth S. Haldane and G. R. T. Ross, 2 vols. (Cambridge: Cambridge University Press, 1970), 1:196.

13. Even the colloquialism "to lose one's mind" implies that the whole thing is gone, not just a separable part of it. So too Freud's idea of an unconscious, which

posits separations between levels of consciousness, leaves the mind intact. Thus, insofar as a thought goes from a conscious to an unconscious sphere, it is not lost, it is simply displaced. In fact, the notion that nothing can be lost from the mind is, in Freudian ideology, what causes trauma to the self, which, as it were, is an accumulation of its experiences.

14. John Donne, "Expostulation XIX," in *Devotions upon Emergent Occasions* (Ann Arbor: University of Michigan Press, 1975), p. 124.

15. This Sir Thomas Browne demonstrates most dramatically by his declaration of independence from any palpable body in his association with a self antecedent and exterior: *"Before Abraham was, I am,* is the saying of Christ, yet is it true in some sense if I say it of myselfe, for I was not onley before myselfe, but *Adam,* that is, in the Idea of God, and . . . in this sense, I say, the world was before Creation, and at an end before it had a beginning; and thus was I dead before I was alive; though my grave be *England,* my dying place was Paradise, and *Eve* miscarried of mee before she conceiv'd of *Cain"* (*Religio Medici,* in *The Prose of Sir Thomas Browne,* ed. Norman Endicott [New York: Doubleday, 1967], pp. 65–66). Later, in New England, in tones similarly ecstatic, Jonathan Edwards was to disassociate himself from his corporeal body. He was to claim to be "rapt up to" and "swallowed up in" God (*Basic Writings,* ed. Ola Elizabeth Winslow [New York: New American Library, 1966], pp. 83–84). If typological extravagances dispense with the body, they also know how to reappropriate it. Thus, Horace Bushnell, Hawthorne's contemporary, suggests that the outer world represents the inner one, is a mere body for the human spirit: "There is a logos in the forms of things, by which they are prepared to serve as types or images of what is inmost in our souls" ("Preliminary Dissertation on the Nature of Language as Related to Thought and Spirit," in *Theology in America: The Major Protestant Voices from Puritanism to Neo-Orthodoxy* [Indianapolis: Bobbs-Merrill, 1967], p. 325). In this standard typological formulation, man in his entirety is the "spirit" or life's inside. The world of corporeal things merely houses our bodies, which, as a consequence, assume the status of spirit or souls.

16. See Doubleday, *Hawthorne's Early Tales,* pp. 192–200, 227–38.

17. In *The Elixir of Life Manuscripts* (XIII), a man kills a soldier and then thinks, by virtue of the other's death, to have escaped death's consequences. As in "Roger Malvin's Burial," Hawthorne continues to state the idea of exchange (another's death for one's own immortal life) with Faulkner-like obsession, never getting the idea either finished or, to his own satisfaction, right.

18. The story is, indeed, about ambivalence, as Frederick Crews suggests in *The Sins of the Fathers,* but it is not about Robin's ambivalence as separate from anyone else's. Rather, ambivalence exists in the characters and characteristics of the world, all doubly complexioned. For example, the processional in the church and the processional in the street are brought together in Robin's query as he is about to leave the former: "What if his kinsman should glide through yonder gate, and nod and smile to him in passing dimly by?"

19. *The Letters of Herman Melville,* ed. Merrell R. Davis and William H. Gilman (New Haven: Yale University Press, 1960), p. 125.

20. Edwin Haviland Miller, *Melville: A Biography* (New York: Persea Books, 1975).

21. *Letters of Herman Melville,* p. 142.